Elizabeth Rundle Charles, Henry Boynton Smith

The Early Dawn

Or, sketches of Christian life in England in the olden time

Elizabeth Rundle Charles, Henry Boynton Smith

The Early Dawn
Or, sketches of Christian life in England in the olden time

ISBN/EAN: 9783337097585

Printed in Europe, USA, Canada, Australia, Japan

Cover: Foto ©Lupo / pixelio.de

More available books at **www.hansebooks.com**

THE EARLY DAWN;

OR, SKETCHES OF

Christian Life in England

IN THE

Olden Time.

BY THE AUTHOR OF
"Chronicles of the Schönberg-Cotta Family."

WITH INTRODUCTION
BY
PROF. HENRY B. SMITH, D. D.

NEW YORK:
M. W. DODD, No. 506 BROADWAY.
1864.

Entered according to Act of Congress, in the year 1864, by

M. W. DODD,

In the Clerk's Office of the District Court of the United States, for the Southern District of New York.

EDWARD O. JENKINS,
Printer and Stereotyper,
20 NORTH WILLIAM STREET.

INTRODUCTION.

IT is the high office of history to restore the Past to a new life. All great events have a twofold life; once, as they actually occurred, and again, as they are revived upon the historic page for the benefit of after times. The historian must first of all give an accurate record of facts in their just order; but more than this is needed, if the Past is to speak persuasively to the Present. It must be so reanimated as to bring to view living men and scenes, that the imagination may be enlisted and the pulse quickened. To the sharp outline of fact, fiction may add its embellishments, and thus allure many who would otherwise pass carelessly by the great lessons of human history.

The author of the *Chronicles of the Schönberg-Cotta Family* is already well known and loved in many households of our land. In that attractive volume, the story of the Great Reformation, its spiritual conflicts and heroes, were so strikingly described, as to deepen our sense of the great debt we owe to those who then contended valiantly for the true faith against the corruptions and despotism of the church of the Middle Ages. In the sketches comprised in the present volume the scene is transferred from Germany to England, and thus comes nearer home to some of our sympathies and associations. The *Christian Life of England in the Olden Time* is here depicted, through several centuries, from its earliest dawn, in its contrasted lights and shadows, down to "the morning star of the Reformation." The Druid is first introduced in converse with the Jew and the Christian. The Two Martyrs of Verulam fall within the period of the Roman domination, full fifteen hundred years ago. The fortunes of an Anglo-Saxon Family are briefly sketched through three generations. The contests of the Saxon and the Norman, and their different traits, are vividly pourtrayed, in the time of the Crusades. And few tales are more interesting and instructive than that in which Cuthbert narrates his experience in the Order of St. Francis and his illumination by the "Everlasting Gospel" of Joachim, and Cicely relates how Dr. Wycliffe, of Oxford, ministered to her spiritual needs and insight.

The undeniable charm of these sketches consists in their simple, truthful adherence to the spirit and traits of these olden times. The author has been a diligent student of the literature, and, through the literature, of the very life of the epochs. This is revealed in many skillful touches of art, in incidental allusions, apt citations and graphic descriptions of scenes and persons. But more than this is her rare gift of tracing the workings of the human soul in its needs and aspirations, its human love, its divine longings. The permanent religious wants, which remain the same under all varieties of external fortune, are so truthfully set forth that the Past becomes a mirror for the Present.

It is a good thing, in such company, to review those contests of our ancestors which have enured to the lasting benefit of mankind. It deepens faith in the workings and power of Divine Providence. Our belief in the final triumph of the Gospel, through its manifold contests, is made more firm, when we see it, as in these Lights and Shadows of its early dawn in England, subduing paganism, planting itself firmly among Britons and Saxons, equally professed by Normans and Saxons and shaping their social and civil life, surviving in spite of the corruptions of the times, and breaking forth anew, in clearer light, with evangelic zeal, among the Lollards, who spake in new tongues the words of the old faith, and became the precursors of the Great Reformation. Our youth should be made familiar with these scenes; for thus may they be helped in their preparation for the great work of life.

H. B. S.

New York, June 15th, 1864.

CONTENTS.

I.—Lights and Shadows of the Early Dawn,	11
II.—The Two Martyrs of Verulam,	29
III.—Annals of an Anglo-Saxon Family Through Three Generations,	75
IV.—Saxon Schools and Homes,	119
V.—Saxon Minsters and Missions,	161
VI.—Alfred the Truth-Teller,	209
VII.—Alfred the Truth-Teller,	247
VIII.—Saxon and Norman,	295
IX.—A Story of the Lollards,	343

I.

Lights and Shadows

of the

Early Dawn.

I.

LIGHTS AND SHADOWS OF THE EARLY DAWN.

ONE Midsummer Eve, more than seventeen centuries ago, the red gleams of a huge bonfire contended with the pale moonbeams in clothing with fantastic light and shade the gigantic piles of granite which crest, as with a natural fortress, that point of the Cornish coast now called Trerhyn Castle. The wild flickerings of the flames leaped high enough at times even to touch with their fiery glow the edges of the mysterious Logan Rock which crowns the summit.

That it was no mere bonfire of merry-makers might be easily seen in the earnest faces and grave movements of the men gathered round it. They were not mingled in a confused throng, nor scattered in irregular groups, but moved solemnly round the fire from east to west, following the course of the sun, now hidden from their gaze beneath that shoreless ocean whose waves thundered ceaselessly against the base of the cliff on which they were assembled.

Their steps were the slow and measured movements of a sacred mystic dance; and as they circled round the blaze they sang a wild monotonous chant, to which the minor intervals gave, not the plaintive tenderness of a major melody broken by a minor fall, but rather the abrupt and savage restlessness of a combined wail and war-cry.

From time to time the song rose with the flames into a defiant shout, and then sank again into the low crooning of a dirge; the steps of the singers changing with the music from a rapid march to the slow tramp of a funeral procession. The sacred music of that old British race resolved itself into no calm, restful, major close.

Theirs was the worship of a conquered race, and of a proscribed religion. Driven by the Romans from their temples in the interior of the island—temples, whose unhewn and gigantic grandeur not even the persistency of Roman enmity could ruin—this little band of the old lords of the land had met in that remote recess, not yet trodden by the conquerors' feet, to celebrate the rites of their ancient faith, under the guidance of one of their own proscribed Druid priesthood.

There, under the shadow of that grand natural fortress, to us so like one of their own Druid temples, they had kindled on May Day the sacred "Fire of God;" and there on Midsummer Eve they now gathered round the "Fire of Peace."

At length the rites, endeared to them as the last relics of their national existence, were finished; the wild chant was silent, succeeded by the ceaseless roar of the breakers; and the torches were kindled at the sacred fire, to relight once more, from a sacred source, the household fires that night extinguished.

One by one the little British company dispersed, and

could be traced along the cliffs, or inland across the unbroken moorland, by the glare of their torches.

The Druid was left alone. A solemn, solitary figure, he stood on the deserted space by the decaying fire, his fine form still erect, although the long beard, characteristic of his priestly office, was snow-white with age. The fitful glow of the expiring embers threw a mysterious light on the folds of his white robe, and gleamed on the rays of the broad golden circlet which bound his brow. Turning from the fire he looked across the sea, scarcely more solitary or wild than the rugged shore on which he lingered.

It was always a dreary moment to him when the solemn rites were over, and the worshippers were gone. A few minutes since he had stood before the awe-stricken throng as one altogether apart and exalted, a medium of intercourse with the unknown supreme powers, a representative of the majesty so dimly understood, so vividly dreaded; and their faith had thrown back a reflected reality on his. But now he stood alone, a mortal man to whom the unseen was indeed as invisible as to the meanest of those worshippers; and he felt he would have gladly borrowed from the meanest and most credulous among them that faith in the invisible which his presence inspired in others, but which he found it so hard to maintain in himself. His people looking with dim and longing eyes into the infinite, at least saw him; whilst he saw only a blank infinity.

Musing thus, he gazed on that restless, boundless ocean, the broad sweep of whose waves measured the long path of moonlight with their perspective of diminishing curves. Could it be possible, he thought, that at the end of that radiant pathway human eyes (were they but pure enough) might see the silvery outlines of that "Isle of the Brave," where he taught his people the spirits of their dead were resting? Could it be that the waves which broke with that wild and wistful music at his feet might sound in human ears (were they but worthy to hear) the echoes of those deathless shores in the far west, where perhaps they had received their first impulse?

Thus he stood musing, until his reverie was broken by the sound of footsteps close at hand. Turning hastily round, he saw between him and the fire a dark form wrapped in a Roman mantle.

"Who art thou," he asked abruptly, "that hast tracked us thus to our last refuge? Thou hast lighted on what may prove to thee a treasure better than any of the mines thy people grudge us. Doubtless, thou seest," he added bitterly, "that I am one of that proscribed Druid priesthood whom, unarmed and defenceless, your Roman armies so much dread. Denounce me to the rulers, if thou wilt. I will follow thee without a struggle. Of what avail to me is life? And who knows what secrets death may teach?"

"I am no Roman," said the stranger sadly. "On my people also the wrath of those irresistible legions has fallen. I also am one of the priesthood of a proscribed religion, and of a conquered race. Far in the East my people had once a city beautiful beyond all on earth, and a temple where white-robed priests, mitred with gold, ministered and sacrificed to Him whose name must not be uttered. Our temple is burned with fire, our city is laid waste, and trodden under foot of strangers; our people are scattered east and west, and I among them. I had lost my way to-night on this wild coast, as I was journeying to the port near this, whither of old our fathers came to traffic, when, seeing the unusual gleam of this fire, I came to learn what it meant. Thou seest no ally of the Romans in me."

The Druid was appeased, and laying aside his priestly vestments, he appeared in the ordinary Celtic plaid worn by his tribe. The two men found a strange link in their isolation from other men; and, piling up the scattered logs on the dying embers, they agreed to remain together there until the dawn should throw sufficient light on their path to enable them to travel safely along those rugged cliffs against which the waves, now hidden in the shades of night, seemed to roar and chafe, like raging and disappointed beasts of prey.

"Your priestly vestments remind me strangely," said the Hebrew, when they were reseated by the fire, "of the sacred robes my forefathers wore of old. Whence did your religion come?"

"The sources of sacred things are hidden in night," replied the Druid. "Some say our religion was taught direct from heaven; some, that it was brought, before the memory of man, from a land in the far East, whence after the great flood the father and mother of our race came forth."

"In those distant ages," said the Jew, "doubtless your forefathers and ours were one. Since you had a priesthood, had you then also a temple and sacred rites?"

"We had many temples," was the reply; "gigantic circles of stone, as unhewn and as enormous as these amidst which we stand. Huge reminders of the solemn cliffs and mountains set up in unrivalled majesty on the solitary sweeps of our great inland plains; roofed by the heavens, and floored by a bare unsmoothed earth. I laugh when I see the pigmy temples in which these Romans bow down before their little men and women gods."

"You had, then, no graven images?"

"Of old we had none; and never any in our temples. We have but one image of the Highest; if indeed," he added, in a low and awed voice, "he is only an image! Our worship is directed to the sun. In his eternal course from east to west our sacred dances move. At his rising we rejoice. When in flowery May his beams once more begin to make the earth fruitful, we kindle in his honour the 'Fire of God,' and begin our year anew. When he has risen in midsummer to his highest seat in the heavens, and reigns in his fullest might, we kindle the sacred 'Fire of Peace,' as to-night, in honour of his peaceful and consummated dominion."

"Since, then, you had temples, had you also sacrifices?"

"We had," was the solemn reply; "but not such as those of the Romans; not only the white steer from the herd, or the spotless lamb from the flock. We offered to our gods costlier sacrifices than these, and dearer life."

"What life, then?" said the Jew, in horror.

"The only life worthy to be accepted for the life of man," was the reply; "the only life worthy to be offered to the Immortal."

"Your altars were stained with human blood!" said the Jew, with a shudder; "your people had indeed, then, a different law from mine. But to whom," he continued, after a pause, "did you offer these terrible offerings?"

"The various tribes of our race had various names for him," said the Druid, in a low voice. "Some called him Hu, and some Dhia or Dhe, and some Be'al, the life of all life, the source of all being."

The Jew started as the name, denounced by his prophets, and abhorred by his race, fell on his ear, yet strangely blended with a word like the incommunicable name he might not utter, the mysterious Jah.

"It is very strange!" he said, at length. "Your words sound to me like an echo of the utterance of the prophets of my people, resounding through the ages as the waves through one of these ocean caverns, and broken into strange discords and wild confusion."

"Had you then no sacred writings?"

"We have none," said the Druid. "Our aged priests teach the sacred words in solemn chants to the priestly neophytes, and initiate them in the sacred rites. So we were taught; so shall we teach those that follow, if the world or our race is to endure."

"But," said the Jew, "did you never shrink from the sufferings of the victims as you sacrificed them, or think whether there might not be some pity in the Eternal which might revolt from such rites."

"Am I not a man?" was the reply. "Doubtless my heart often ached at the sufferings of those we sacrificed, especially at first. But the sufferers were, for the most part, criminals, or captives taken in war; and what was I, to be wiser than the aged who taught me?"

The remembrance of the sacred name, revealed to the law-giver of his nation, rushed in on the heart of the Jew—of "Jehovah Jehovah Elohim," the eternal and the mighty, "merciful and gracious, long-suffering, abounding in goodness and truth, yet by no means clearing the guilty;" and with it came the recollection of that ritual so stern in its demands for the acknowledgment of sin, and of the forfeited right of the sinner to life, yet so jealous in its guard for that human life it declared forfeit.

"Are you sure that your god hears you when you thus invoke and sacrifice to him?" he said, after a pause.

"We assure the people of these things," was the evasive reply; "and also of rewards and punishments in the world beyond. The people need the barriers of such belief to keep them from crime."

"But you do not teach what you do not believe?"

"Belief is not so easy for the instructed," was the reply. "Who that has looked into the depth of life can rest and believe like the ignorant?"

"Our faith," said the Jew, mournfully, "was a faith for all; our most sacred truths were for the peasant as well as the priest. Among us the seers revealed what they had seen, and the prophets believed what they taught."

The Druid listened long with grave interest as the Hebrew spoke of that God who was revealed to his people as at once so awful and so near; before whom, the prophet said, "The holy hosts above veil their faces," and yet of whom the shepherd-king could say, "He is my Shepherd."

At length he said,—

"But since you had such revelations, and such a faith, and were a nation so honored by the Highest, how can it be that you are a banished man like me? Did you not speak of the city of your people as laid waste, and their sanctuary as desecrated? What does this mean?"

"I know not, or, at least, I can only partly conjecture," was the sad reply. "Our people had sinned, and our God is one who will not clear the guilty. Once before, our fathers were driven from their homes into that yet further East whence first they came, and our holy and beautiful house was burned with fire. But then, in their exile they had prophets and promises, and a limit fixed to their disgrace, at the end of which they were indeed restored. But now we have no prophets, nor any who can interpret. Scattered hither and thither we lose the record of our lineage. Our glory is all in the past. In all the future I can see no vision of hope. It seems to me, sometimes, almost as if our nation had made shipwreck in the night on some unknown sunken rock. Around us and before us is no shore, nor any light in view, save in that distant past to which the blazing ruins of our temple warn us we may not return."

"Yet," resumed the Druid, "had it been otherwise with your nation, scarcely would your prosperity have brought hope to the world, to other races, or to mine. You say it was to your nation only God spoke; to your nation alone the promises were made, which in some incomprehensible way you have lost. The world, then, has lost little in your fall."

"I know not," replied the Jew. "Our prophets spoke of the veil being rent from all people, and of all nations coming to the brightness of the rising of a King who was to reign over ours."

"Did this King then never come?"

"How can he have come?" said the Jew, with a strange impatience. "How should I then be here, an exile without a country? And was not our King to come as a Conqueror and a Redeemer for our nation,—as a Sun, flashing his unquestionable glory on all nations? There is, indeed," he added, a fanatical sect who sprang from our race, who assert that our King has come, and that it is for rejecting him we are rejected. But who can believe this?"

"It would be terrible, truly, for your people to believe

it," said the Druid. "Those amongst you who think thus must be a mourning and wretched company."

"Nay," was the answer, " they are not. Their delusion leads them to profess themselves the most blessed of men. They think that he whom they call King and Lord, who not much more than a hundred years ago was crucified by the Romans in our city, has arisen from the dead, and lives in heaven. And they say they are glad to die to depart to him."

"Their hope extends then beyond death," said the Druid, abstractedly. "There are then some who think they know of one who has visited the 'Isle of the Brave,' and has come back to tell what he saw!"

As they spoke, the dawn began to break over the green slopes of the shore on a promontory of which they sat. One by one the higher points of that magnificent series of rock-bastions which guard our country from the Atlantic, like a fortress of God, caught the early sunbeams. Soon the ocean also was bathed in another ocean of light, broken only by the shadow of the cliffs, or by the countless purple cups of shade, which gave an individual existence to every one of those wonderful translucent green waves.

The two priests of the two religions moved slowly across the pass between the rocks which separate the natural castled bulwark, where they had passed the night, from the green slopes of the coast within.

"See," exclaimed the Druid, "how the fire, which during the hours of darkness was all our light, now lies a faint red stain on the daylight; whilst the waves, which all night roared around us like angry demons, quietly heave in the sunshine. The earth has her dawns renewed continually. Will no new sun ever rise for man? Must the golden dawn for us be always in the past?"

Too deep a shadow rested for the Jew on the glorious predictions of his prophets for him to give any answer; and silently they went along the cliffs.

When they had walked inland thus for some time, they saw before them a labourer, in an earth-stained and common dress, going to his work in one of the mines which of old had tempted the Phœnicians to those very shores.

This miner was evidently young, and had the lithe grace of the South about his form and movements. As he walked he sang, and the tones of his rich Southern tenor rose clear and full through the clear morning air. The cadence was different from any music the Druid had ever heard. There was a repose about the melody, quite foreign to the wild wails or war songs of his people. And as they drew near, the language was to him as strange. They stepped on softly behind the singer, and listened.

"Strange words to hear in such a place," murmured the Jew at length. "They are Greek—the language of a people who dwelt of old, and dwell still, in the East, near the home of my forefathers."

They drew near and greeted the stranger. There was a gentle and easy courtesy in his manner as he returned their salutations, which, in a son of the North, would have betokened high breeding, but in him might be merely the natural bearing of his acute and versatile race. He willingly complied when the Jew asked him to repeat his song, which he translated thus to the Druid :—

> Glory to God in the highest,
> And on earth peace,
> Good-will among men.
> We praise Thee,

We bless Thee,
We worship Thee
For thy great glory,
O Lord, heavenly King,
O God the Father ruling all,
O Lord the only-begotten Son,
Saviour, Messiah,
With the Holy Spirit.

O Lord God,
Lamb of God,
Son of the Father,
Who takest away the sins of the world,
Receive our prayer.
Thou who sittest at the right hand of the Father,
Have mercy on us,
For Thou only art holy—
Thou only art the Lord,
Saviour, and Messiah—
To the glory of God the Father. Amen.

"Ask him if he has any other such sacred songs," said the Druid; "the words sound to me beautiful and true, like an echo of half-forgotten music, heard long ago in some former life from which perchance my soul came into this."

"I will chant you our evening hymn," said the miner; and he sang again—

Joyful light of heavenly glory,
Of the immortal heavenly Father,
The holy and the blessed
Jesus Christ!
We, coming at the setting of the sun,
Seeing the evening light,
Hymn the Father and the Son,
And the Holy Spirit, God.

> Worthy art Thou at all times to be praised
> With holy voices, Son of God,
> Thou who givest light,
> Therefore doth the world glorify Thee.

"Wonderful words," said the Jew, after translating them. "They seem almost like a response from heaven to what you said; like the promise of the dawn for man for which you longed. Friend," he said to the miner, "how camest thou hither? Thy learning is above thy calling."

"Not so," replied the other meekly. "I was never other than a poor man. These truths are common to the most unlettered among us."

"To whom does he allude by 'us?'" asked the Druid when he understood.

"We are the Christians, the men of Christ," said the stranger, replying to the Druid's question in his own native Celtic language, although with a foreign accent. "I was a vine-dresser on the sunny hills near Smyrna. My father learned the faith from the Apostle John, the Beloved; and I was exiled hither to work in the mines in the far West because I could not deny my Lord."

"Bitter change," said the Jew, "from those vine-clad southern hills to toil in the darkness on these cold northern shores."

"Where I am going there will be no need of the sun," was the calm reply; but the ominous hectic flush deepened on his hollow cheek.

"How, then," said the Druid, "is your faith maintained in this life of exile and bondage? Here you can have no temple and no priest."

"We have a Temple!" was the joyful reply, "not made

with hands; and a Priest, though not seen now by mortal eyes."

"He speaks in parables," said the Druid.

"I speak no parables," said the Christian, "but simply matters of fact, of which we are all assured."

"Have you then also sacrifices?" asked the Druid.

"We *have* a Sacrifice," was the low and reverent reply; "One, spotless and eternal, never more to be repeated. The Highest gave his Son. The Holy One yielded up himself. *God has provided the Lamb.* The Lamb of God and the Son of God are one."

"He speaks of the promise made to our father Abraham," exclaimed the Jew.

"Life for life," murmured the Druid, "life of man for life of man."

"Nay, it was not man who made the sacirfice," said the Christian, "but God. Not the sinner's life was required; the Son yielded up his own."

"You have then no sacrifices to offer now," said the Druid.

"Not so," said the Christian joyfully; "we have a daily, ceaseless sacrifice to offer—a living sacrifice, acceptable to God through Jesus Christ; even *ourselves*, to do and suffer all the holy will of God,—we ourselves, body, soul and spirit, to fulfil the will of Him who loved us and redeemed us with his precious blood to God."

"But," resumed the Druid, "is that holy life, which you say was willingly yielded up for man, extinct for ever? Shall the holy perish and the guilty live?"

"Nay," was the reply, in a tone of concentrated fervour, "that immortal life could not perish. The Son of God is risen from the dead, and dieth no more. And now," he continued, speaking eagerly, as one who has good news to tell, "He sitteth enthroned at the right hand of God, the Sun of the City above."

"Have you then also a sacred city?" said the Jew in a tone of surprise.

"It lieth toward the sun-rising," replied the Christian, in the words of an early martyr, "Jerusalem the heavenly, the city of the holy."

"Your golden age, your holy city, are then in the future, not in the past," said both.

"You speak of an immortal life for each man," added the Druid, "but is there never to be a good time for mankind?"

"It is written, that the King, the Christ, will come again in glory, to judge the wicked and to raise the just," was the reply; "and that then truth and righteousness shall reign on earth, for he is holy, and just, and true, and in Him all the nations of the earth shall be blessed."

Often, during the months that followed, the Hebrew and the Druid sought that lowly miner's hut. There Jew and Gentile learned together concerning Him who is the Hope of Israel and the Desire of all nations.

The blank wall of darkness, which to the Jew had seemed so strangely and abruptly to close the long path of prophetic light and promise, parted and dissolved, displaying to his adoring gaze the Sacrifice to whom all sacrifices pointed, the Priest in whom all priesthood is consummated, the King of whom Hebrew kings and prophets sang, in whom all dominion centres.

To the Druid the dim desires of his heart were at once explained and fulfilled. Sin and falsehood were discovered and brought to shame. "Life and immortality were brought to light." And on both gradually dawned, as the power and the wisdom of God, not a doctrine merely, nor a ritual, but the Christ, the Son of the living God.

Thus along the rocky shores of the Atlantic rose in threefold harmony the Christian hymns to Him who heareth always; the Sun whose presence is day to faith, the Glory for which Israel waited, the Redeemer for whom all nations blindly groped and longed, the Lamb of God who taketh away the sin of the world.

There also, ere long, in that lowly hut, those strangers watched as brothers by the death-bed of the Smyrniote exile, now one with them in Christ. And there, on that bleak shore, they buried him, in a quiet nook, consecrated by solitude, and thenceforth by the immortal seed of "the body that shall be."

Races have passed away since then, and civilizations; rituals and religious systems have grown up, run to seed, and perished; but from those early ages to this that new song of life and hope has never been entirely silenced on our British shores.*

---

* Tertullian speaks of Christianity as having in his day penetrated to regions of Britain which the Roman legions had not reached. And subsequent history proves that the ancient British Church derived its faith and its customs from the Eastern Church. (Neander's Church History; Milman's Latin Christianity, &c., &c.)

II.

THE TWO MARTYRS OF VERULAM.

II.

THE TWO MARTYRS OF VERULAM.

THE history of Romanized Britain seems scarcely to have more connection with the history of England and Englishmen, than the history of the geological convulsions which preceded it. Indeed, in some respects it has much less. The succession of fishy and vegetable occupants of our shores have left their indelible traces on our fossil rocks, our coal-beds, our alluvial plains. The Roman possessors of our country swept over it like a passing wave, leaving no traces imbedded in the foundations of our social life. We are in no sense their descendants or their heirs. A great historical chasm separates those centuries of foreign and superficial civilization from the rough and real Saxon times which followed them. Convulsed, and invaded, and devastated, as our country continued to be for many centuries, the continuity of its history is never again utterly broken after the establishment of the first Saxon kingdom. Those Northern seamen, those Kentish, and Northumbrian, and West Saxon kings, are substantial living men to us. They are our flesh and blood. But Boadicea and Caractacus are almost as shadowy to us as the Roxane or Andromaque of the French stage. If even, by a severe mental effort, we succeed in convincing ourselves of their existence, their existence has little more to do with us than that of their contemporaries in Rome or Alexandria.

Neither the conquerors nor the conquered of those dim, ancient days, touch us with a sense of kindred. Our inheritance of Roman civilization has descended to us indirectly through its mediæval interpreters, rather than directly from the Cæsars who reigned in Britain. Whatever of Celtic thought or life has interwoven itself into ours, flows rather from the legends of King Arthur than from the history of Caractacus, king of the Trinobantes, or Boadicea, queen of the Iceni.

Partly, perhaps, this feeling is caused by the inaptitude of the Roman historians for rendering native names. How is it possible for Englishmen to feel any relationship with the inhabitants of Camalodunum or Verulamium; with the Iceni, the Silures, or the Ordovices? Through the pages of Latin historians, everything is Latinized. Caractacus speaks like a senator of austere old Rome—Boadicea harangues like a matron of the early republic; or rather, like the representative of such a matron on the stage. Had a few fragments reached us of the British records of Roman conquest, they might probably touch our hearts more than all the encomiums or the reprehensions of Tacitus. But, as it is, Romans and Britons—conquerors and conquered—are almost equally foreigners to us.

Unfortunately, the early history of Christian life in our country, which might have supplied the missing link, is too irretrievably mixed up with legend effectually to do so.

Even St. Alban, the martyr of Verulam, is a far more shadowy being to us than the Smyrniote Polycarp, the

African Perpetua, or the martyrs of Vienne. And the first name that emerges into plain historical distinctness in the ecclesiastical annals of our land is, unhappily, the chilling name of Pelagius.

Yet of the existence and martyrdom of St. Alban there seems little reason to doubt. His sufferings are not elaborated into any of the frightful torments with whose ghastly illumination monastic chroniclers delighted to dazzle their readers. Legend has indeed garlanded the narrative with flowers of wonder, but it has not sullied it with horrors. Fifteen hundred years ago, on the green heights now crowned by the Abbey Church of St. Albans, we may believe a Christian martyr did actually give up his life for Christ—not indeed an English martyr, yet truly one of our spiritual kindred, truly our brother in the family whose ties are for eternity.

Fifteen hundred years ago, and once again since then!

The last sunbeams were lingering on the hill now crowned by the Abbey Church of St. Albans, then crested with native forests; but twilight was fast creeping over the river, and the town on its banks, when a bridal procession passed through the streets of Roman Verulam, from the house of the bride's father to that of the bridegroom.

There were the flashing of torches, the songs of the youths, the escort of veiled virgins, and all the picturesque pomp which has become to us so allegorical.

Many pronounced aloud their good wishes for the bride, as she stepped by, her face hidden, like Aurora's, in her flame-coloured veil, and the little crimson-slippered feet peeping out from beneath the purple border of her white robe. The household of Valeria, and her father, and the old soldier Caius Valerius, was much respected in Verulam as an exceptional household, on the virtuous old Roman model.

Valerius being thus a Roman of the old type, the old Roman customs were more strictly adhered to in this instance than was usual in those degenerate days.

The maidens carried the distaff and spindle after the bride, and the boys waved the pine torches. At the door of the bridegroom's house, he met her with the ancient challenge, "Who art thou?" to which she murmured the prescribed reply, "Ibi tu Caius, ibi ego Caia"—"Where thou art Caius, there am I Caia."

Then after reverently anointing the garlanded door-posts against the spell of malign demons, and binding them with woollen fillets, she was lifted over the sacred threshold, on which it was inauspicious for her to tread.

The sheep-skin, typical of household industry, was placed beneath her feet, and the keys, typical of household authority, were gravely given into her hands. Together bride and bridegroom touched the sacred primal elements of fire and water, "source of all things," and late into the night echoed through the street and along the river the sounds of feasting, and the songs of the virgins chanting the nuptial songs.

There was weighty meaning in all these ceremonies, a recognition of the sacredness of marriage and the religious capacities of womanhood, of incalculable social value, when contrasted with the Oriental degradation of women, or the monastic Manichæan misapprehension of marriage.

In those simple words, "Where thou art Caius, there I am Caia," were implied a whole world of sacred social rights. Ancient Rome did not rise above the nations by her corruptions, but by her virtues. By her corruptions she fell.

How fallen, however, from this ancient ideal the manners of the times in which Valeria lived she little knew. To her the words and the rites were invested with a deep sacredness. Her father had brought her up in seclusion and simplicity, and in a reverent attention to the religion of her ancestors.

Before the marriage she had been present at the sacrifices, and had anxiously watched the auguries. On the next day she shared in offering libations to the household gods, and garlanded them with flowers.

She then proceeded to order everything for the feast her husband was to give that evening, and in the afternoon the matrons came with presents and salutations. It was not till the following day that she found herself alone after the supper with her husband in the dwelling room, when she took her distaff, and seating herself on a low stool near his couch, began to spin in silence.

For some time he watched the white hands flashing to and fro at the distaff, and the serious expression which rested with such a charm on the girlish face.

He might have watched her for hours in unbroken silence. It was quite contrary to Valeria's ideas of domestic etiquette to speak to the lord of the household until she was spoken to. Besides, she knew nothing of her husband's tastes or ways of thinking, never having spoken to him, except in formulas of compliment, before their marriage. At length he rose, and laying his hand on hers, stopped her busy fingers, and said,—

" Valeria, talk to me."

She coloured, and looked up with a startled expression. " About what, Aurelius?"

" About what you were thinking of."

The suggestion did not assist her. She was not clear

that at the moment she had been thinking of anything, and she was quite clear that a few moments before she had been thinking of what she would have been afraid to mention to him.

She therefore looked down and said nothing.

"Tell me, Valeria, what you were thinking of. You looked grave enough for your namesake when she was meditating the deliverance of Rome, besieged by Coriolanus. What were those grave thoughts?"

Valeria decided that conjugal duty required her to speak, and Roman veracity to speak the truth, and therefore, colouring deeply, in a low tremulous voice, she said,—

"I was thinking, Aurelius, why you omitted the prayers to the immortal gods before and after the meal!"

He looked perplexed. Hitherto he had watched her quiet methodical movements with an amused interest, much as if she had been a precocious child playing the matron. Valeria was not sixteen, and there was a girlishness in her light movements, and a childlike unconsciousness in her expression and in all her ways which made her seem even younger. Therefore the question startled Aurelius. It awakened the memory of his own religious perplexities, and he wondered if she shared them. But he answered lightly,—

"It is plain, my Valeria, that you have taken eternal leave of the dolls and playthings which you sacrificed in the temple the day before yesterday. What put such grave questions in your head?"

"Only because it is different from what my father did," she replied simply. "He was always very exact about the libations and invocations, and he always told me reverence for the immortals was the foundation of the Roman State and of every virtuous Roman household."

It was plain that Valeria's faith had never desired any further sanction than her father's word. Aurelius saw that the great chaos of doubt, in which his thoughts often recklessly tossed hither and thither, was a region entirely unknown to her; and, as a sensible man, he respected her principles, on which, unfounded as they might be, he felt the sacredness of his home was better founded than on anything else he knew.

"I can never be grateful enough to your father," he said, "for bestowing on me a wife fair as Hebe, and religious as a Vestal."

Valeria was encouraged to say,—

"It was then a mistake about the invocations?"

"It is an omission that shall occur no more," he replied.

Valeria was satisfied. She had no suspicion of religious rites being practised without a certain measure of religious reverence; and thenceforth the pious customs of her father's house were transferred to her own. The Lares and Penates were duly crowned and honoured, the temples visited at the festivals, the libations and sacrifices duly made at the meals at home. Caius Valerius rejoiced in his daughter's household as one worthy of days of primitive virtue and religion; and Aurelius rejoiced in his wife as a grafting of all that was gentle and loving in womanhood on the severe stock of old Roman virtue. Often, however, he wondered at the nature of the faith which thus influenced her, and once, when she returned from sacrificing in one of the temples, he said to her,—

"Valeria, what did your father teach you about the immortal gods?"

"That they are pleased with us when we do right,"

she said, "and displeased when we do wrong; that they accept our sacrifices, and reward those who worship them."

"Do you worship them all equally?" he asked.

"No," she said; "you know there are the great gods and the lesser; the gods of the Roman State, and the household gods; and the immortal goddesses, the mothers of the gods; and Diana, and the rest of the Olympians; besides the nymphs of the rivers and the woods."

"What do you know of their history?" he asked.

"Not much," she said. "I only know they care for us, and have sometimes been seen on earth, and that they hear us when we invoke them."

"How do you know that?" he asked.

"My father told me so," she replied, with a wondering look.

"You never, then, met with any who had seen or heard them?" he rejoined.

"No," she replied; "except, perhaps, in dreams. I have had dreams of them myself," she continued, with some hesitation.

"What kinds of dreams?" he asked.

"I saw the mother of the gods once," she said, in a low voice, casting down her eyes; "seated on a beautiful flowery hill, dressed in purple like the Empress, with a face like my mother's on the cameo, and she smiled on me very graciously."

He smiled, and smoothed her hair with his hand.

You do not think, then, that the immortal gods walk on earth now."

"Not often, I think," she said; "but they used to come often, you know. Do you not wish they would come again?"

"I am not sure," he replied, rather absently; "that is,

I am not sure about all of them. You have never, then, read their histories?"

"No," she replied; "my father said they were not written in a way for young girls to understand."

"Your father, no doubt, was right," he said.

"But now that I am a matron," resumed Valeria, inquiringly, "perhaps I ought to know more?"

"I hardly think so," he replied, drily; "you seem to me to know enough."

"Then there are the Lares," she resumed; "I have an especial devotion for them, Aurelius; and often when I crown the images of the ancestors, I fancy the shade of my own mother may be hovering near and smiling on me."

"Do the shades then leave the fields of the dead below?" he asked.

"I think they must," she replied; "because some wicked people are afraid of them, you know; besides, I have certainly seen my mother in a dream. Do not you think so?"

"I do not know," he replied; "I never had such dreams. But I like your history of the immortals very much."

"Is it not, then, the same as yours?" she asked simply, looking up.

"We are both Romans," he replied, evasively. "Of course our gods are the same. What do you pray to the immortal gods for?" he resumed.

"I used to ask them to protect me and my father, and to make us prosperous. And lately I have asked them more than all to be favourable to you."

"But suppose the immortal gods were *not* to make us prosperous, Valeria?" he rejoined, after a pause.

"I never thought of that," she said.

And so the conversation dropped.

Every kind of prosperity was showered on that household. Health, and peace, and love reigned there. Valeria went again and again to offer her sacrifices of thanksgiving in the Temple of the Mother of the Gods, bearing her infants in her arms. In all her house and in all her life there seemed no shadow, unless it might be occasionally on the thoughtful brow of Aurelius. But the caresses of the little ones seemed able even to charm that away.

And yet there was an exception that sometimes caused the one religious perplexity to the gentle heart to Valeria.

From her childhood her father had owned a British slave, named Gwendolin, who had been her nurse, had accompanied her to the house of her husband, and had now become the nurse of her children.

Kindly treated, she had served her young mistress with affectionate fidelity. But there was a settled depression in her demeanour, which no efforts of Valeria could long dissipate. And since the birth of the children, Gwendolin had often been found weeping silently as she rocked them to sleep, whilst sometimes tears would even choke the low lullabies she crooned to them in her own wild Celtic tongue.

At length, one evening, Valeria questioned her why she wept.

"I have sung these lullabies by the cradles of other little ones before," sobbed the slave, all the pent-up feeling breaking through in one wild burst of agony; "my own! my own!"

Valeria gazed in wonder at the weeping woman, as if a whole new unknown world had opened with an earthquake beneath her feet.

Gwendolin had been to her the faithful slave, the tender nurse, an appanage and portion of her own happy life ; and now she sat weeping before her, a woman, a mother, with a whole hidden life-history of her own, and that a history of sorrow !

Valeria had little comfort to offer. She could only murmur,—

"The immortal gods are wise and mighty, Gwendolin. We must submit."

"*Your* gods!" exclaimed the slave. "The gods of your Rome!—what are they to me? Yes, I know too well that they are mighty ;—or, at least, I know your legions are mighty. Have they not torn from me husband, father,—all I had? Have I not stood in your Roman slave-market—I, a chieftain's daughter, and a chieftain's wife? Have I not seen my babes sold from me there? What care your gods for me?"

Valeria was silent. She did not clearly know whether this was blasphemy, or whether it was not true. Different nations, she had been told, had different gods ; and she felt a dim sense that the gods of the conquered could not be any very effectual help. She, therefore, fell back on the power of human sympathy.

"Gwendolin," she said, "I am very sorry for you. If I had known, I would not have had you torn from your home for the world!" And with a mother's faith in the omnipotence of her children's love to soothe and cheer, she added, "These little ones shall be to you, as far as may be, as your own. Have not you been as a mother to me, a motherless child?"

Gwendolin's tears fell more freely and less bitterly. "Yes, you are very good," she replied. "Forgive me if I seem ungrateful ; but these little ones were different,— they were my own. I had a right to their love!"

Valeria sat for some time in silence, and then she said—

"But have you not also gods whom you can invoke? Have not your dead also regions where they meet in the lower worlds?"

"What do I know?" Gwendolin replied, bitterly. "My people's gods have not saved them nor me. The priesthood of my race is gone, slain or banished far by your legions. The sacred fires glow no more through the midsummer night; the temples are silent; the sacred groves are deserted. No longer is the sacred mistletoe gathered, with the golden knife, from the oak by moonlight, while the white bulls are sacrificed below. And," she murmured in a low voice, "no more do the cries of the conquered rise from the burning piles, to propitiate the spirits of our dead and the gods of our race."

"Had you, then, temples?" asked Valeria.

"Temples to which your little buildings of brick and shapen stone were as the toys of children."

"Where?"

"In solitary places—on the great silent hills—by the sea-shore; huge circles of unhewn stone, circle within circle, each stone in itself a tower; the floor, the green herbage; the roof, the great sweep of heaven."

"And you had sacrifices?"

"Yes," was the reply "real sacrifices! Not of lambs only, and flowers, and heifers—such offerings as children might bring—but living men!"

"Did they offer themselves willingly?" asked Valeria, shuddering.

"Willingly! No. Sometimes, indeed, our women chose to die with their husbands; as who would not who could choose? Our warriors brought the victims, and our Druids sacrificed them. Life for life; human blood for human blood. What do the gods care for sheep, and goats, and garlands of summer flowers?"

Valeria shuddered.

"Your gods must be hard to please," she said. "And what welcome do they give your dead?"

"Who among the dead has come back to say?" replied Gwendolin, bitterly. "Some say their spirits are born again in other bodies; some, that they wander in an unseen world below, where all debts are paid and all crimes avenged. But I," she said, mournfully, "I, a slave woman! what do I know?"

Then they fell into a long silence, and listened to the soft breathing of the children as they slept.

At length Valeria said,—

"Why did you never tell me this before, Gwendolin?"

"I did not mean to tell you now," was the reply. "The words broke from my heart with the tears. Do not you remember Africanus?"

"Africanus, the Christian slave, who was sent to the mines for blaspheming the immortal gods?"

"Yes, lady. Why should I have risked his fate by speaking to you of the gods of my people?"

"But that is quite another thing," said Valeria. "Your gods are the gods of your race, and you cannot help it if your race is not mine. But Africanus, my father said, was of an abominable sect, who blaspheme the gods of all nations, and want every one to worship instead a man who was crucified three hundred years ago in Palestine. Crucified! a death no just or honourable man ever dies! Besides, my father says the Christians are not only fanatical and impious atheists, but they are seditious men, and have a net-work of secret societies throughout the empire, endangering everywhere the public peace."

"Africanus seemed a harmless creature," said Gwendolin, listlessly. "He was the only one who ever cared to speak a comforting word to me."

And so the mistress and the slave talked in low voices by the sleeping children, until the little ones awoke and brought back their thoughts from the shadows of the past and the invisible; to both of them so shadowy, to Gwendolin so dark. Kisses on soft, baby cheeks nestled to theirs—caresses of baby arms—how warm and how real beside those cold and unseen worlds! Why had they wandered thither? Valeria felt as if awaking from a dark and troubled dream.

But, for Gwendolen, one whole such sunny, woman's world of love had actually faded and vanished away into that land of shadows. And Valeria could not shake off from her a sympathetic sense of darkness and terror. A shadow had been thrown over the present, and an element of perplexity into the future, which, for the first time, made a rent in the small perfect world of her life, rounded off with its own green, flowery circle of earth, and its own blue, sunny arch of sky. She began to have a dim perception that the arch of heaven was something more than the roof, sun-lit or star-spangled, of her home.

Valeria was strictly a keeper at home. It was therefore quite an event to her when, one bright day in early May, she and Gwendolin, with the children—the prattling boy who was her first-born, and the baby-girl—set off in a lectica with silken curtains, drawn by two mules, with her husband riding beside her, and an escort of armed slaves, to pay a visit to an old friend in a villa on the Thames, near the station of London.

With an eager delight, almost as great as her boy's, she pointed out to him the white and red cattle grazing in the meadows by the rivers which they crossed. Here and there Aurelius pointed out to her the scene of a battle, where, in days now past by three or four generations, the Britons had been defeated; and she saw Gwendolin's face grow rigid, and turned the subject.

Now, along the firm level of the well-paved Roman road (the well-known Watling Street) on which they travelled, there was nothing to remind them that they were not travelling in the neighbourhood of Rome itself.

The people they met for the most part returned their Latin salutations. Roman mile-stones marked the distances on the road. The British chieftains whom they met were not to be distinguished by their dress from the conquerors. In the recesses of the forests through which their way sometimes lay, no doubt they might have found native herdsmen; huts and villages scarcely reached by the slight surface-culture of the Latin civilization. But to Valeria the journey was as easy, and as much on Roman ground as if she had been travelling from Rome to Capua. On the broken heights of Hampstead Heath, glowing with gorse and heather, they paused to look down on the colony of London. The long summer day was declining, and from the burning sky behind them soft rosy lights kindled up the white walls and temples of the city in the valley beneath—unconscious cradle of the metropolis of an empire wide as that of Rome itself. The little boy, wakening from his sleep, laughed to see the wild birds dipping their wings in the pool on the very ridge of the height as it shone golden in the sunlight; and to watch the deer which had come to drink, bounding away down through the green glades, till they were lost among the perspective of the massive trunks. So they descended through the oak woods to where the Thames reflected on its broad smooth surface Roman temples, baths, and porticoes, through an air, on that summer evening, clear and pure as that of Rome.

The experience of those few days—the first she had ever spent from under her father's or her husband's roof—was as an earthquake to all Valeria's ideas of the world.

If her conversation with Gwendolin had opened her eyes to some of the sorrows of life, those days in Londinium disclosed to her the sins and corruptions of the corrupt society amidst which she had been innocently and ignorantly living, in a way which appalled and disgusted her beyond utterance, and made the whole ground of life seem to her as a slippery and treacherous ice concealing an abyss of foul and stagnant waters.

On the first evening after her return to her home, Aurelius asked how she had enjoyed her visit.

"Oh, Aurelius," she said with a quivering lip, "let me never leave my home again!"

"Has my dove been so terrified by this one flight out of her nest?"

"Of course I was safe with you," she said; "but the world is too wicked! The theatres, it was an insult to have been asked to go and hear what was said there! But the houses and the very temples seem no better, and they even venture to tell scandalous stories of the immortal gods!"

"These things are not new, Valeria," she replied; "and at Rome they are worse."

"But who dared to invent evil things concerning the gods, as if they also lived not to do what is right, but what is pleasant for the moment; and as if they made no distinction between the wicked and the good? Of what avail would immortality be if the next world is to be such as this, and if the very gods were not as good as virtuous men? Aurelius," she asked suddenly and passionately, "what do you believe?"

He paused a few minutes.

"I think," he then replied, "that the infinite and the divine exist in the world opposed to the blind force of matter and of nature. I think also that spirit is eternal, and that in some form or other, all that is spiritual in us must, therefore, ever continue to exist."

"But is that all?" she said with a shudder. "You *think*. I want to *know*. I want, not 'the divine,' Aurelius, but a God. I want not to exist on as the air does, I know not how or where; but to live on with you, and my father, and the children."

"Live on then now, my beloved," he said, with mournful tenderness. "Have you *not* me, and your father, and the little ones? Why should we not hope that to-morrow, and to-morrow, and countless to-morrows will be as bright for us as to-day?"

"I think of Gwendolin," she said, sighing. "What compensation have the morrows brought to her?"

Then suddenly changing the subject, she said, "Aurelius, what are those Christians? They seem everywhere. They spoke in London of their being persecuted, tortured, imprisoned, slain in every region of the empire, and yet springing up everywhere as if they were indestructible; and," she added with some hesitation, "one morning early, as I was returning from the temple I heard low sweet singing in a house which I passed. I stopped to listen, and the words were something like this, 'Glory in the highest to God, and on earth peace, goodwill among men,' and then followed praises to the 'heavenly King, the Father who ruleth all,' and strangely blended with these were words which seemed to me very lofty and beautiful, were praises of Jesus Christ, whom they seemed to call the Son of God, and to speak of as 'sitting on the right hand of the Father.' What did it mean? There was a sacredness and solemnity in their way of singing, which seemed so different from the careless levity of those in the temple I had just left. Aurelius, tell me more about these Christians. Are they really so bad? Since much I thought good seems so evil, may not they be better than I thought?"

"They are not bad, I think," he said, perhaps not even dangerous to the state, but only fanatical and superstitious—'infructuosi in negotio, in publico muti, in angulis garruli,'" he added, quoting an opinion of his time. "I have two books about them by the learned Lucian and Celsus. If you like I will read you some things that these authors say."

From a little niche with carved cedar doors he drew two manuscripts, unrolled them, laid his hand on the passages, and read. Lucian says,—

"They (the Christians) still worship that great man who was crucified in Palestine, because it was he who introduced into human life the initiation into these new mysteries. These miserable creatures have persuaded themselves that they are immortal, and will live for ever. For this reason they despise death itself, and many even give themselves up to it. But again, their first lawgiver has persuaded them that as soon as they have broken loose from the prevailing customs, and denied the gods of Greece, reverencing in their stead their own crucified teacher, and living after his laws, they stand to each other in the relation of brothers. Thus they are led to hold everything equally in contempt, to consider as profane whatever does not agree with their own notions, which, however, they have adopted without any sufficient warrant."

And Celsus writes, "They refuse to give reasons for what they believe, but are ever repeating, 'Do not examine, only believe; thy faith will make thee blessed. Wisdom is a bad thing in life, foolishness is good. Let no educated, no wise man approach, but whoever is ignorant and uneducated, whoever is like a child, let him come and be comforted.'" And again, "Those who invite us to be initiated into the mysteries of other religions begin by proclaiming, 'Let him draw near who is pure from all stains, who is conscious of no wickedness, who has lived a good and upright life.' This is their proclamation who promise purification from sins. But let us hear the invitation of those Christians, '*Whoever is a sinner*,' they cry, '*whoever is foolish, is unlettered, in a word, whoever is wretched, him will the kingdom of God receive.*'"

"Quite a fanatical set of people, you see, my love," observed Aurelius, laying aside the manuscripts, "at once base and proud, contemptible, and despising others; with some good ideas, no doubt, borrowed from philosophy, but not at all people we could wish to learn of."

"I see," replied Valeria, with some disappointment, awed into acquiescence by the double authority of her husband and of a written book, "they must be very presumptuous and foolish. But," she added musingly, "it does seem as if it were a religion that might do for Gwendolin. With so many temples for the prosperous, and so many philosophies for the wise, perhaps the immortal gods may have meant that there shall at last be one religion for the wretched and the unlettered. I wonder if this Christianity might comfort the slaves."

Valeria had brought back other reminiscences from Londinium besides that dark glimpse into the world.

A pestilence had broken out there before their departure, and a week after their return to Verulam the mother and the slave sat watching by the sick-beds of the two little children.

The little rosy faces were flushed with fever, the bright eyes were wandering and meaningless, the hot lips, but yesterday fresh as dewy rosebuds, moaned incessantly, and the little arms that used to cling so tenderly tossed restlessly about in helpless entreaty.

Night and day the mother watched and prayed to the immortals, and tried every remedy she could hear of, but, one by one, she saw every effort to relieve the little sufferers fail, until at last the mother's passionate struggle with death ceased. The infant lay lifeless in its cradle, the boy lay dying on his mother's knee.

Valeria would not have the precious remains reduced to ashes. Wrapped in these holiday garments she had woven for them and so often dressed them in with kisses and laughter in the happy days gone by, she laid them in little wooden coffins, such as many of the native Britons used, and had them enshrined in a marble mausoleum in a garden by the river, near the town.

For many weeks she utterly refused all sympathy, not with bitter words, but in silent irresponsive despair. No words penetrated into the heart of her grief. She had no hope, and she sought no comfort. Her grief was the dearest thing she had left, for it was all that remained to her of her joy.

She made no visits to the temples. The household gods remained uncrowned. No libations and prayers turned her bread of tears into sacrifices and feasts. But daily, morning and evening, she visited the tomb of her lost darlings, and garlanded it with flowers, and perfumed it with "ointments very precious." She had no hope even there; the fair precious limbs she knew would perish—were perishing—into undistinguishable dust; but she had nothing besides.

Sometimes her husband went with her, and more than once he said, "My beloved, is not this sorrow also mine?" She admitted his right to weep with her, but still in spirit she wept alone. Despair knows not participation. The world was for Aurelius; but her world had been those little ones, and they were gone, for ever and for ever gone.

Nor did this grief bind her more to Gwendolin. It brought them nearer indeed to a level, but not nearer each other. With the selfishness of hopeless sorrow, Valeria shrank with uncontrollable dread from that widowed and desolate woman, as if she had been the evil genius of the house; whilst Gwendolin, in her heart, bitterly compared the grief which still left Valeria so much, with her own utter desolation.

At length one day her father felt it necessary gently to reprove her grief.

"My child," he said, "thou art not the first who has known sorrow. The immortal gods live still and are almighty. We must bow to their decree. Does not the supreme Jove himself bow to the decree of Destiny?"

"I do bow," she replied, "who can help it? But I cannot pray. Of what avail is it? Will the gods bring me back my dead? Or can they?"

"But think," he said, "have they nothing more to take?"

"Father," she replied with a calm bitterness, "when they please they will take all I have. I know it. I cannot move them. I do not say they are cruel, and you say they are wise; but if the supreme Jove himself cannot turn back or anticipate the decree of Destiny, why should I pray to him? I might as well seek to stop the wheels of Fate with my feeble hands as with my prayers."

"But the gods have their rights," he replied, "and whether it avails or not, we must render them their due."

"Father," she replied, "I will obey. But do not ask me to pray."

Thenceforth she repaired with offerings to the temples as of old, and garlanded the household gods; and the old man was satisfied. But one bright, warm summer evening, when the twilight brightened longest on into the night, on the 21st of June, as she and Gwendolin were returning from the garden in which was that precious tomb, the city was in a tumult, and Aurelius came to guard them through the excited crowd.

"What does this mean?" she asked.

"Amphibalus, a Christian priest, has been found concealed in the house of Alban," he said, "and Alban has assumed the Christian's clothes, and given himself up to punishment instead of his guest."

"Were they strangers to each other?" asked Valeria.

"Until these last few days it seems they were; but now both are Christians; and no Christians are strangers to each other, but brothers, for the sake of Him who died in Palestine."

"I remember," she said, "that was what you read me

from the book. But Alban was a worshipper of the gods. I have seen him in the temples with his parents."

"He has become a Christian."

"How? who persuaded him?"

"I do not know," he replied rather carelessly. "These Christians have great powers of persuasion." But Aurelius himself was infected with Valeria's interest. Since the death of the children she had scarcely asked a spontaneous question, or cared to listen to any tidings. He hailed her curiosity as a sign of returning life, and took pains to procure her all the information he could.

In the evening, after making inquiries in the town, he returned to her, and said, "It seems that this guest of Alban's was, in his way, a good and devout man, and the young host was much struck by the time he spent in prayer, both night and day, especially as those Christians have no images, but kneel down and speak aloud, as if to some one who, though unseen to others, was visible to them. Alban entered into conversation with his guest, and at length gave himself to his teaching, and became a worshipper of his God."

"What will they do to him?" asked Valeria.

"I scarcely know," was the reply. "Our rulers in Britain are tolerant to all, but the decrees of the emperors are very severe, and this young man refuses to sacrifice."

"*You* will have nothing to do with punishing him!" said Valeria eagerly.

"I have no need," he replied. "I am not the governor."

"But my father need not imbrue his hands in the blood of this youth," she said. "What evil has he done?"

"If there is an execution," he replied, "your father, as an officer of the legion, must be present."

The morrow dawned.

The martyr was brought before the governor, and after being reprimanded for concealing a sacrilegious and seditious person, was required to sacrifice.

He steadfastly refused.

"Then," said the judge, "of what family or race are you?"

"What does it concern you of what stock I am?" the young man replied (probably seeking not to implicate his kindred). "If you desire to hear the truth of my religion, be it known to you that I am now a Christian, and bound by Christian duties."

"I ask your name, not your religion," said the judge; "tell it me immediately."

"I am called Alban by my parents," he replied; "and I worship and adore the true and living God, who created all things."

Then the judge, sternly interrupting him, commanded him to delay no longer to sacrifice to the great gods.

Alban rejoined, "These sacrifices, which by you are offered to devils, can neither benefit the subjects, nor answer the desires of those who offer up their supplications to them. On the contrary, whosoever shall offer to these images shall receive everlasting pains for his reward."

"He called the immortal gods devils!" exclaimed Valeria, as her husband related this to her. "Yet was not what he said about prayer too true, Aurelius?"

He was silent.

"The prayers of the Christians do not, at all events, seem to save them from suffering," he said at length.

"Perhaps they ask for something else," she said thoughtfully. "You say they seem so willing to die!

Perhaps they ask for things in the other world. But, Aurelius, do they all call the gods devils? Perhaps," she added doubtfully, " they are thinking of the dreadful things I heard about the Olympians at Londinium."

"Probably," he said absently.

"What will they do to him?"

"He will be scourged, and probably then beheaded."

"When?"

"To-day."

"And where?"

"On the wooded hill across the river."

All day Valeria watched from her upper chamber in the tower of the house, which looked over the town and the river, towards the hill, to see what would happen. Towards evening the bridge became crowded, and she saw a solitary figure ford the little stream near it. The crowd gathered round him when he reached the opposite bank, and all went up the hill together. There was an eager buzz and murmur, succeeded by loud, tumultuous shouts, and then by a dead silence. After that, soldiers, citizens, women, and children, came slowly down the hill again. But there was no noise. An awe seemed to have fallen upon all; and in the dusk Valeria thought she saw two bodies borne across the bridge. The people returned silently to their homes through the streets, as if from burying their own dead.

Soon afterwards she heard her father's voice in the house below—the silent house, where now no little ringing voices echoed.

The old man was strangely moved. "I have heard of these things," he said, "but it is another thing to see. That boy died with the firmness of a senator of old Rome. But with a joy," he added, "that seems to me something beyond! These men do indeed believe they are immortal."

"Were there not two bodies borne across the bridge?" asked Valeria.

"Yes; these doctrines penetrate everywhere. The very executioner refused his office, and chose rather to die as a Christian with the condemned. And indeed, if what supported that boy in death were true, perhaps he could not have done better."

"Father," said Valeria, laying her hands in his, "would it not be well to see if this doctrine can be true? Everything else seems so dim and so uncertain!"

"My child, it is death to believe this. Death even for thee! The edicts spare none."

"*Death* spares none!" she said mournfully; "and if this immortal life should indeed be certain, and we could only know it! Aurelius," she said, as he came in, "I want to know more of this religion which speaks to the wretched, and makes men to whom life might be dear rejoice to die."

"It is a perilous inquiry now," he replied. "And what can any tell us, more than you learned from your early ancestral faith: that the virtuous dead exist in unmolested tranquillity on the shores of the blessed?"

"That was enough for me once," she said, "before the babes had been taken thither from my bosom. Before that dreadful day, those shadowy shores seemed real enough. But now that those precious ones are there— those darlings that have nestled to my heart and smiled into my eyes—all seems dim, empty, and unutterably cold and dark. It is not so much even of immortality I want to be assured, as of some immortal beings who are there on those shadowy shores, to warm that cold world with their presence—to take my little ones by the hand, from my heart to theirs, until I may go to them. The immortal gods are on Olympus. If I could only learn of some god who welcomed the dead, and would be the sunshine of the worlds below. Without that, what is immortality itself but a blank abyss, without light or limit? It is not enough for me even to hear, 'Thy babes still exist.' I want a voice I could trust, to say, 'Thy babes *live with me.*'"

"But how will you learn this from the Christians?" Aurelius asked.

"I have heard," she said, "that some of the sufferers speak of death as 'going to be with Christ;' and I should like to know what that means. Aurelius, can no one teach us?"

"They have sacred books," he replied; and almost glad to see Valeria once more interested in any subject, however perilous, the next day he brought her a Gospel of St. John, and deposited the dangerous treasure in the niche with cedar doors, beside the volumes of Lucian and Celsus. By that time the enemies of Christianity had discovered that its strength lay in those mysterious sacred books; and the persecution of Diocletian was distinguished from all preceding ones by the search for these prohibited Scriptures, to ensure their destruction.

Evening after evening, when all was quiet in the house and in the town, Aurelius spread the roll on his knee and read, while Valeria, forgetting her distaff, sat on a cushion at his feet and listened; and her father, for the first time in his life, was rivetted by any writing, not an imperial edict, or a record of military achievement.

For some time they made few observations. Aurelius was the first who seemed to grow uneasy. On the second night, after reading the interview with Nicodemus, and with the woman of Samaria, he said,—

"It is what I thought. A blending of the later Platonism with some mystical Jewish ideas."

"But," said Valeria, eagerly, "it is Platonic doctrine brought down to *me !* I could never understand your Platonism, but I seem to understand this. See, it speaks not of the Divine and the Infinite, but of a Son of God, who was also a Son of man, and dwelt among us, and healed the sick, and answered quite plainly and simply all those who came to learn of him, even that poor, lonely woman!"

But when they came to the parable of the Good Shepherd, her large dark eyes opened with an expression of wondering joy, and she said in a low, deep voice,—

"Now I understand it all!"

And taking off her signet ring she kissed it reverently.

It was an intaglio of a shepherd carrying a lamb in his bosom.

"Aurelius," she said, "this is Christ! And the lambs must mean the little children. Father," she exclaimed, solemnly, "this ring was my mother's! Was she then a Christian?"

"I scarcely know," he replied with some hesitation. "She died among strangers in a strange city, while I was with the army. Christian women nursed her; for she died of a pestilence, of which none else would risk the infection. And after her death they sent me this ring as her last memorial. I could not tell what gloomy superstitions might have seized on the dying, and I never heard anything more."

"But this is not a gloomy superstition!" Valeria said. The old man made no opposition, and Aurelius read on.

Sentence by sentence the divine words sank into that childlike and broken heart; until when Aurelius came to the words, "Blessed are those that have not seen, and yet have believed," she clasped her hands, and looking up to him with a smile, such as he had not seen on her face since their babes were smitten, she said,—

"See, there is a message left exactly for us. We have not seen, and we will believe!"

"You believe?" he said doubtfully.

"How can I help it?" she said. "It is exactly what I want, what every one must want, and what no one ever thought of before. Is it not all that all men have always been longing for; and yet what no man ever discovered? Whence then could this message come but from heaven; from Him who knows? Father, is it not so?"

"The character of Christ is very wonderful," said the old man. "Severe as a Roman of the noble old times against falsehood and injustice; tender as a woman to the suffering of others, yet uncomplaining as Regulus amidst suffering of his own! If God is like this," he continued, "heaven is worth dying for; and if man can be made like this, life is better worth living, than in late evil years I have thought."

Much yet remained, however, before Valerius and Aurelius would yield up the prejudices of years. Intellectual pride in Valerius struggled long against a religion which denounced all intellectual caste, and admitted all on equal grounds, only as little children. Pride of a pure life, and an honest dread of confounding the stern distinctions between right and wrong, repelled the old soldier from a Gospel which received none, except on their knees, as penitent sinners.

It was only gradually, through a continuous study of

the sacred writings, that the vision of the truth revealed in them rose and expanded before the mind of Aurelius, until he learned to rejoice in bowing as a little child before a wisdom, beside which all other wisdom seemed but as the chance guesses of children, or the dim gropings of men half blind. He comprehended at length that when the Son of God requires men to become as little children, he does not do so that they may be dwarfed and stunted; but that laying aside all the follies of precocious manhood, they may grow to be truly men.

And gradually, through those same Scriptures, the ideal of holiness rose and expanded before the conscience of Valerius, until he listened with a gratitude as great as that of any publican to the words, "I came not to call the righteous, but sinners to repentance."

It seemed very strange to Valeria that Gwendolin, who seemed of all to need the words of divine comfort most, was the slowest to receive them.

"The more I want it to be true," she said, "the more afraid I am that it may not be." She wondered why, if it was indeed true, God had been so long in sending the Comforter to a world so steeped in wretchedness and crime. Sorrow to her had been an embittering and hardening pressure. There was a kind of desolate pride in the isolation and completeness of her griefs; and it was long before she could admit the ideas of love and joy. At length, when the Gospel reached her, it was not so much as a refuge from sorrow as a deliverance from sin. It was not so much with the cry, "I have suffered,—heal me!" as with the confession, "I have sinned,—forgive me!" that this lost sheep came back. "I have hated, envied, and despised all the happy. I have hated and resisted Thee!" she learned at last to say, with penitent, child-like tears. And, being forgiven, she grew to believe she might yet be blessed. It was long before the rain and dew from heaven could penetrate that parched and dried-up heart; but when once the softening influence was felt, it seemed as if she could never receive enough; and the transformation was more manifest in her than in any of the rest,—as from the desert to the garden of the Lord.

Years passed on. The persecution (which had on the whole fallen but lightly on Britain) ceased. The emperors, who had triumphantly added to their other titles the glory of "having destroyed the Christian name and superstition throughout the east and west," confessed at length that their "benign efforts to bring the Christians back to the religion of their fathers had failed," and that henceforth, "provided they did nothing contrary to Roman discipline, they might continue to hold their assemblies;" and concluded with exhorting them, after experiencing this proof of imperial indulgence, to pray to God "for our prosperity, and for their own."

Other children were born to gladden the hearts and home of Aurelius and Valeria. But the little tomb in the garden by the river Ver continued to be the sacred spot of the household. The little ones were early taught to garland it with flowers, and to anoint it with perfumes, according to the Christian customs of those times; for the mother had learned that the dust of her beloved was precious, not merely as a sacred relic, but as an immortal seed of life; and none of the prevalent controversies concerning the destinies of unbaptized infants could shake her simple trust in the Good Shepherd who, she was persuaded, had carried her lambs home in His bosom.

What that tomb was to her, the death-place of the martyr Alban became to the whole Church at Verulam. Solemnly, on festival days, the little Christian band went across the bridge, and up the wooded slopes of the opposite hill, "adorned, or rather clothed, with all kinds of flowers, having its sides neither perpendicular nor even craggy, but sloping down into a beautiful plain, worthy, from its lovely appearance, to be the scene of a martyr's sufferings." There, in a green forest-glade, on the crown of the hill (afterwards called Holmehurst, or the Woody Place), those early Christians delighted to meet, and to chant the praises of Him to whom their city had sent one of her sons to join the noble army of His martyrs. And there also, probably, they gave thanks that the last persecution had swept over the Church, and the last martyr-blood had stained the land.

More than twelve hundred years passed over the martyr's grave on the hill, and with them swept away Romans, Britons,—even the Roman Empire itself,—burying not only the inhabitants, but the very walls and dwellings of Verulam.

On the woody slopes, up which the martyr had gone to his death, rose the houses of a new city, called by his name; and the crest of the hill where he suffered was crowned by an abbey, believed to be made doubly sacred by the presence of his relics.

Yet up that hill once more a martyr was to be led to die; and once more the authority by whose bidding he was to suffer claimed its sanction from Rome.

Early one summer morning little Margery Joyce and her widowed mother were rambling on the banks of the river Ver, just below the old town of St. Albans,—the mother culling medicinal herbs, and the child as busy gathering wild flowers, which she was skilled in making into posies, to sell, and so eke out their scanty living. When the sun began to rise high, they rested, to take their mid-day meal of bread and cresses, under the shade of a fragment of old Roman wall.

"Mother," said the child, picking up a broken piece of tesselated pavement, "what are these strange old stones?"

"They say they were the work of the Romans, who had a great city here hundreds and hundreds of years ago!"

"What! the Pope of Rome?"

"No; another kind of Romans,—great soldiers, who once conquered all the land; and heathens."

"What! where these docks and nettles grow, and where the cows graze in the meadows, were there once streets and houses?"

"Yes. I have heard your grandfather, who was a learned man, say there were palaces here, with beautiful floors of many-coloured stones; and temples of the old heathen gods."

"What! the false gods we read of in the Bible?" asked the child; "the gods they burned little children to please?"

"I am not sure, Margery; I think they were the gods St. Paul and Barnabas were mistaken for, when they burned oxen and garlands, and would have sacrificed to them."

"And here, on these meadows, there were really streets and houses, and men and women living in them, and little children playing in them? Mother, it is better than a fairy tale. Tell me more."

"The hill opposite us, where the town stands now."

continued Widow Joyce, "was then, they say, a green wooded hill, covered with wild flowers."

"That must have been beautiful!" said the child.

To her the city of a thousand years ago seemed like an enchanted place; and the flowery fields of a thousand years ago like a garden of dreams. It never occurred to her that old Verulam was as every-day a place to its inhabitants as St. Albans was to her; or that the flowers the children of long ago gathered on the wooded heights, now sobered into streets, were neither more nor less fair than those which she had gathered that morning from above the buried temples and palaces of the old city.

"How beautiful it must have been!" she said. "I should like to have lived then, mother,—should not you?"

"I hardly know," said the mother; "those also were cruel times. On the crest of the hill where the cathedral stands, those old Romans once put a good man to death, striking off his head because he would not deny the Lord Jesus Christ. His name was Alban. And long afterwards, when the country became Christian, they gathered the martyr's bones, and built the abbey over them. And so in time the city of the old Romans perished, and the new city grew up around the martyr's grave."

"Then I would not indeed have lived in those times, mother!" said Margery. "Yet," she added, thoughtfully, "I thought you said they burned a good man the other day because he would not do what God had told him not. And burning must be worse than beheading. There must then be some wicked men in the world now, mother."

The widow sighed, and, gathering up her herbs, took the child's hand, and walked back towards the town.

"There are always wicked men, child," she said, "but

God is mightier than the devil. See, the grass grows over the ruined palaces of the persecutor, and the grave of the martyr is the crown and glory of the land. It says this shall be so in the Bible; and we see it with our eyes."

As she spoke they came near the narrow bridge. They found it occupied with a cavalcade, which they waited to let pass. There were a few soldiers, and several of the county yeomanry. The high sheriff himself rode at the head of the company, and the mayor of St. Albans had just come down the hill to meet him. But Margery saw her mother's eyes rivetted on a pale, quiet-looking man, who was bound and closely guarded in the midst of the throng; and when the horsemen swept up the hill she asked who it was.

"I think it must be George Tankerfield the Gospeller," was the whispered reply. "It was reported they would bring him here."

"What for?" asked the child; "what has he done?"

"What St. Alban did long ago, my child," said the widow in a low voice.

"What will they do to him, mother?"

"What they did to the old martyr; or worse!" was the solemn answer. "They are leading another martyr, Margery, up that hill to die!"

"Oh, mother!" said the child, "will God let them?"

"He may let the martyr suffer," said Widow Joyce, mournfully. "But," she added in a firm voice, "He will not let the enemy prevail."

As they went up the street, the people stood on their door-steps looking after the cavalcade; and many a murmured "God bless him," and also some muttered curses on the heretic, fell on Margery's ear.

The high sheriff, with the prisoner and the escort, put up at Cross Keys Inn.

Many thronged to see the condemned man, both friends and foes; and among them Widow Joyce took her little Margery. As in the early Christian times, men and women in those days again and again courageously risked danger and even death only to say a word of reverent sympathy to their suffering brethren, or even to give a friendly grip to the hand so soon to be reduced to ashes for the Master's sake.

Many a contradictory opinion Margery heard as she stood with her mother just outside the door. "Some were sorry to find so pious a man brought to be burned; others praised God for his constancy and perseverance in the truth. Contrariwise, some said it was pity he did stand in such opinions; and others, both old men and women, cried against him; one called him heretic, and said that it was not fit that he lived. But Tankerfield spake unto them so effectually out of the word of God, lamenting their ignorance, and protesting unto them his unspotted conscience, that God did mollify their hardened hearts, insomuch that some of them who had doubted him departed out of the chamber weeping."*

Among those who wept was little Margery Joyce; and she wept so bitterly that at last her mother had almost to carry her home.

For a long time the child sat sobbing on her mother's knee, until at last the sobs came at longer intervals, the large tears stood on her crimsoned cheek, and she lay quite still with her head on her mother's bosom, the little frame only now and then heaving with the passing storm of emotion.

* Fox's Martyrs.

"Poor little one!" said the mother at length very gently, 'I should have known better than to have laid such a weight on thy tender heart."

"Oh, mother," said the child, "it was so different from what I thought! I thought his face would have shone as the Bible says that first martyr's did, or that he would have looked so grave and solemn, it would have felt like being at church to see him. But *he is just like one of us!* His voice was so gentle, and he looked so kind, I cannot bear to think he must be put to all that pain. Oh, mother, the old martyrs could not have been like that, so like father used to look, or the people never could have made them die."

The widow took the Bible and read aloud, as well as her tears would let her, the fourteenth chapter of St. John. "There, darling!" she said, "it is to *Him* the good man is going! It is to Jesus. And it will not be long."

So she soothed the child until, weary with excitement, she fell asleep, and the widow gently laid her on the bed, and taking her distaff, seated herself quietly at her spinning-wheel, whilst she listened with eager interest for every sound in the street outside. Before long the latch was lifted, and a decent-looking woman came in, with a child in her arms.

"This is a sad business, Neighbour Joyce," she said.

"It is long since our town has seen such a day," was the low reply.

"But most of all," rejoined the woman, "my heart aches for his poor wife. It seems that she, not knowing what she did, delivered him up to his foes. He had had a heavy sickness, and had lain long in the house, when on a certain day he rose and walked into the Temple fields by the river Thames, to take the air and see the shooters. In the mean time, Mr. Beard, yeoman of the guard, came to his house and inquired for him, pretending to his wife (the false knave!) that he came only to have him dress a banquet at the Lord Paget's. His wife, poor soul, because of the yeoman's apparel, which was very rich, took him to be some great friend, and with all speed prepared herself to fetch her husband. And lest this gentleman should be tired with tarrying, she fetched a cushion to sit on, and laid a fair napkin before him, and set bread thereon, and came to tell her husband. But when he heard it, he said, 'A banquet, woman! Indeed, it is such a banquet as will not be very pleasant to the flesh! But God's will be done.' When he came home, he saw too plainly who it was, and called him by his name. And the wife, poor body, perceiving wherefore this gay gentleman had come, grew well-nigh frantic (as well she might), and seized a spit, and would have run him through, had not the constable chanced to come in and rescue him. Yet she sent a brickbat after the traitor, and hit him on the back. But all in vain; her husband was delivered to the constable, and brought to Newgate.* Poor, helpless woman's hands! what could they do against the queen's officers?"

"Let us pray she may have patience," said Widow Joyce.

"My husband says the country has need of something beside patience now," replied the neighbour, "and that men will not much longer hold their peace at these things. London is growing fractious already, and that is why they have sent him to die here. I trow they will not find that we at St. Albans like such doings much better than the

* Fox.

Londoners. Not that we are Gospellers," she continued hastily; "but who with a man or a woman's heart can stand such treacheries and cruelties as these?"

"It is said that George Tankerfield himself was no Gospeller until these persecutions drove him to it," replied Widow Joyce. "Seeing the great cruelty which the Papists used, he was brought into a doubt of their doctrines, and began in his heart to abhor them. Concerning the mass, especially, he had much doubt; and at length he fell to prayer, desiring God in mercy to open to him the truth, that he might be thoroughly persuaded therein, whether it were of God or not; if not, that he might utterly hate it in his heart. The Lord, as I believe, mercifully heard his prayer. He was moved to read the New Testament, whereby the light was poured into his mind; he grew to detest the ways of the Papists, and came no more to their doings. Moreover, the truth kindled such a flame in him, as would not be kept in; but he spoke to his friends, entreating them likewise to repent and turn to the truth with him."

"Yes," said the neighbour, uneasily, "that is the worst of those new doctrines—people cannot be quiet about them. But I would liefer be Tankerfield or his poor wife than the yeoman who took him, or even, for that matter, Master Edward Brocket the High Sheriff, who brings him here to die."

So saying, she arose, and left the widow once more alone with the sleeping child.

Meanwhile the day was slowly passing away, and the martyr, knowing that the hour was drawing nigh that he should suffer, desired the wine-drawer that he might have a pint of malmsey and a loaf, that he might eat and drink in remembrance of Christ's death and passion, because he could not have it administered to him by others in such manner as Christ commanded. And then he kneeled down, making his confession unto the Lord, with all who were in the chamber with him. And after he had prayed earnestly, and had read the institution of the Holy Supper by the Lord Jesus, out of the Evangelists and out of St. Paul, he said,—

"O Lord, thou knowest it, I do not this to derogate authority from any man, or in contempt of those who are thy ministers, but only because I cannot have it administered according to thy word."

When he had spoken these and such like words, he received it with giving of thanks. Then he was entreated to strengthen himself by taking some meat; but he said he would not eat that which should do others good that had more need, and that had longer to live than he had.

He prayed his host to let him have a good fire in the chamber, which was granted him. And then sitting on a form before it, he put off his shoes and hose, and stretched out his leg to the flame; and when it had touched his foot he quickly withdrew his leg, showing the flesh did persuade him one way, the spirit another. The flesh said, "O thou fool! wilt thou burn, and needest not? The spirit said, "Be not afraid, for this is nothing in respect of fire eternal." The flesh said, "Do not leave the company of thy friends and acquaintance, which love thee, and will let thee lack nothing." The spirit said, "The company of Jesus Christ and his glorious presence doth exceed all earthly friends." The flesh said, "Do not shorten thy time, for thou mayest live, if thou wilt, much longer." The spirit said, "This life is nothing unto the life in heaven, which lasteth for ever."

And all this time the sheriffs were at a gentleman's

house at dinner, not far from the town, whither also resorted many knights and gentlemen out of the country, because that gentleman's son was married that day; and until they returned from dinner, the prisoner was left to the care of his host, by whom he was kindly treated. And, considering that his time was short, his saying was,—

"Although the day be ever so long,
Yet, at the last, it ringeth to even song." *

So the martyr waited, and the sheriffs dined, and Widow Joyce sat spinning beside her sleeping child, the low whirr of the wheel sounding through the silent chamber as she prayed and repeated sacred words of divine promise, and listened for the terrible sounds she expected in the street without.

At length the quiet was broken. There was a hum of many voices, and a hasty moving to and fro of feet, and then the heavy tramp of armed men stepping evenly.

Widow Joyce laid aside her spinning-wheel, and went to the window and looked out. The street before her window was quite deserted and silent, as if it had been a city of tombs. Not a face at window or door. All who cared or dared to see that day's doings were gathered at the place called Romeland, a green spot near the west end of the abbey church, where the stake was set. Mothers had gathered their little ones around them within their houses, lest they should see or hear some dreadful thing. Many would gladly have closed the shutters as for a funeral. For on all the town an awe rested, like the shadow of death in every household.

* Fox.

Widow Joyce knelt and looked out, and prayed, until a strange glare lighted up the windows of the house at the opposite corner, which faced the abbey green, a strange dull glow reddening the quiet summer daylight.

Then she hid her face and looked no more into the street, but looked in her heart up to God. For she knew too surely that another martyr was in his death-agony at that moment on the crest of St. Alban's hill.

She was aroused by the sound of footsteps in the street. The light of the long summer day still rested on the town, no longer broken by the terrible glare from the opposite windows. As the people were dispersing quietly to their homes, speaking little as they went, and that little in low tones which did not reach the ears of any but those to whom they were addressed.

Thus the long day passed away, and the abbey bells rang the even song, and many went from the martyr's stake to say their vespers as usual in the abbey church.

Margery awoke, and was sitting up gazing in a bewildered way around her, when Widow Joyce arose from her knees by the window.

"Was it a dream, mother?" said Margery. "I thought I saw the kind face of that good man shining, like Stephen's, above the flames. And when I awoke, you were quietly kneeling by the window; and I heard the church bell, and I thought it must be time to say my morning prayers."

"It *has* all passed like a dream, my child," said the widow, "for that good man; and he is singing his even song, or rather his first morning hymn, in heaven, and to him the day will never darken more. See, Margery," she added, "you have scarcely been asleep two hours, and in that time the martyr has passed through this fiery trial from the beginning to the end, and has entered on an eternity of joy."

All that evening the people crept quietly about the streets, and on the morrow many awoke with a weight of awe on them, as if the old familiar streets had been hallowed into the solemnity of a cathedral; as if the common incidents of life and time had been fused into transparency, and eternity was shining through.

Many stole quietly that day to the abbey green, the spot called Romeland, and among them, at the dusk, Widow Joyce and Margery; and as they looked at the little heap of ashes and the blackened circle on the grass, an old man drew near and told them how yesterday, when the mayor and others were reviling Tankerfield for his courageous confession, "a good knight went up to him, bound as he was to the stake, and spake softly, and said '*Good brother, be strong in Christ.*' And Tankerfield replied, '*Good sir, I thank you; I am so, I thank God.*' And then the fire was set unto him, and he desired the sheriffs and all the people to pray for him, *and most of them did*, and so embracing the fire, he called on the name of the Lord Jesus, and was quickly out of pain."

As the widow and the child went home again, Margery said in a low voice,—

"Then, even *in those two hours*, mother, the good man was comforted!"

Days passed on, and things resumed their every-day aspect in St. Albans. Little children went eagerly about their play, and men and women about their pursuits. The sounds of mirth, and debate, and traffic, and of all life's cares, and joys, and sorrows, were heard again in the streets. The grass grew as green over the death-place of the martyr of that year as over that of the martyr of twelve hundred years ago.

Years passed on. The unhappy queen died, the persecution ceased; and in the church built over the relics of the first martyr of Verulam, and in the houses of the town, was read and reverenced the precious English Bible, for whose truths the last martyr of St. Albans suffered.

And in England, from that time to this, the Word of God has held the place won for it throughout the land by the deaths of many martyrs, rooted deep in the hearts of the middle and labouring classes, which are the heart of a nation, and from which most of the English martyrs sprang.

III.

ANNALS

OF AN ANGLO-SAXON FAMILY

THROUGH THREE GENERATIONS.

Story of the Abbess Frideswide, recorded by Deorwyn, the Nun, Daughter of Alfhelm and Astritha.

III.

AN ANGLO-SAXON FAMILY THROUGH THREE GENERATIONS.

STORY OF THE ABBESS FRIDESWIDE, RECORDED BY DEORWYN, THE NUN.

IT must have been in the very night when the great Abbess Hilda died that Frideswide, our mother, Prioress of our Abbey of St. John's, on the Derwent Lake, related to me the things which I am about to write.

For I remember the winds howled fiercely down the valleys, and the waves of the lake dashed against the banks like the waves of the great sea, and tearing the convent fishing-boat from its moorings, broke it in pieces. And with the sounds of winds and waters came other sounds,—voices, wild wails, and low faint moans, other than winds can make. And three days afterwards a monk came from the Abbey of Streaneschalch (Whitby), and told us how the Lady Hilda, mother of so many congregations, was dead; and then we knew why such strange terrors had seized us on that stormy night; for, doubtless, there had been great tumult among the powers of the air when that great spirit went its way through storm and cloud to God.

The night was very wild. It was a comfort when we looked across the foaming waters to see the little lamp still gleaming from the island where Herbert dwelt, the holy anchoret. Because we knew his heart also was lit, and girded, and that throughout the storm he was defending us all with his holy vigils of prayer. But the hearts of many of the younger sisters quailed. More than once the dormitory, which was only built of oak and thatched with reeds, quivered as if it would fall; and the rain came through the roof. Therefore we were all rejoiced to obey the order to rise and chant the midnight psalms in the church; and afterwards Frideswide, the abbess, permitted me, when the rest had retired, to sit with her by the fire in the great hall, while she spoke to me of the past, of the men and women she had seen, and of the dangers and deliverances of her life. Her voice could always calm us, as the voice of a mother quiets the little ones. She always spoke and looked the truth. Fear and falsehood could not find a nook in which to hide on her broad white brow, or in the blue depths of her eyes. She seldom said endearing or commendatory words; but a softening of tone in her voice, or a sign that she had observed, was more to us than countless phrases of tenderness or praise from another. She did not always insist on the minute monastic rules, as they have been enforced amongst us since. But while she lived, there was the firmest order in the convent, both among the brothers and the sisters; for ours was a double house. Not the most timid among the sisters would have dared to be a coward in her presence; nor would the boldest among the brethren have dared to question her commands. And yet she seemed to me more like one of the great women of our Saxon people than like a holy woman in the legends of the saints,—more like a wise house-mother than a saint. She prayed much, indeed, and read the Gospels; but her prayers seemed chiefly the girdle which kept the duties of her active life together; and she had no miraculous visions, and heard no wonderful voices; nor when she died were there any wonders wrought at her tomb.

But then she had been married. And I am not sure that miracles are ever wrought save at the tombs of consecrated maidens; at least it is very rare.

But of this I am sure: since then I have never seen one who loved God more; nor have we ever met with one who loved and served us as well.

Tears bedew her tomb, if it is hallowed by no sacred supernatural odours of sanctity.

She was my father's mother. And she spoke to me thus on the night that the great Abbess Hilda died:

"The good Bishop Aidan is dead, and Oswald the holy king, and many of the best men and women I have known; and more are aged, and must soon be gathered home. The memory of the aged is as a casket of treasures. Death locks it close forever, and throws the golden key into the dark waters under the foundations of the earth, whence, till the last fires are kindled which shall lay that boundless ocean bare, no man can recover it. Wherefore, child, it may be well that thou shouldst learn what happened to thy people of old.

"Our kindred came from beyond the sea. From the days when Woden led the Asæ forth to conquest from the golden halls of **Asgard** in the far East, a longing has ruled in the hearts of our race stronger than the longing of the exile for home, compelling us ever westward, westward, towards the resting-place of the sun. And here, in this island, it may be, we have reached our goal. Have I not stood on the rocky western shores and seen him sink to rest, where nothing lay between us and him but countless, boundless waves? Further west our race cannot wander. Therefore, in this island, I deem we have found our home.

"Our fathers did not find the country a desert. They had to dispossess the people of the land; to drive them from their fields and cities into the barren fastnesses, where even now they linger on the shores of Wales and Cornwall. For strength is the gift of Heaven; and it is the destiny of the strongest to rule."

"But was that right, mother?" I said.

"It was fate," she said; "and our fathers were heathens."

"But the people who were robbed of their homes must have suffered grievously," I said.

"They did, doubtless," she replied. "I have heard that the land was full of the wails of the widow and the fatherless."

"But what if any stronger still should come, mother, and do to us even as our fathers did to them?"

"Then our children would suffer," she said, "and the wail would go up, not in the Welsh, but in our own Saxon tongue,—the wail of the widow and the fatherless and the wronged. And so it will be until the strongest comes; and then the strong will rule, and the weak will serve, and the land will have rest."

"But," I said, "is the wail of the widow and the

oppressed lost in the wide air? Does it not go up to God?"

"It does, child," she said. "The strongest possess the land; but the oppressed are purified in the fire, and made holy, and are blessed in heaven."

"Then," I said, "it seems that God reigns in heaven, and strength on earth."

"God reigns in His kingdom, in heaven, and trains for His kingdom on earth," she said.

"Then the earth is but as the smith's forge," I said, "where the weapons are made. No wonder it is so full of confusion."

"Nay," she said; "it is also the battle-field where the weapons are practised."

"Then for earth itself," I said, "there is no hope. God is training men and women for heaven; but the devil is reigning among the nations, and making them rage like wild beasts."

"Not altogether so, I think," said the abbess; "I have a glimmering of hope that even for the nations on earth God has his training; only the battle is too close around us for us to understand how the day is going,—we are not high enough to see. If that wild impulse had not brought our fathers hither, they might have lived like heathens still; and, I may err, but I believe God would never suffer a nobler race to be subdued, or utterly rooted from the earth, by one less noble. Not only for their strength, but for something in them that was nobler than strength, I think our fathers possess the land. For, child, although wrong and falsehood may triumph for a time, as the sudden onslaught of a savage horde may overpower the sons of the heroes, true strength is based on right and truth. Etzel, the foul Hun, might overrun the nations; but Dietrich, the Goth, reigned after him, and the Huns were driven back from the west. And our fathers, I trow, were of nobler life than those they displaced, who had taken up the lesson from great Rome, when she herself was sinking into her premature degraded dotage. Nay, further, I deem that not only cannot the nobler be rooted up by the less noble, but that what is noble in the feeblest cannot perish. If the world is to be better for the triumph of our Saxon race, our Saxon race itself, I trust, will become nobler by the conflict, and by the mixture with the conquered. Do we not owe even our Christianity to the vanquished Roman and the enslaved Briton?

"Much evil is done under the sun, and the powers of darkness are strong; but since God, the good, is almighty, right must be mightier than wrong, not only in heaven, I deem, but on earth, and even in hell. For hell itself is no kingdom of the lawless, but the eternal prison-house of all who break the eternal laws. In the light God rules by love; in the darkness by chains; in this twilight of the earth by both.

"Had not even our heathen forefathers a glimmering of this? Does not the Völa sing of the days to come:

> 'There are fields without sowing;
> All things against us turn for us;
> Baldur, the sun-god, will come again;
> The Asæ will dwell without evils:
> Do you yet understand?
>
> A hall stands brighter than the sun,
> Covered with gold in Gimle;
> There the good will dwell,
> And enjoy all good through the ages.

> She sees arise,
> A second time,
> The earth from ocean,
> In verdant shene.'"

"Mother," I ventured to say, "who taught the heathen their wisdom? and why, since they remembered so much, did they forget so much more?"

"Every day begins in light, child," she said; "and beyond the light the strongest sight is blind. Every child can ask what no sage can answer. Hereafter, the sacred books say, there will be no night. The young say, 'We are strong, and the earth is vast; we will scale the mountains, and then we shall see into the stars.' The aged say, 'We have climbed the mountains, and the stars seem no nearer; but the earth is small, and we are feeble. We will wait.' Therefore child, we will turn away our eyes from the great world, and you shall hear the way God has led me through my little life. For a child can make a drawing of the round earth and the ocean round it, and the great Midgard serpent encircling both; but of ten men who have lived among the mountains, only one can guide you safely through them; and I deem we learn more of the ways of God by observing what he has done, than by reflecting what he might have done.

"We were born beyond the seas, I, and your father, and my brother Leofric. In our home amidst the lowlands of the German coast, near the mouth of the Elbe, we heard marvellous reports of the conquests our kindred had achieved in the fair island to the west. From one and another of the younger sons of our great families, starting in the ship which was all their heritage, with a band of adventurers, had come back in a few years rumours of victory and spoils, and of conquered cities to which our towns were mere mud villages. One and another of our race, we heard, were seated on the thrones of the vanquished, crowned kings, with captive princes kneeling as slaves at their tables, and corn-fields tilled, and flocks and herds tended by the vanquished slaves who had once been their owners.

"It seemed as if the days of the Asæ—the heroes and the founders of our race—had come back again. The tales of conquest from the island in the West rivalled, in our childish fancy, the legends of the golden halls of Asgard in the far East. Our world had two Edens. Before as well as behind us, towards the sunset whither we must go, as well as towards the sunrise whence we came, rose the royal halls of feasting, and smiled the fields green and golden, watered by the living streams.

"At length our time came. The longing which comes on the noblest of our race, the passion for wandering, strong as the love of home, came also on Wulfric, our father. One of our kindred, an ealdorman in Wessex, also sent us a call to join him against the Britons. Our mother knew what she might have to encounter when she married a brave man. Without a struggle she left her kindred and her birthplace, and, with no attendant but an aged nurse, embarked with us for the west of this island. To Leofric, my brother, and to me, the day of our embarkation was a day of the proudest and wildest delight. Our father we trusted in as the bravest and wisest man of our tribe. Proud and severe to others, the awe of his slaves, he was honoured and loved by his soldiers; and to my mother, and to us all, his pride was the pride of affection, and all his austerity but a strong shield thrown around us. The sea was as familiar to us as the land; from infancy we had steered our little boats among the creeks, and we had deemed it our greatest joy to accompany our father in his shorter voyages. And now we believed we were to sail straight into a world beautiful as the first earth which rose green from the ocean, and to reign in cities glorious as Asgard.

"On our way we were driven hither and thither by storms; but to us the storm seemed but the wilder mood of our old play-fellow. I remember how my heart throbbed, and my whole soul seemed to rise and grow as our ship plunged through the great waves; and rejoicing in the fierce might of the sea, I laughed to see how our little bark was mightier than they. For my father's hand was on the helm, and his eyes were on the waves, and as he steered us among them, although again and again the ship staggered with the blow, in another moment the broken billow was foaming powerless behind us. The hand and eye of my father I thought had mastered the waves; and thenceforth let them curvet, and shake their white manes as they would, they were but our war-horses to bear us on in a chariot of victory whither we chose to go.

"At last we landed in a creek on the western coast. I remember at first a vague feeling of disappointment at finding this new earth, with the short grass on its cliffs, not more different from our own. The grass perhaps was greener, and instead of our low sandy shores, steep cliffs rose breasting the waves. But we were treading for the first time the shores of our dreams, the land of the new Asgard, or golden city of our race; and it seemed to us the rocks ought to have been of something else than stones, and the green something more than that of common grass. However, we soon began to take delight in our new country, and we had little time for dreaming, for a stronghold had to be made at once, of turf and stones, as a refuge for the women and children of our company, and as a treasury for the stores of which we were to despoil the natives.

"Our preparations were soon finished. Some of our men had returned from an exploring expedition, and had met messengers from the Saxon kinsman who had invited us thither. The Celts also were around awaiting us. The next day our forces were to unite with our kinsman's, and a battle was to be fought. Early in the morning we rose, the sacrifices were offered to Woden, and the wise men who came with us declared the flowing of the blood of the victims to augur well. My mother herself girded on the sax, or short sword, to the tunic she had woven for my father. I see it now. It was of purple linen, embroidered with golden eagles. My father embraced us, and promised to bring us home gifts from the fight. We had no doubt of the result. All day my brother and I played on the sands below the cliff on which we were encamped. Leofric was eight, and I was twelve; and we talked of the palace to which our father would bring us, and of the way we would behave to the captive princes and princesses, our slaves. Leofric thought they would make delightful playfellows, and we would teach them Saxon. I intended not to speak much to my maidens. I would be kind to them; but they should wait on my looks, so that I only had to wave my hand, and they would obey my will. But most of all we spoke of our father on the throne, and our mother with the silken robes and the diadem of gold. For we both thought our mother the fairest woman in the world; and I loved my father as perhaps one should only love God.

"The night came; but not my father. For some days we watched eagerly for every footstep with the longing eagerness of hope deferred.

"And then one of our men, wounded, and faint from loss of blood, brought back a fragment of the purple tunic to us, and my father's sword.

"The women of our company surrounded him with bitter wailings, and some with bitter reproaches.

"'The brave have perished,' they said. 'All the brave have perished, and thou only hast fled.'

"But then our mother's spirit rose, as befits the spirit of women of royal race. She did not wail nor upbraid. She said simply,—

"'How did your lord die?'

"'As only one of his race should die—in the thick of the battle.'

"'Doubtless,' she said, 'it could not be otherwise. But not one word? did he not leave one word?'

"'Before the fight,' was the reply, 'he spoke to me, and said, "Those against us are many; and a brave man should not despise his foes. If I fall, my body will be buried among the heaps of the slain, my spirit will journey to Walhalla. But do thou take my sword and my tunic, and bear them to the camp to thy lady, and let the women and children embark again for our native shores."'

"The words came faintly in broken sentences from the wounded man's pale lips; but my mother's face was whiter than his, and her lips were white as death; yet she pressed them silently together, and uttered not a moan. All the life seemed to have passed from her body to her soul, and her soul shone through her tearless eyes.

"'My lord's commands shall be obeyed,' she murmured.

"In a few hours, the little camp my father had so carefully chosen for us was deserted, and we were all on board two of the ships manned by the few men who had been left to guard us.

"As we turned from the shores we had landed on with such exultation and hope, a wild despairing wail broke from the women. I shall never forget it. To my dying day that helpless, hopeless, bitter cry will ring in my ears; the funeral wail for the dead we might never see again, nor even bury; the cry of anguish, which was not a prayer, but only a cry, echoed back by the rocks of this land of our dead, echoed back by the golden walls of Walhalla, and by the iron gates of Hela, the death-goddess,—but reaching no heart of pity, responded to by no voice!

"We children were at first appalled into quietness. Then, as our first terror passed, the sobs of the little fatherless ones came mingling with the deeper agony of those who knew what they had lost.

"My mother only sat motionless and mute. At first when she had given our father's sword to my brother, his eyes had kindled, and he seemed to think it was a great gift and trust from his father. It was not until we were in the ships again, and turning from the shores, that he began to comprehend that it was Death, and not my father, that had given him this sword.

"'Shall we not wait for father?' he asked.

"'Your father waits for you, my boy,' was her reply, 'in Walhalla, in the halls of the heroes.'

"'But when will he come to us?'

"'Never!' she said. And then for the first time he understood, and he turned aside with a quivering lip. For it was instilled into us from infancy that brave men must not weep, least of all the sons of Woden. I do not remember feeling any disposition for tears. There was nothing in this sorrow to soften the heart. No tender pressure of a dying hand, no tender words from dying lips; only a wrench of hopeless separation, and a bitter agony of indignation, and loss, and revenge, and hatred, and despair. I was appalled, tossed like the spirits some have seen in visions, from the ice to the flames; from the benumbing pain of hopeless bereavement to the burning indignation of powerless hatred. There was nothing in that to make me weep, or to make me better.

"The only tender thought left in me was for my mother. But, unhappily, her grief was too much like mine, with all the added intensity of her womanhood, for me to comfort her. She endured, but she refused all comfort.

"The depth of her sorrow was best understood by me through the passiveness which had fallen on her, now that the first necessity for action was over.

"More sorrows awaited us, but they seemed not to move her. She had reached the depths, and all the blows of Fate could sink her no lower.

"The ship we were in was driven on the coast of Wales, and wrecked there.

"The British wreckers came thronging to the shore, and we were taken captive.

"As we were driven through the land to the great slave-market at Chester, our captors stopped at a stone building, where we were met by a procession of men with black robes and shaven heads (shaven wholly, in the Eastern mode, not with the coronal tonsure of the Latins). To these they gave my mother's amber necklace, and some golden bracelets, which had been my father's last present to me. They were laid on the altar with solemnity, I understood, as offerings to the gods of the land.

"That was my first glimpse of the Christian religion. Henceforth I included what our enemies worshipped in my detestation of them.

"Hitherto we three had not been separated. At Chester this also awaited us. We were penned like cattle in an open place of the city for sale. Two men approached us, who spoke to each other in a dialect quite sufficiently like our own for us to understand. And before long we understood that they were intending to purchase us separately.

"Then my mother's calmness gave way; and she, whose voice I had always been accustomed to hear in calm command, knelt to those strangers, and implored them with passionate tears to let us be together. She said we should be better worth having; she would do the work of two women if they would let her remain with us.

"But it was in vain. They did not seem cruel or unmoved. But they were agents for others. They were only bargaining. Leofric and I were purchased by one purchaser, and my mother was bound and led away by the other.

When she saw that appeal was useless she regained all her old dignity; and embracing us once, she suffered herself to be led away.

"But I could not so easily understand the hopelessness of our fate.

"With my childish hands I seized the cord that bound her wrists from the man who was leading her away, and said,—

"'You do not know what you are doing. We are great people at home. We are of the royal race of Woden.'

"'Of a good stock, doubtless,' said our purchaser, 'or I should not have bought you. My lord has I know not how many princes tending his herds, and my lady as many princesses serving in her bower.'

"Then, not cruelly, but roughly, as he would have seized a refractory animal, he turned me from my mother, bound my wrists and Leofric's with strong cords, and drove us before him.

"I dare not even now dwell on the bitter humiliation of that day, or on the frantic schemes of vengeance which flitted through my brain.

"I wonder often when I hear people speak of sorrow as if it must make us better. Sorrow without God, sorrow without the knowledge of the Man of Sorrows, seems to me to make the heart bitter and savage,—not like the angels, but like the wild beasts, or the fallen angels who sorrow for evermore.

"It was only Leofric, my little brother, that kept me human.

"It was long before I learnt that resistance was quite in vain, and only bound the yoke more firmly on me. Then I subsided into sullen subjection, and disputed nothing; but chiefly I learned to do this for Leofric's sake, because my rebellion brought down blows upon the boy, or separated us. Had it not been for him, I think, I would have resisted to the end, and died.

"At last they thought my spirit was sufficiently broken; and being (they said) fair in face, and quick in understanding, I was given to the Lady Ethelberga, the young queen of King Edwin of Northumbria—his second wife, but lately married, and come into the North from her royal home in Kent,—to be her thrall. Leofric was still employed outside in tending the royal herds.

"I might have been considered fortunate. The young queen was not unkind to me; and some of the ladies admired my cleverness, and my blue eyes, and abundant flaxen hair. But it seemed to me they petted me as they would a bird or a favourite hound; and my pride revolted from their caresses more than from the blows and rough words to which I had been used before.

"Therefore, before long, I was allowed to pursue my duties unnoticed and unreproved. I learnt to embroider and to play on the lyre. But no threats or persuasions could induce me to sing. Should I profane the ballads of my people, learned from my mother's lips, by singing them to divert these strangers? My worst care, however, began to be for Leofric. His disposition, always gentler than mine, seemed to me to be losing all its fire, and I feared his very soul was growing to be a slave's soul.

"Over this I shed many bitter tears.

"Again, at King Edwin's court, I came in contact with the Christian religion.

"There was a tall monk from Italy residing in the palace, Bishop Paulinus. He had come from Kent with the queen.

"He preached often concerning the faith; and also spoke in private to any one who would listen. But at first he did not make many converts. And I (God forgive me) hated the very name of Christianity. Was it not the religion of my captors? Had not the treasures of which we, the widow and fatherless, had been robbed been accepted on Christian altars? Moreover, the life of those monks seemed to me base and unmanly. I hated the sight of their smooth, long, foreign faces, and their shaven crowns. It seemed to me a miserable, slavish existence, for a man to glide in and out of houses clothed

in a long robe like a woman's, and droning out prayers
and psalms. I thought the stern virtues of my people
nobler than these.

"There was great pomp at King Edwin's court. The
great hall and the queen's chamber were hung with
tapestries; the floors were strewn every day with fresh
rushes. The state dresses of the queen and her ladies
were of silk from Asia, embroidered with gold; and both
men and women wore jewelled necklaces and bracelets.
The king, wherever he went, was preceded by standard-
bearers flaunting the royal banners, or the Tufa—the
globe fixed on the spear.

"We were seldom long in one residence, but travelled
from one royal house to another, for the king to adminis-
ter justice and receive tribute.

"We, the attendants, commonly went before, and hung
the walls with the silken hangings, and strewed the floors
with fresh rushes, and set the tables with the golden and
silver cups and dishes, in readiness for the arrival of the
court.

"Wherever we went, the Archbishop Paulinus had a
Christian chapel, where he and the good deacon Jacob,
the beautiful singer from Rome, chanted the church ser-
vices; and Edwin, the king, made his offerings to the old
Saxon gods of our fathers in the temples;—to Thor, the
Thunderer; to Frea, the Beautiful; and to Woden, the
All-father, our royal forefather, and chief of all the gods.

"At length a change came over the court. We were
living at the royal city on the Derwent, near the remains
of an older city, Derventiona, built by the Romans. I
liked to be there. It was a kind of bitter comfort to me
to see the ruins of the old palaces and temples. I thought,
'Why should we make such ado? Not only men, but

nations pass away. The palaces of yesterday will be folds for flocks to-morrow.'

"It was the holy Easter-tide, and Paulinus and the Christians had made such festival as they could in a heathen palace.

"On that day the king also sat in all his pomp, to receive an embassy from the king of the West Saxons.

"Suddenly we in the queen's apartments heard wild war-cries and a confused shouting from the hall where the king sat; and soon after the king himself appeared at the door, white and silent, and then a body was borne out covered. And we were told that the supposed ambassador was an assassin, who had been sent, armed with a poisoned dagger, from the West Saxon king; and that, to save his lord's life, Lilla, the brave nobleman, had made a buckler of his own body, receiving the fatal thrust in his breast. Then all the men had fallen on the assassin, till he sunk pierced with many wounds.

"The king was saved, but Lilla, the noblest, was slain.

"That night the young queen bore her first child, the Princess Eanfled.

"The king gave thanks to the gods of his fathers—to Frea and to Woden; but Paulinus rendered praise to Christ, and told the king how he had prayed to Him for the queen's safety.

"The king was moved, and vowed that in case God would grant him victory over the perfidious West Saxon king, he would forsake his old gods, and thenceforth serve and worship none but Christ.

"The victory was given. King Edwin forsook Woden and Thor, but would not hastily adopt a faith of which he knew so little.

"But the babe Eanfled was baptized with twelve

others of the royal family. And among those was the royal maiden, Hilda, daughter of the king's nephew, who afterwards became the great Abbess Hilda.

"At that time the Pope Boniface sent letters to the king, exhorting him to become a Christian; and to 'his illustrious daughter,' the Queen Ethelberga, admonishing her to labour for her husband's conversion. With the letters came presents: to the king, a shirt, a golden ornament, and a garment of Ancyra; to the queen, a silver hand-mirror and a gilt ivory comb. To me these seemed presents little suitable to the dignity of the Northumbrian royalty. But from many expressions dropped by the Italian monks, I gathered that at Rome they look on us Saxons as a kind of rude and simple savages. As if not being able to read, like the monks, out of books, made men to be children, or prevented their knowing the world and the wisdom of the aged. For I deem that men were before books, and that those who can speak wise words of their own are wiser than those who can read or copy the wise words of other men.

"It was not the Pope's letters which fixed King Edwin's purpose. It happened thus:

"Paulinus had been permitted to preach in public, and the deacon Jacob to chant his psalms. For many days the king had withdrawn much from his usual amusements and occupations, and had wandered moodily about the chambers, or sat alone, evidently pondering many things in his heart. At length his resolution was taken, and he summoned the Witenagemot—the great council of the wise men of his nation—to consider the great question of religion, to the end that if they were also of his opinion, they might all together be cleansed in Christ, the Fountain of Life.

"Leofric was there among those that kept the door. What he saw and heard moved him much.

"The king sat there on his oaken chair of state, with the elders of his people gathered around him, and Paulinus beside him. Not one among them but had heard of the new doctrine. King Edwin asked them one by one what they thought of it. He sought not the clamorous consent of a crowd, but the counsel of each one.

"Coifi, chief of the priests of the old Saxon gods, answered at once:

"'O king, consider what this is that is now preached to us; for I verily declare to you, that the religion which we have hitherto professed, has, as far as I can learn, no virtue in it. For none of your people has applied himself more diligently to the worship of the gods than I; and yet there are many that receive more favours from you, and are more preferred than I, and are more prosperous in all their undertakings. Now, if the gods were good for anything, they would rather forward me, who have been more careful to serve them. It remains, therefore, that if, upon examination, you find those new doctrines which are now preached to us better and more efficacious, we immediately receive them, without any further delay.'

"But another of the king's chief men spoke more nobly, and said: 'The present life of man, O king, seems to me, in comparison of that time which is unknown to us, life to the swift flight of a sparrow through the room where you sit at supper in winter, with your chief men and counsellors, and a good fire in the midst, whilst the storms of rain and snow prevail abroad. The sparrow flying in at one door and out at the other, whilst he is within is safe from the wintry storm; but after a short space of fair weather, he straightway vanishes out of your sight, into the dark winter whence he came. So, this life of man appears for a short space; but of what went before, or what is to follow, we know nothing. If, therefore, this new doctrine contains something more sure, it seems justly to deserve to be followed.'

"Then the Italian priest arose at the king's command and spoke. A strange contrast with his audience. They, stalwart and large in form, with bearded faces and fair hair, with broad open brows and honest wondering blue eyes; he, tall and spare, with a slight stoop in his otherwise majestic figure, robed in a long black robe girded with a cord, his dark brilliant eyes flashing from the thin palid face, like a visible triumph of the spirit over the flesh. And the contrast in his speech yet greater. The rich flow of his persuasive eloquence bore the hearts of the wise men with him; and when he ceased, Coifi the priest exclaimed that he had long known there was nothing in what they worshipped, but now he plainly saw that in this teaching were life and salvation, and eternal happiness. Therefore he counselled that those unprofitable altars where he had so long served in vain should be destroyed with fire, and proposed that he himself should be the first to light the pile.

"This took place in the council-hall, and not long afterwards, before we heard what had passed, to their amazement the people beheld Coifi the priest, violating all the customs of our race, armed with unpriestly arms, and mounted on one of the king's war-horses, ride forth from the palace to the ancient temple of Woden, the All-father and Thor the Thunderer at Godmundham. There he launched the spear into the sacred precincts, desecrating them by the act. No vengeance followed; wherefore all the people said the gods were nothing ; and Coifi and his men destroyed the temple and all its buildings with fire.

"The flames burnt on into the night. Leofric and I gazed on the dread unnatural glare from a field near the palace. while he told me what he had heard in the council-hall.

"'See, Frideswide,' he said, 'no avenging fire from heaven meets those fires of defiance from earth. Little cause have we to mourn the downfall of the gods who tempted my father on by false auguries, and then abandoned him to death and us to bondage.'

"'Yet,' I said, 'it seems to me ignoble to serve or to forsake the gods for such reasons. What king would care for loyalty such as this Coifi's, measured only by a calculation of his gifts! If the prince is good, and *our* prince, I deem we should follow him, not only to victory, but to exile. If Woden and Thor are true gods, and *our* gods, the fathers and lords of our race, though all the world abandoned them, I would not. The life of the gods is long, and their eyes see far into the past and the future, and how should I dispute their wisdom or their will?'

"'But,' answered Leofric, 'if, as the other counsellor said, any light is in this new faith which would show us what is beyond this life, it would be worth watching. For truly to us here this short space of life is no warmed and lighted hall of feasting. but cold and wintry as the world outside.'

"'That may be,' I said ; 'to me it matters little. What to me is any world beyond, unless our father and our mother are there? But as to the reasonings of this Coifi, I despise them in my heart. These are not the motives which move any brave man, any man with free blood in his veins. They are the wretched calculations of a hireling or a slave.'

"Great changes followed. All the nobility, after being instructed, were baptized with the king, and many of the common sort, on Easter Day, in the spring over which has been built since then the church at York. The national temples were destroyed, the national religion was changed. Wherever the court journeyed, Paulinus and Jacob, the deacon, journeyed with them. Paulinus preached, and Jacob chanted the Psalms to the listening people. Especially was this the case at Adgefrin, the royal seat in Glendale. There for thirty-six days the people flocked in to listen to the new doctrine from all the towns and villages around. From morning to night Paulinus, the archbishop, instructed and catechised them, and then those who embraced the faith were baptized in the little river Glen.

"Leofric, being of a gentler temper than I, listened and believed; but I felt as if this new faith would raise up another barrier between me and my dead father, whom I loved beyond all dead or living; and I would not listen. Besides, it always seemed to me—as Paulinus sought to win converts by promises of victory and prosperity to those who would believe—like a mere question of strength between two rival chiefs. I cared little which prevailed; but I honoured the old heroes better than the new monks, and I would not desert my father's gods. And being of 'the common sort,' I was left to myself.

"Days of peace and prosperity followed. In river after river throughout the fair valleys of Northumbria, multitudes of people were baptized; in the Glen, the Derwent, the Swale, and the Trent. In town after town the white-robed converts kept their baptismal festival. There was gladness and peace throughout the land. It became a proverb that wheresoever the dominion of King Edwin extended 'a woman with her new-born babe might walk from sea to sea without harm or peril.' And so strong was the law, and so great the love of the king, that the brazen cups which he caused to be suspended on stakes near the clear springs in the highways, for wayfarers to drink, were safe as in the royal treasure-chests. In Lindsey (Lincoln) also, and the province of the East Angles, the faith spread.

"Not that there was no sorrow in the palace. Well I remember the weeping of the queen when two fair babes, Ethelhun and Etheldrith, lay lifeless in their white christening garments, and were buried in the new church at York, where the king had been baptized. But I saw there was a hope in these Christians, which made death not the same to them as to me. *And that was the first thing which moved me towards them.* But this was only a passing cloud. All the land had rest. All men held Paulinus to be a prophet; every month was full of the peace and prosperity the new faith had brought.

"Then suddenly, like a dream, the whole bright scene vanished, and instead came ruin, and defeat, and death.

"King Edwin was slain in battle. Paulinus and the queen, with the orphaned children, fled to Kent. Cadwalla, king of the Britons, called a Christian, came from the west; and Penda, the heathen king of the Mercians, joined him from the south; and together they ravaged the land far and wide. None were spared for any merciful reason, and few of the slain escaped with only death. It was a war of vengeance. If all the Asæ had descended from Asgard to avenge their insulted temples, the desolation could not have been more cruel.

"Many, indeed, believed it was so, and abandoned the faith which had been proclaimed to them with earthly promises, when these promises failed. The foreign clergy fled, with golden cross and chalice, over the seas to Canterbury; the churches were destroyed as the heathen temples had been.

"One night in that terrible time, when Leofric and I were wandering in the fields round the village of Akeborough, near the city of Richmond, we heard sweet sounds of solemn music from a dwelling near—not the wild cadences of heathen music, but sustained and grave, such as the Gregorian chants the Italians had brought from Italy.

"We found it was the good Deacon Jacob, who, being only a deacon and a singer, had yet remained to keep the flock together when bishop and priest had fled. He had not, perchance, wit to preach, or strength to rule; but he had a voice to sing God's praises, and a heart to serve. Throughout the storm he abode steadfast, keeping up the courage and nourishing the faith of the few who clung to him and to Christ, with Christian hymns and old prophetic psalms. That was the second thing that moved me towards the Christian faith. A faith which could give hope in death, and inspire hymns of praise amidst such ruin, seemed to me worth listening to. For the first time I asked Leofric to speak to me of Christianity; but we had little time then for speech or thought.

"Battle followed battle, one king after another was slain. Wherever we went we came to the blackened ruins of towns and homesteads, or trod the wasted fields.

Yet those times were not utterly miserable to me. Leofric and I were free to wander whither we would.

"At length King Oswald came, son of the ancient kings of the land, and rightful heir from his birth, and set up the wooden cross before his army in the place called Heavenfield (Hallington), near the old Roman wall. And kneeling before it, he said aloud to all his men, 'Let us all kneel, and jointly beseech the true and living God Almighty in his mercy to defend us from the haughty and fierce enemy; for He knows we have undertaken a just war for the defence of the nation.'

"Then, with the first dawn of day, advancing on his foes, the victory was his. The tide of conquest was turned, and the foe was once more driven from the land.

"Our rescue, however, was not yet come. Leofric and I were once more taken captive, and sold as slaves to the conqueror. The little glimpse of liberty we had enjoyed might have made the bondage bitterer; but the hymns of the good Deacon Jacob rang through my heart, and I felt less desolate than before.

"We were thralls of Oswald the king. But at last, in my bondage, the word reached me which set my heart for ever free.

"King Oswald sent for Christian teachers from the North, where he had received the faith; and they came from the sacred island of Iona, on the western shores of the land of the Scots—holy and humble men, who would accept no gifts for themselves, nor assume any state such as the Italians deemed their due. They would not ride in ease or pomp through the land, but walked from village to village, conversing with such as they met, searching out the wants of the poor, comforting the afflicted, and reproving the oppressor.

"Greatest and humblest of all these was Bishop Aidan. In him first I learned to understand how a Christian monk may be nobler than any hero of the race of Woden, and win nobler victories.

"Never shall I forget the first time I heard him, when first he came, and Oswald the king sat at his feet and interpreted his words to the people.

"He promised nothing, on earth. How should he care to do so whose life so plainly showed that his hopes and joys belonged to quite another sphere?

"He spoke of the Lord Jesus Christ, the 'gentle-hearted Saviour, who came from heaven to this middle earth to open heaven to sinful man;—who, not ceasing to be God, became also man, that he might, by his passion and death, make men sons of God.'

"Much of this I must have heard from Paulinus before, but the words seemed new to me from Bishop Aidan's lips. God the Almighty had been slowly loosening the bars of my heart, as the sun loosens the ice-bars from the earth; and when He himself, through the word of his servant, came to the door and knocked, it opened softly, without resistance, and the closed door of my poor, dark, and narrow heart, became a window into his world of love and joy; the threshold of my heart became to me the threshold of his kingdom.

"But most of all I rejoiced for the name the holy Aidan gave our Lord—the name of *Redeemer*, Himself the Redeemer and the Ransom. Then and there it flashed into my heart, as I stood far back in the throng among the other slaves, '*I am free.* Christ the Lord has made me free. Henceforth men may claim the service of my hands in this short life, but my heart is free; *I* am free. The Redeemer has redeemed me with his precious blood. I am his freed woman and his willing thrall for ever, and his alone.'

"I cannot tell the thrill of liberty that went through my heart at that moment. I did not speak to any one then about it. It is not the way of our race to speak quickly of that which touches the depths of our hearts. And I understood so little what I felt; how could I speak?

"For the first time in my life my spirit ceased to chafe against my bondage. I felt I had an inner, imperishable freedom, none could touch. The next day I went about my work with a heart as light as if it had been for my mother. Bishop Aidan had said we were all 'redeemed servants of the Lord Christ.' My fears for Leofric also were gone. If he believed this ennobling doctrine, which enabled all men to become, as it were, household servants of the Lord of all, I felt no slavery could enslave his soul.

"This was at Bishop Aidan's first visit. Then for a time he departed to the island of Lindisfarne, which the king had given him to build a monastery thereon, as on the holy island of Iona whence he came.

"Neither Leofric nor I, nor any we knew, could read; but many around us had heard one portion or another of the history of the Redeemer, and piece by piece we learned the story of his wondrous birth; of Mary, the most blessed maiden mother; of His painful life, His journeyings, and His teachings; of the sick he healed; of the sinners he forgave and made saints; of his bitter passion and death on the shameful cross for us; of his resurrection, and his ascension, in the sight of those who loved him, into heaven; of his sending the Holy Ghost to teach and comfort us who still stray on this dim middle earth.

When, therefore, Bishop Aidan came again and catechised us, he deemed us fit to be baptized; and we went down into the river Derwent at Easter, and were baptized, even as our souls were bathed in Christ, the Fountain of Life.

"Then came the eight days of holy festivity, sacred and festive to slave as to freeman; while we kept on the white baptismal robes, and were much in the church listening to holy discourses, and learning by heart and chanting hymns in our native Saxon—the Te Deum, the Apostles' Creed, the Our Father.

"Not long afterwards, the good bishop himself called us to him, learning that we were brother and sister, and asked us of our kindred. He had a way of finding out the oppressed and sorrowful, and his face was full of tender pity as he listened to our story. He asked us straitly also of the name of our mother, and whither she had gone into bondage. But we could tell him little; long before this, we feared, she must have sunk beneath her griefs, and died. Then he said he had money given to him to liberate those who had been unjustly made slaves, and he offered to ransom Leofric, and teach him, among other youths he was training, to be a priest and a learned man.

"Leofric hesitated long. He could not bear to leave me; but at length I prevailed on him, and he went with the holy bishop.

"The days were lonelier than I had thought they would be when he went. I had been used to guide him like a mother rather than a sister, being older, and having the stronger will of the two. It was not until he went that I found out how often his good sense and gentle strength had led me, when my more vehement purpose had seemed to be ruling him.

"Such separations are needful in life, sometimes, to make us understand what our beloved are to us, and we to them.

"But the lesson was hard. As regards earth I felt like one of whom I have heard, who was healed of a fever, but left deaf and blind. Such a blank the world seemed to me without one familiar voice, or one beloved face for which to watch.

"Had it not been for the Our Father and the Creed; had it not been for the Redeemer and his presence, what would have become of me then?

"And, alas, this was what our mother had borne; this, without heaven to hope for! without knowing the suffering Lord and his cross!

"It did not last long. God was pitiful to my impatient heart.

"One summer evening, I had been sitting spinning among the maidens and directing their work, which was my task, till it grew dusk; and then, when the others had gone to their work in the house and farm, and I had gathered up the cloth and wool, the distaffs and the wheels, and made all ready for the evening meal, I went to the door for a few minutes restlessly, as if I had some one to watch for, as I had been used to watch for Leofric.

"I knew too well there was nothing for me to wait for; but that night there were strange yearnings in my heart, wherefore I lifted up my heart and said the Our Father. But I did not get beyond '*Thy will be done*,' for while I was thinking if I could say it truly, my eye lighted on two figures in the distance moving slowly through the deepening twilight; one bowed and feeble, the other erect and tall.

"And in another minute I had folded my mother in

my arms. Yes, she was folded to my heart, not I to hers! So little power seemed left in her who had left us so fair and strong. The old bitter passion of revenge glowed up again in my heart. Yet I do not think her bondage had been cruel; it had only been hopeless. Mechanically she had been driven from task to task, unresisting and uncomplaining, until all the light of her soul seemed to have shrunk into a time-lamp to measure the hours of labour.

"Nervously, as we sat beside her, weeping, with our hands in hers, every now and then she looked up and said gently, and with a kind of wistful tenderness, 'I must not keep you; we must not be late.'

"Bishop Aidan had purchased her freedom. Leofric had found her after a perilous search, and had brought her to me. The good king Oswald himself had pity on us and set me free. A little land was given us on the coast, near Whitby, the abbey of the Abbess Hilda. Leofric deemed it his first duty—and so did Bishop Aidan—to abide with our widowed mother and with me. Before long, he made a fishing-boat, and we three once more dwelt together in our wooden hut looking over the Eastern Sea.

"Thus passed many years.

"Slowly a little light came back into our mother's mind. She ceased to count the hours with such restless anxiety. She suffered us to caress and tend her as we would a petted sick child; and by degrees the great bitterness passed from our hearts, and we loved her as she was. Sometimes she would be watching for me or for Leofric when either of us came back from field or sea, and her face would light up with a feeble smile, like the sunshine dimly struggling through the mists of the valley.

And now and then she would stroke my hair, and say,—

"'Little Frideswide's hair was fair and soft like this.'

"But how far she connected us with those dim, tender recollections we never knew.

"Meantime the abbey of the Abbess Hilda rose before us on the height of Streaneschalch, the Bay of the Lighthouse,* above the sea; and now and then Leofric would go in his boat to carry an offering of fish to Lindisfarne, the Holy Island, and bring back tidings of Bishop Aidan and his work; how the oaken church was rising, cased with lead, on the summit of the island; and the humble wooden huts of the good monks were clustering round it; and how men and women were being gathered by the preaching of these holy men throughout Northumbria into the Church. For, while the Scotch built their churches of wood, they built countless costly living stones into the Church.

"Leofric would usually stay some days at Lindisfarne. He felt it like an opening into the heavens; where the messengers of God, like the holy angels, ascended and descended between God and man; linked to heaven by prayer, and praise, and study of the sacred Scriptures; and to man by ceaseless ministries of love. The brethren owned no property whatever. What money they received was spent at once in relieving the poor, and in ransoming slaves and captives. Kings, and ealdormen, and thanes, visiting their island for instruction or for worship, contented themselves with the frugal fare of the monks. Lindisfarne was a place of continual movement and activity, and yet of deep repose of heart. Thither continually missionaries were returning, with

* Whitby.

tidings of how their work had sped throughout the land, even beyond the limits of Northumbria and Lindsey, East Anglia, Mercia, and even in Wessex; of kings bowing their necks to the yoke of Christ; of humble men enlightened by the truth; of monasteries founded; of eager crowds flocking to listen to them in the towns; of solitary crags which they scaled to tell the holy Gospel to robbers and outlaws. And thence, after a period of repose beside those still waters of life, spent in reading the Scriptures, committing psalms to memory, or storing the mind with sacred hymns, the monks would go forth again two and two, on foot, with no provision but such food as they could carry, to traverse the land east and west, north and south; crossing the pathless moors, penetrating into the remotest valleys; ever as they went addressing all they met, noble or peasant, heathen or Christian; seeking to lead the unbelievers to Christ, the Fountain of Love; and to invite the believers to alms and works of love.

"Leofric would often remain many days with the brethren; but I rejoiced in these visits, for he pursued his studies there, learned to read and write, and always brought back in his memory some new hymn, or psalm, or sacred history, of which he would discourse to us and to the neighbours long afterwards.

"On the summer evenings, when I was watching for him, I used to know he was coming by the floating of the well-known chants across the sea in the intervals between the breaking of the waves.

"Well I remember one evening the awe that shadowed his face when we thus met, and I feared to question him dreading whether some terrible chance had happened to Bishop Aidan, our dear father in God; when he told me that a new and dreadful kind of infidels had arisen in the East under the guidance of one Mahomet, who had laid the ancient churches waste with fire and sword, and that now the very sepulchre of our Lord, and Mount Zion itself, had fallen into their hands. This had happened in 633, the year after our father Aidan was appointed bishop, but it was only now that the certain tidings had reached us.

"A great weight rested on us long after that, and on all the neighbours when they heard it. We remembered how we had seen the sun and the moon darkened not long before, and the stars falling from their places in the sky, and beheld awful glares of lightning across the sea in the eastern sky, and we thought the Anti-christ had surely come, and that God would not suffer the world to last much longer.

"But that was fifty years ago, and his long-suffering endureth yet. So little can we measure his times.

"These tidings, however, made time and its joys and cares seem very brief, and the thought which I had had before gained strength in me, that I was withholding Leofric from the service of the Lord.

"I cast about much in my mind to find how I could support my mother without him. I did not think her maintenance would be difficult to secure. The sea was as familiar to our race as the land, and I felt sure that with the fisher-boy who accompanied my brother I could have cast the nets and also tilled land enough for our nourishment. But the difficulty was that I could not leave my mother alone.

"In this perplexity I at length resolved to consult the Abbess Hilda, that loyal lady whom all that knew her called mother for her singular piety and grace.* She

* V. Bede.

seemed to me, from all I heard of her, to be like one of the ancient priestesses or wise women of our people, only enlightened from heaven, and hallowed by Christian love; such insight was in her to discern the right, and such decision to pursue it.

"All in our neighbourhood prized her counsel above that of any, detached as she was from all things of mere earthly interest, yet linked to all men by warm, womanly sympathy.

"My difficulties vanished when I saw her. She had no doubt that if Leofric had indeed a call from our Lord to follow him and teach men, being himself instructed and approved by Bishop Aidan (who was to her as a father) he should be ordained and go forth to preach.

"We could come, she said, and reside near her monastery, and when I must be absent one of the sisters could watch my mother. Thus the way was made smooth; Leofric went with a joyful heart to join the brethren at Lindisfarne, and our mother and I removed to a cottage near the monastery of Whitby, the Bay of the Light-house, and worked in the fields or cast the nets from our boat into the sea.

"We were near enough to be present at many of the services, and often in the night we heard the nocturnal praises of the brethren and the sisters. The quiet music seemed to soothe my mother wondrously. Sometimes, as she held up her finger and listened, the light of thought seemed to dawn faintly in her eyes, like one half awaking from a troubled dream. And those were blessed and fruitful days for me. In my spare hours I learned to read in our Saxon tongue. We used also to hear wonderful tidings from pilgrims who had been beyond the seas,— of the infidels who had taken Jerusalem, of the sepulchres of the apostles and martyrs at Rome, of the heaving to and fro of the nations, of ancient churches swept away in the East, of heathen tribes of our race converted to the faith of Christ, of holy hermits lighting the candle of the Lord among the barbarous people in the wild forests, and sometimes of martyrdoms. Marvellous stories also we heard of miracles wrought by the bones of holy men, and even by the earth on their graves; of storms calmed by prayer and by the holy oil poured on the waves; of visions of heaven and hell seen by dying men and women.

"For not only from the region about us did people come to consult the Abbess Hilda; kings and princes and noblemen came from far and near to learn of her and to see her holy life. Such zeal also did she inspire in the brethren and sisters under her guidance for the study of Holy Scriptures and for good works, that five bishops renowned for wisdom and sanctity issued from her monastery, namely, Bosa, Hedda, Oftfor, John, and Wilfrid.

"To her also was brought Caedmon the herdsman-poet, who sang to our people of the creation, of the departure of the children of Israel from out of Egypt, and their entering into the land of promise, of the incarnation, passion, resurrection, and ascension of our Lord, and of the coming of the Holy Ghost.

"Sometimes I used to think, when our own mother was taken from us, I should like nothing better than to live a religious life under the Abbess Hilda. But when I thought of this I generally pictured myself as an abbess rather than a nun. The Abbess Hilda's life was indeed varied and rich in interest, but it seemed to me my spirit would chafe under the regular round of monotonous occupations which occupied most of the sisters; I feared that I might grow worse instead of better under such a discipline.

"And therefore, when Alfhelm the Thane asked me to become his wife, and offered to take my mother to be his, I thought it best to do as he said.

"After that we divided our days between a farm he had near Whitby and his sheep-walks among these mountains.

"When our first child was born our mother took a wondrous delight in it. She seemed to consider it her own, and would nurse it for hours, lavishing the tenderest endearments on it. For the first time she seemed for hours together to come out of her dream; and from those days her mind gathered a little strength, so that she even learned by degrees the Our Father, and such simple words of prayer and praise to our Lord and Saviour as we could teach the little ones, and with them was baptized.

"So it went on until one summer her strength failed, and we carried her into the Abbess Hilda's monastery, to see if the nursing of the sisters might restore her. All remedies, however, failed, and at midnight she passed silently away with her hand in Leofric's and mine, breathing faintly old familiar names, our father's and ours; and we thought, among them, the name of Christ. So she closed her eyes, and we thought she was gone, when once more they opened with a look of conscious wonder and awe and joy in them that we can never forget. And so she fell asleep, while the sisters in the church were singing—

    'We are thine Israel;
      We joy in thee, O God;

And we the ancient foe repel,
   Redeemed by Christ's own blood.

'At midnight bursts the cry,
   (So saith the Evangelist),
"Arise! the Bridegroom draweth nigh,
   The King of Heaven, the Christ."

'At midnight's season chill
   Lay Paul and Silas bound;
Bound and in prison sang they still,
   And, singing, freedom found.

'Our prison is this earth,
   And yet we sing to thee!
Break sin's strong fetters, lead us forth,—
   Set us, believing, free.'

"And as they sang, her fettered spirit, long since ransomed, was set free for ever.

"After that, troubles came upon the Church. Our father Aidan, the apostle of Northumbria, died. Foreign priests arrived again from Italy, and disturbed the minds of the simple people, saying that the holy Aidan and his Scotch monks had taught schismatic practices; namely, shaving the heads of priests wholly, instead of leaving a crown of hair, in imitation of the sacred crown of thorns; and observing Easter on a different Sunday from all Western Christendom.

"The Abbess Hilda opposed this foreign teaching and dictation with all her might, as a free Saxon lady and a true disciple of Bishop Aidan, who had been consecrated a nun by him.

"However, in the council held at her abbey of Whitby, King Oswy (the good King Oswald being dead) decided that the foreign monks, with whom his Kentish queen

Eanfleda agreed, held the right. Many, deeming these questions of less moment than peace and union, submitted; but Bishop Colman, Aidan's successor, withdrew with his Scotch monks into Scotland. That was a grievous day for us, and for all who had learned to know and love the Saviour from their teaching. Many a weeping eye followed those good men as they left Lindisfarne, and, crossing the sands left bare by the ebbing tide, bent their steps homeward to Scotland, poor as they came; bearing nothing with them but some of Bishop Aidan's bones, and the love of all good men; leaving nothing behind them but their few humble huts on the island, and the precious seed of God which they had sown in the hearts of our people.

"Leofric would have willingly accompanied them, as did some even of the English monks, but Bishop Colman did not counsel this. At his request (for King Oswy honoured him much), Eata was consecrated abbot in his room, a meek and reverend man—one of the first twelve English boys whom Bishop Aidan had received and instructed in the faith of Christ.

"Leofric therefore continued to labour among our people in Northumbria. Like many of the Culdees or priests from Iona, and most of the secular priests even among the Roman party, he married.

"Good men were sent us also from beyond the seas, and among them the zealous and learned Archbishop Theodore, who was born at Tarsus, the city of the Apostle Paul, and established schools of Latin and Greek throughout the land, and did much good. But to me none of these strangers could ever be like good Bishop Aidan and the great Saxon Abbess Hilda.

"And thenceforth my husband and I loved more and

more to dwell among the quiet of these hills, away from strife and tumult. And here we built this priory on the border of the lake, that whichever of us should survive might retire thither as to a refuge, to pass the solitary evening of our days in prayer and praise. For my husband thought it good rather to regard the monasteries as a place of rest and vesper quiet when the day's work is done, than as a retreat from the toil and burden of the day."

So spoke the Abbess Frideswide, our mother. And two days afterwards the monk came with the tidings of the great Abbess Hilda's death.

And not long after this the Abbess Frideswide, our mother, also fell into sickness. After lingering some days, she called all those in the monastery around her bed, and admonishing them to lead a life devoted to God, and full of charity to each other, and speaking to each of us apart some special word of faithful, motherly counsel, to which, weeping, we listened, and which we never can forget, she received the Eucharist, and after that did not speak through the night, so that once we who were watching almost thought her spirit had fled. But as we knelt beside her, waiting to receive her last breath, she opened her eyes, and said, in a voice faint but quite distinct,—

"How near is it to the hour when they will arise to chant the Prime?"

We answered,—

"Not far off; but there is too much weeping in the house for many to be able to sing."

Then she said, "They sing to Christ! Let me hear his praise again before I go;" and signing herself with the sign of the cross, she laid her head on the pillow, and lay still until the sweet sounds rose to us from the church of the voices chanting the hymn of the Holy Hilary:

> "Thou art the world's true Morning Star;
> Not that which o'er the edge of night,
> Faint herald of a little orb,
> Shines with a dim and narrow light.
> Far brighter than the earthly sun,
> Thyself at once the Light and Day."

And as she listened, she desired us to raise her so that she might look out on the dawn.

And so her spirit passed away to be associated with the blessed. And "her light came to her at the dawn of the day," when the sunrise glowing over Borrodale lighted up Skiddaw and Blencathera with a soft crimson.

Some in our convent were disappointed that no visions were seen when she died, nor any marvels wrought at her tomb. In so many other monasteries glorious sights have been vouchsafed, and heavenly sounds have been heard:—of "a body, shining brighter than the sun, drawn up to heaven in a white sheet by cords brighter than gold;" of "celestial music floating up the way the soul is to go;" of perfumes of Paradise at the tomb.

Doubtless (except in as far as these marvels are only bestowed on those who die unwedded), this is to humble us, whose eyes and ears are not worthy to be thus opened.

But as regards our mother, the Abbess Frideswide, I am content. It seems to me more fitting to her that she should have entered thus calmly on the other life, as if death were to her but another step in the path God was leading her day by day; caring to the last for those committed to her charge. With open eyes, as it were, she descended unshrinking into the cold waters of death, and seemed scarcely to feel them; for her heart was to the last engaged in guiding home the flock who watched her weeping from the brink, until she turned her gaze finally to Him who had trodden those pathless waves before, and was with her now.

To me such a death, so calm and fearless, seems nobler than that of any of the old heroes whom our race honoured of old. They confronted death boldly and defiantly as a foe. She, as a vanquished foe, scarcely regarded him, but looked beyond him to the redeeming Victor who plucked out his sting.

More suitable to her memory than perfume of roses, or visions, or any marvels, were those wise and quiet words of love and faith, the daily morning hymn, and the common light of dawn paling before her dying eyes into the light of the unveiled presence of Christ the Lord.

IV.

Saxon Schools and Homes.

STORY OF THE LADY ADELEVE,

RECORDED BY HILDELITH, THE NUN.

IV.

SAXON SCHOOLS AND HOMES.

STORY OF THE LADY ADELEVE, RECORDED BY HILDELITH THE NUN.

THE ABBESS HILDA'S MINSTER.

"DEORWYN and I," said Adeleve, my mother to me, "were the daughters and only children of Alfhelm and Ostritha his wife; and Alfhelm, our father, was the son of Frideswide the abbess.

"Our childhood was spent chiefly on our father's farm, near the lake of Derwent, at the foot of the castle crag, in Borrodale. Deorwyn was feeble in health, like our mother, and required tender nurture. She was also a wise and religious child, and delighted in nothing so much as when, on Sundays and holy days, we crossed the lake, and heard the monks and nuns chant the praises of God in our grandmother's minster.

"I, on the other hand, often enjoyed the crossing the lake more than the sacred services; especially when the wind came rushing down from Scawfell, and tossed our boat on the foaming waves. For I was strong and fearless; and whilst Deorwyn desired only to be a nun, I regretted that I had not been a boy, to climb the hills in the storms with my father, to bring the flocks into the fold, or to scale the crags in search of the eagles which destroyed the lambs. She liked the calm evenings when the light gleamed softly on the lake and glowed a deep rose on Skiddaw, and the green islands lay cradled in the lake, as dream-like and still in the golden waters as the rose and lilac clouds above them in the golden sky.

"I liked to be awakened in the night by the great winds rushing down from Scawfell like an army with war-shouts. While Deorwyn nestled close to me like a frightened bird, I seemed in some way to belong to the mountains, and to feel them part of me, and to rejoice in their strength. I had no more thought of being afraid of the winds and the storms which came to us from our mountains than of my father's voice when he called angrily in the chase.

"Our grandmother, the Abbess Frideswide, said that I was more like what she had been, and Deorwyn like her brother Leofric—only that he was a boy.

"In one thing Deorwyn and I both delighted equally, —namely, in our visit to the holy Herebert, who then lived in his cell on the wooded island which bears his name. We generally bore with us some little offering of fish and fruit, or of bread—the choicest of our mother's baking.

"He ever welcomed us tenderly, and told us sacred stories from the Gospels and the Acts of the saints. It was a great holiday for us when we could persuade our nurse to launch our little skiff, and with her stout arms to pull us to the island. Often the saint would see us from the shore, and be on a rock at the edge to help to draw the boat to land, and then lift us out of it.

"Sometimes, however, we heard his voice from afar, rising in a sacred chant; and then our nurse would not suffer us to land, but would row us slowly round the island, and take us back again.

"In our nurse's stories Deorwyn had not nearly as much delight as I had. These were chiefly of the old gods and heroes; of Loki the Black-hearted, who slew Balder the Beautiful, for whom every living being wept —even earth, and trees, and stones—so that the heart of Hela, the death goddess, was all but moved to let him go from her dark dwellings; of Thor the Thunderer, who fought with the earth giants; of Adumbla, the sacred cow, who licked the salt-rocks into the shape of Bor, the father of Odin; of the frost world, the fire world, and the cloud world, and their inhabitants; of the wolf Fenris, which pursued the sun goddess and the moon god. To me these stories were all the more enchanting because there was a delightful uncertainty about them, through which they loomed like Skiddaw through the morning mists. I was not at all sure how far these things were fables and how far they were true, and had often a vague thrill of mingled hope and fear—wondering whether the sudden thunder-claps which burst among the hills in spring might not be the strokes of Thor's hammer, or the golden clouds at morning the glitter of the golden walls of Asgard in the far east. I knew, indeed, that all power to hurt was taken away from the old gods; but our nurse was not at all sure, nor was I, how far they might be still lingering around their old worshippers of our race, to display their giant power in freaks of strength, or to show their good-will in friendly gifts.

"Deorwyn felt otherwise. She thought the old gods and heroes fierce and cruel sprites, and never liked to hear their names.

"So our childhood passed until our father was killed in a fight with a British prince, near Chester; and our mother soon after died of grief. Then Deorwyn was taken into the minster of our grandmother Frideswide, to devote her life to God; and I was sent to the abbey of the great Abbess Hilda, at Whitby, to learn all learning and accomplishments befitting a maiden of noble birth, and to be sheltered until my marriage with my cousin Osric—the son of Leofric, our grandmother Frideswide's brother—to whom I had been betrothed in infancy.

"The Abbess Hilda's monastery was no seclusion. It was the very centre and spring of the good which was done in the land. It was a school for the young, a college of clergymen, and especially of missionary clergymen, and a refuge for the oppressed and the aged. Whilst the kings and nobles were continually journeying from one estate to another to receive their rents, their sons and daughters could be educated in the abbey, free from all the dangers and unsettledness of this wandering life.

"The minster (monastery) formed quite a town in itself clustered around the church, which was built after the Scotch method with wood, and was roofed with thatch, and had slits for windows, which were made very narrow, and with deep sides sloping outward, that the rain and snow might not beat in on the worshippers.

"It was, however, the most beautiful building I had then seen; and on the altar, covered with its fair white cloth, lay a wondrously costly copy of the Gospels in Latin, with a large sapphire set in the golden cover.

"The dwellings appropriated for the sisters were for

the most part scattered wooden buildings—some for dormitories, some for schools, and one for the refectory. The brothers had their little village apart from ours. In the church also we sat in separate parts, although our voices blended in the praises of God.

"There were also guest chambers for the many noble and royal visitors who came to see our mother the abbess; and there was a house of refuge for the aged, and another for poor wayfarers.

"These buildings stood on the brow of the hill looking far over the sea. Down the green and wooded slopes rose many huts of the mechanics and farm-labourers who worked on the abbey lands; and below, on the banks of the river, was the fishing village, inhabited by the many fishermen who supplied the community with fish. We were all employed to the full. The Abbess Hilda suffered no drones in her hive.

"With the first break of day in summer, and before it in winter, we were all aroused by the convent bell. Then most of the brothers and sisters assembled in the church at the cock-crowing, and chanted, such of us as knew Latin, the hymn, *Eterne rerum Conditor*—'Eternal Maker of all things.'

"I remember to this day how beautiful it was, as we left the church, to watch the dawn breaking slowly from grey to gold over the eastern sea. At matins, three hours later, we assembled again, and sang the praises of Him who is 'the brightness of the Father's glory.' And to this day those hours seem to come back to me musical with God's praise. For the many who cannot read, I think it is a most worthy custom thus to make the very hours of the day so many pages of a sacred hymnal, which memory illuminates with her fairest colours.

"Much of the day was spent by us, the young maidens, in the school, learning to read Anglo-Saxon gospels and hymns, to spin and weave, and to embroider.

"Arithmetic was not taught us, although some of our number learned to read Latin, and a few also to write.

"We were always much astonished at the learning of the boys, when the bishop, or a learned priest, came round and examined them, and they solved arithmetical problems with what seemed to us the most magical skill, such as this,—

"An old man met a child. 'Good day, my son,' he said; 'may you live as long as you have lived, and as much more, and thrice as much as all this, and if God give you one year in addition to the others, you will be a century old: what was the lad's age?' And the lads actually answered it, so the learned priests said.

"My old longing to have been a boy came back to me when I heard such wonders, and more especially when I heard them discourse concerning the firmament, with all the stars revolving round us, and the earth in the centre shaped like a pine nut, with the fountains and rivers running through it like the veins through a man's body. Most especially, however, did I envy them when the young nobles among them swept by to the chase, on foot or on horseback, to follow the harriers over the hills, or to hunt the wild boars.

"After that I turned with some discontent to my distaff in the narrow chamber, or to the recipes against the bites of adders, or against burns and scalds, so many of which we had to learn by heart. Often, however, the nun who instructed us would relate histories of the marvels wrought by the faithful in their lives and deaths; especially of the holy bishops Aidan and Chad; of Fursey, the holy Irish anchorite, who preached the faith in Lindsey (Lincoln) and among the East Angles, and was vouchsafed such wondrous visions of the other world; of Cuthbert, bishop of Lindisfarne, the great friend of Herebert, the anchorite of Derwent-water, so dear to Deorwyn and me.

"She told us also of Hii, or Iona, the holy island of the western seas, which was the mother church of almost all our English churches north of the Thames; of the perpetual prayer and praise that went up from its humble cells and churches; its grassy heights and wave-washed rocks to God; and how one after another issued thence to proclaim the redemption of mankind through every village, and lonely hamlet, and busy town, throughout this land of ours.

"To me, as we listened, that lonely island seemed as holy as Rome, or Jerusalem itself, and more like heaven; since at Rome we heard there were great sinners as well as great saints; and Jerusalem being now dumb in the hands of the heathen, living prayer and praise must surely, I thought, be more heavenly and dear to God than any graves.

"This nun had also marvellous histories which she used to tell us as it grew dusk, about the deaths of many holy men and women; how when Bishop Chad was reading the Holy Scriptures and praying in the oratory of his monastery, he heard suddenly the voice of many persons singing most sweetly and rejoicing, and appearing to descend from heaven, from the southeast (where the throne of Christ is), until it drew near the roof of the oratory, and filled it; and then, after listening half an hour, he perceived the same song of joy ascend and return to heaven the way it came, with inexpressible sweetness. After which, having assembled the seven brothers of the house, and bidden them farewell with fatherly counsel, in seven days he went to heaven the way the music came. She told us also of the young boy Esica, who was brought up among the nuns, and falling sick, called three times as he died, 'Eadgith! Eadgith! Eadgith!' which summons that holy virgin, though absent, obeyed at once, being seized the same day with the same distemper, and 'following the child into the heavenly country whither he called her' before the sun had set. And of another dying nun, who entreated those who were watching round her bed to put out the candle, 'for I tell you,' said she, 'that I see this house filled with so much light, that your candle there seems to me to be dark.' And as they still hesitated to extinguish it, she added, 'Let it burn; but take notice that it is not my light, for my light will come to me at the dawn of the day,'—which was fulfilled, for then she died.

"I liked better, however, the stories of what the saints did in their lives;—how once Bishop Aidan, from his solitary retreat in the rocky islet of Farne, saw the flames encompassing the city of Bamborough, from the great pile of planks, wattles, and thatch, which the heathen Penda, king of the Mercians, had kindled; and lifting up his hands and eyes to heaven, he said '*Behold, Lord, how great mischief Penda does!*' which words were hardly uttered when the wind changed, and turned back the flames from the city on those who kindled them;—how Bishop Cuthbert scaled the robbers' nests, and preaching the glad tidings to the outcast, won them to the fold of Christ;—how Bishop Chad, when storms of wind or thunder and lightning came, would immediately call on God to have mercy on him and all mankind; and if it lasted, would repair to the church, and watch through the tempest, praying and repeating psalms until the calm was restored; 'for,' said he, 'the Lord thunders in the heavens, moves the air, darts lightning, to excite the inhabitants of earth to fear him, to dispel their pride by reminding them of that dreadful time when the heavens and the earth being in a flame, He will come in the clouds with great power and majesty, to judge the quick and dead. Wherefore we should answer his heavenly admonition with fear and love; that as often as he lifts his hands through the trembling sky, yet does not strike, we may implore his mercy, and searching the recesses of our hearts, cleanse them from the pollution of our sins.' It was good also to hear of Oswald, the king, meekly sitting at the feet of Bishop Aidan, to interpret his words to the ignorant people; or of Owini, the courtier, quitting the world for the convent, with the axe and hatchet on his shoulder, that 'not being capable of prolonged meditation, he might yet use such gifts as he had, and labour with his hands for God.'

"These things interested me always more than the visions at death-beds or the miracles at the tombs, because if it pleases God to pour a flood of light into our chamber when we die, or to make our coffins diffuse perfume like the richest balsams, it may be very edifying and sweet to those who survive us; but I do not see how we can do anything to bring it about. Whereas when I heard of Aidan simply commending the sorrows of others to God, and being heard, I used to think I might try to do the same. Often through life that strong, quiet prayer of his, has encouraged me to pray, as, beside the bed-side of my sick children or near the battle-field where my husband fought, I have knelt and said with weeping eyes, '*Behold, Lord, this my sorrow!*' and felt that was enough.

"Often also in the storms at sea or on land I have remembered Bishop Chad, and bowing at the voice of God, have prayed, not only for myself, but for all men in need and peril, and have found that the prayer for others wonderfully quieted my heart as to my own danger.

"And all through life the good Owini, with his axe and hatchet, has seemed to walk before me, who have so little faculty for contemplation, saying, 'There are gifts for each, and there is a path for each to heaven.'

"Again and again from lonely, perilous moors and dens of robbers, the voice of Bishop Cuthbert has seemed to call on me to labour for the lost, to bring them into the fold.

"Dearer than any of these worthy names to me, however, is that of our mother, the Abbess Hilda, true mother to me the motherless girl; patient counsellor, and never-failing friend. It was she, above all others, who taught us to revere the holy men from Iona—to mourn the day when, after the great synod held at her abbey, when the King Oswy decided for the Romans, good Bishop Colman left the cradle of so many churches, the lowly but most glorious monastery of Lindisfarne, and departed northward. She had contended earnestly for the Scots—not, I think, that she deemed it of much moment whether the monks were shaven wholly, according to the Scotch and Oriental method, or coronal-wise like the Romans, in imitation of the crown of thorns; but the free Saxon lady, daughter of Odin, and of the kindred of kings, did not easily brook that Italian priests should lord it over our free Saxon Church, or that the party who fled with Paulinus from the storm should return when the storm had passed, to reap what they had not sown.

"Much debate about these matters I heard in my youth, and much I wondered that these good Scots should thus be humbled; but since our Lord says, 'He that is chief among us is he that serveth,' I in my old age have learned to think that the Scotch monks have done well not to part with their Christ-like crowns of service and lowliness for the Latin crowns of exaltation and rule, and the Roman palls.

"There was little monotony at the minster. The presence of the warm heart and clear mind of the abbess was felt everywhere. Cædmon, the Christian poet, was one of the Abbess Hilda's monks. The elder nuns used to tell us how one night, when the harp was passed round to him at the feast, he knew no song to sing, whereupon, rising, he left the table, and went to the stable to feed the horses under his charge. There he composed himself to sleep, when in a dream one appeared to him and said, 'Cædmon, sing some song to me.' He answered, 'I cannot sing, and for that reason retired from the feast.' Then said the voice, 'Nevertheless, you shall sing.' 'What shall I sing?' he rejoined. 'Sing the beginning of created things,' said the voice. Then in his dream he began to sing, in words he had never heard before, the praises of the Creator, the deeds of the Father of glory. Awaking, the songs he had sung in his dream rang through his heart; and others, hearing of his gift, led him to our Abbess Hilda, to whom, in the presence of many learned men, he told his dream and repeated his verses.

"They all concluded that heavenly grace had been conferred on him by our Lord, whereupon the abbess, embracing the grace of God in the man, instructed him to quit the secular habit and enter the monastery. And there he lived thenceforth, meekly listening to the sacred stories of Holy Writ from the lips of the learned—for he could not read—and then singing the same for his people in Saxon verse.

"To Cædmon, the herdsman poet, we delighted to listen, gathering around him, in the great minster-hall on winter evenings, or on summer evenings on the cliff above the sea, while the quiet waves rippled faintly far below, as he sang to his harp, in our own mother-tongue, of the fall of angels in the far-off ages: of the birth of the world, and then of the birth of the Holy Child at Bethlehem: of his agony for us in the garden and on the cross: of his glorious rising and soaring into heaven: and of the Holy Ghost the Comforter, whom Christ sends to us, that we may not be orphans though bereaved of the sight of him. Heart-stirring it was to listen how, in the beginning,—

'The children of glory,
  The hosts of angels,
  The glorious thanes,
  Feeding on bliss,

'Knowing not sin,
  Praised the King,
  Willingly praised the Lord of Life.'

"How then,—

'When there was nothing
But cavernous gloom,
And the wide ground
Lay deep and dim,
And the dark clouds
Perpetually pressed
Black under the sky,
Void and waste,
The eternal Lord
Reared the sky.
When the earth was then

Not green with grass;
Covered with the ocean,
Ever black,
Far and wide,
The desert ways,
The Creator of angels,
The Lord of life,
Parted life from darkness,
Shade from shine.
But he, once made fairest of all,
Highest of angels,

Like the brilliant stars,
He who should have thanked
  his Lord
For the brightness he shared,
Began to be over-proud,
And would not serve God,
But said he was his equal
In light and shining;
And thus spoke to himself:—

"I cannot have
Any creature above me.
Why should I
Sue for his grace?
Or bend to Him
With any obedience?
I may be
A God as he is."'

"And how then,—

'He who had been made so fair,
Of angels most shining
Fell out of heaven,
During the space
Of three nights and days,
Into black hell,
And the angels who followed
  him,
And became devils.
There have they for ever
Fire, ever renewed,
The east wind,
The cold frost,
Mingling with the fires.
And seek they other land,
All is void of light
And full of fire,
A great journey of fire.
While he who has been the
  whitest in heaven,
By his Master beloved,
Said with sorrowing speech,
"Is this the narrow place,

Unlike what erst we knew,
That my Master sets me in?
Knots of chains press me down,
Hell's fetters
Hold me hard,
This fire never languishes;
Biting manacles
Arrest my course,
My army is taken from me,
My feet are bound,
My hands imprisoned,
I am kingdomless!
Yet is it ever to me the bitterest
  sorrow
That Adam, the earth-made,
Possesses my mighty throne;
That he is to be happy,
While we suffer misery in hell;
That from him once more
God will people
The kingdom of heaven
With pure souls."'

"Often, through the night, after we had listened to our herdsman poet, those wild laments, or those songs of joy and praise, lingered through my heart, mingling with the breaking of the waves on the rocky shore.

"Happy the poet who learned the art of poetry not from man, but God; whose heart was never tuned to any but sacred songs; who sang the truth of God into the hearts of so many of his people!

"Often, also, we had guests of noble or royal birth, pilgrims from Rome or Jerusalem.

"But more encircled with wonder to me than any of our guests, was Archbishop Theodore of Tarsus. He was an old man when first I saw him. Greek, the language in which St. John wrote, and St. Paul, and St. Peter, was his mother tongue. He had lisped in the very words of the original New Testament. In his childhood and in his youth he had studied in the very city where the Apostle Paul was born.

"Our England owned her first Greek, and many of her first Latin schools, to a fellow-citizen of St. Paul himself.

"As I looked at his white hair, contrasting so beautifully with his dark, keen eye, and as he spoke to us of apostles and evangelists, around him they seemed to rise no longer pictures and shadows, but living men of our flesh and blood.

"Bishop Wilfrid of York also occasionally came to our monastery, not on foot, in humble guise, like the Scotch bishops, assisted by two or three humble missionary priests, who spent their time in reading or transcribing the Scriptures, in preaching and in praising God; but followed royally by a train of horsemen, clad in rich array. Wonders were told us of the church at Ripon, which he had lately built, after the Roman model, with lofty walls and countless arches, foundations like those of the everlasting hills; adorned with gorgeous paintings, and costly plate and books, and with the windows paned with pure, transparent glass. He himself had marvellous tales to tell of the splendours of Rome, which he had visited often. But more than of all this magnificence, I liked to hear what he had done among the wild heathens of Friesland (as afterwards among those of Sussex) when shipwrecked on their coast; how he had taught them at once how to worship Christ the Lord, and how to keep off famine by a better mode of fishing, so that the simple people honoured him as one sent express from heaven.

"Visits such as these were our great festivals. But every Sunday it was a festive sight to see the people flocking to the church of our monastery on the cliff; from the fishing-hamlet by the river, from the cottages on the hill-side, from villages miles away, the labourer, that day free from labour, the thrall, that day free from thraldom; thrall and thane, clerk and warrior, prince's son from the school, peasant's son from the country, meeting under one roof to hear and sing the praises of one redeeming Lord. Some of the service was chanted by the choristers in Latin, and to this the unlearned seemed to listen as to strains of dim but heavenly music. But the Lord's Prayer and the Creed all the people repeated in our Saxon tongue, and many joined in the Saxon hymns and the Te Deum. The Abbess Hilda also always had the holy Gospels read and explained in our mother-tongue, so that each might depart to his home with some new light kindled in his heart and understanding.

"Great was the joy of Easter at the Abbess Hilda's abbey. Then the new converts won during the year from the heathenism which still lingered in the recesses of the land, were baptized in the river below the hill, and, clothed in their spotless baptismal robes, joined for the first time in the services of the church.

"And frequently another rejoicing company were gathered in the church on that day. The slaves, redeemed from the hard and unjust bondage by the alms which Bishop Aidan and his disciples delighted to devote to that purpose, were assembled at the altar at Easter, and there solemnly set free; that evermore they might thank one ransoming Lord for liberation both from temporal and spiritual bondage. Then, indeed, was heard at once the voice of weeping and rejoicing—mothers sobbing for joy to win back their captured children; the sons of freemen thanking God, with trembling voices, that once more they and their sons were free.

"One Easter, I remember, our alms were desired to ransom some Christians who had been taken captive by the heathen Saxons in Old Saxony, the land from which our forefathers came. The priest who thus sought our aid had himself escaped from the same captivity; and terrible were the tales he told us of those our heathen kinsmen,—of their fierce forays on each other and on their neighbours; of the cruel religion which glorified such slaughter; of the shrieks echoing at midnight through the black forests, where they sacrificed human victims to their cruel gods. Then I learned what Thor and Odin were in their power, and I grew to hate their names as much as my gentle sister Deorwyn. Yet, more than ever did these tales make me wish I had been a boy, that I might go and tell these cruel slaves of false spirits by what a lie they were held in thraldom. Death on such an errand seemed to me nobler than even my father's death for his people on the battle-field. Often, also, my spirit chafed against my father's destination of me to the cares of married life, instead of what seemed to me the far loftier calling of a consecrated nun. But since this could not be otherwise, I resolved that if ever I had sons of my own I would train them, and pray our Lord to train them, for such work as this. Such purposes the Abbess Hilda by God's grace, inspired in numberless hearts besides mine. From her schools and her congregations went forth Christian nobles and ladies, Christian poets and clerks, anchorites, bishops, missionaries, and martyrs. Thus the abbey of Whitby, like that of Lindisfarne, was no quiet pool, gathering into itself the lives of holy men and women, to rest still and peaceful in this quiet shade; but a fountain-head of noblest enterprise, and of wide-spread blessings throughout the land.

THE ORDEAL.

"THE time drew near for me to quit the Abbess Hilda's minster, on my marriage, according to my father's will, with Osric, the young Thane.

"The day was fixed for our wedding, the morgen gift which he was to bestow on me on the day after our marriage had been arranged and set down in writing, when a great difficulty arose.

"A monk, whose severity had made him unpopular with the boys, was found one morning in a meadow, wounded and sorely beaten. Suspicion fell on Osric and on a lad named Edwy, who alone had been seen on the previous night walking near the spot where the wounded monk was found.

"The poor monk could remember nothing but that a figure draped in black, whom he took to be a demon, had knocked him down from behind, and, after belabouring him with a club, without uttering a syllable in answer to his cries, had fled at the approach of footsteps.

"Both Edwy and Osric denied the accusation on oath. Before the congregation both stood up and swore solemnly,—

"'In the Lord, I am innocent of the charge whereof they accuse me.'

"Edwy's voice was bold and rapid, and his look defiant. Osric's tones were low and clear, deliberate and steady; and the look of his honest eyes frank and open as usual, neither shrinking from, nor courting any one's gaze.

"It was ruled that the matter should be tried by the ordeal of hot iron, in the church.

"On the day appointed, prayer was made throughout the monastery that God would defend the right. Then the fire was lighted in the church, and the priest, accompanied only by the two accused, went in to see that the irons were duly heated. Meantime, many of the community waited without, until we were summoned inside to witness the ordeal. The Abbess Hilda went first, bearing a silver cross, and followed by the professed nuns, and the young maidens of the schools. When we had ranged ourselves on one side of the church, the monks and youths entered and stood in a line opposite to us. Between us glowed the fire in a large brazier, its dull red glare reflected on the faces of the accused and the priest.

"All of us had spent the day fasting, as also the accused.

"Both repeated the collects imploring the Judge of all to make the truth clear.

"To me it was as clear as daylight already. The bold, defiant stare had passed from Edwy's face, and although his eyes wandered around the church, their unsteady gaze rested on no one. He stood rigidly erect; but his hands nervously clutched his sword.

"Osric stood with head slightly bent during the prayer—pale, and with compressed lips; but when the last word of the collect ceased he looked up, a flush of joyous resolution lighted up his cheek, he glanced at the Abbess Hilda, and then at me, and his eyes smiled trustfully into mine.

"Before that I had almost feared to look; but from that moment I feared no more.

"When the prayer had ceased, the priest sprinkled both the accused with holy water, and also moistened their lips with it. Each kissed the book of the holy Gospels, and was signed with the cross. All this time the irons were lying upon the burning coals. Then one of the pieces was laid, red-hot, on Osric's hands. His lips were slightly compressed, but unshrinkingly he carried the burning mass the nine prescribed feet, from the fire to the stake, and there dropped it. A murmur of sympathy and admiration ran through the church. The priest bound up his hands, and sealed them—to be opened on the third day and examined, to see whether they were healing soundly or not.

"After that the priest raised the other iron with pincers, and slowly prepared to place it in Edwy's hands. But those slow moments overcame the last remnants of his false courage; and, falling on his knees, before the iron had touched him, he confessed, before the whole congregation, his base and cowardly crime.

"Then the guilty was led away ignominiously to

endure his punishment, and all the congregation pressed around Osric and did him honour; but to me, his betrothed, it was permitted to dress his scarred hands. Thus I learned to know the worth of my husband; and also to appreciate the value of the recipes I had learned so reluctantly for the healing of burns and scalds. And thus my heart was won to the lot which I think God appointed for me.

"The scars were on his hands still when he placed the marriage ring on my finger and the mass-priest blessed us at the altar. Glorious scars I thought them, and ever after honoured the trial by ordeal. But Osric, your father, thought otherwise.

"An innocent person, he considered, might want the kind of courage which enables a man to bear pain, and a rogue might possess it. 'Besides,' he said, 'if Edwy's courage had held out a little longer, and he had carried the iron safely from the fire to the stake, the test of innocence would then have been no other than the readiness of the skin to heal, which might fail in a saint.'

"But criminals, I think, are mostly cowards; and if not, is not cowardice in itself a crime? Besides, does not the Almighty answer prayer? Not always, however, my husband thought, in the way or at the time we wish. Besides, since God himself has endowed man with judgment, he deemed it mere idleness to substitute the test of accident for patient search into the truth.

"Some of the clergy, I know, think with him; but at all events that proved a true ordeal for my Osric, as the years that followed abundantly showed; and if it be unlawful for men to try each other by fire, it is certain, from holy writ, that the Lord himself often useth this ordeal to test us.

THE LADY ADELEVE'S HOME.

"It was a great change to me from the Abbess Hilda's monastery to my husband's home.

"There was much for me and my maidens to do in providing for our large household. Every day a score of men sat at our board; and often my husband would bring a hunting party back with him, for whom a feast had to be ready as quickly as Abraham prepared his calf for the angels. And our guests were not angels, nor were calves in our climate so easily made ready. Therefore we had always large store in the house of salted meat, and fruits, and more especially of ale and mead; for no Saxon would drink water if ale was to be had.

"These hunting feasts were very strange to me at first. The guests commonly abode the night, and sometimes drank through the night. My boys, as they grew old enough, served them with horns of mead and ale; and I, and any matrons who might be with me, began the feast by pledging the principal guests. But as the harp and the horn were passed around, and the mirth grew wilder, and the songs more unsteady, we withdrew with the lads. And often through the night, as I listened to the sounds of drunken revelry, I longed for the songs of Cædmon, the religious poet, and the midnight chants of the nuns. For although Osric himself was temperate, he could not for hospitality's sake stint or moderate his guests.

"When the children were able to understand, I taught them as well as I could to chant the vesper and sunrise hymns; and sometimes a hope lighted up my heart that, perhaps, those infant lispings of His praise were as dear to Him who took the children in his arms as the richer music of the holy brotherhood.

"Yet those were days of many lessons, I think, to me, and of almost unbroken happiness, whilst I learned to love the lowly joys of a woman's life of daily service. Around our homestead arose the dwellings of labourers, mechanics, and fishermen; and around our children grew up the children of our faithful thralls.

"The first shadow that was thrown across our married life was the great Abbess Hilda's death; if I may call that a shadow, which was but the passing of a blessed spirit to its own place in the light, the place of bliss to which she belonged.

"I remember, as if it was yesterday, every circumstance around me at the moment we heard the news.

"It was the dewy dawn of a summer morning. We and our household had sung together as best we could the matin hymn, which I had learned at Whitby. The servants were preparing the morning meal of meat, wheaten bread and honey, ale, and mead, in the hall where we all ate together; and we with the children had gone into the garden, which as much as possible I had made like the convent garden. The bees were buzzing around us; I was pointing them out to the little ones, now lying in the honey-bearing leaves of the marigolds, or in the purple flowers of the mallows, sucking the nectar drop by drop with their beaks; now flying around the yellowing willows and purplish tops of the broom, carrying on their burdened thighs the plunder from which they build their waxen castles; now crowding about the round berries of the ivy which climbed over the house, or the light flowers of the lime trees which shaded it,[*] when Osric came to me with a clouded face, and said in a low voice, taking my hands in his, 'Adeleve, our mother, the Abbess

[*] *Vide* Aldhelm, quoted in Sharon Turner.

Hilda, is at rest.' Long as she had been ill, it came on me like a sudden blow benumbing my heart. For when does death not come suddenly? When is the moment when he can smite some precious life into silence, and we who are left shall not moan for one touch, one blessing, one loving, forgiving look more?

"We sent the children into the house, and he told me all he knew of her departure.

"After governing her monastery many years, it had pleased Him who makes such merciful provision for our salvation to try her holy soul for six years with the trial of a long sickness to the end that, after the Apostle's example, her strength might be made perfect in weakness. During all that time she never failed either to return thanks to her Maker, or publicly and privately to instruct the flock committed to her charge, for by her own example she admonished all to serve God dutifully in health, and always to return thanks to Him in sickness and bodily weakness. In this, the seventh year of her sickness, the Abbess Hilda approached her last day; and having received the holy communion to further her on her way, and called together the servants of Christ that were within the same monastery, she admonished them to preserve evangelical peace among themselves, and with all others. And as she was thus speaking, she joyfully saw death approaching, and passed from death into life.

"That same night it pleased God, by a manifest vision, to make known her death in another monastery at a distance from hers, which she had built that same year. There was in that monastery a certain nun called Begu, who, having dedicated her virginity to God, had served him upwards of thirty years in monastical conversation. This nun, being then in the dormitory of the sisters, on a sudden heard the well-known sound of a bell in the air, which used to awake and call them to prayers when any one of them was taken out of the world, and opening her eyes, she thought she saw the top of the house open, and a strong light pour in from above. Looking earnestly upon that light she saw the soul of the servant of God in that same light, attended and conducted to heaven by angels. Then awaking and seeing the other sisters sleeping round her, she perceived that what she had seen was either in a dream or a vision. Rising immediately she ran to the virgin Frygyth, who presided in the monastery instead of the abbess, and told her with tears and sighs that the Abbess Hilda, mother of them all, had ascended to eternal bliss. Frygyth having heard it, awoke all the sisters, and all night they prayed and sang psalms for her soul. And at break of day the brothers came with news of her death from the place where she died.*

"It is reported that her death was also in a vision made known the same night to one of the holy virgins who loved her most passionately in the same monastery where the abbess died. This nun saw her soul ascend to heaven in the company of angels, and being at that time in the remotest part of the monastery (where the women newly converted were wont to be on trial till they were regularly instructed and taken into the congregation) she awakened them to pray for her soul before the rest of the community had heard of her death.

"We and our children and household assembled with thousands of weeping men and women at her funeral, and saw her laid in the church on the cliff where the breaking waves shall chant her dirge till the resurrection of the just.

* Bede Ecc. Hist.

"Then we all scattered to our dwellings, feeling well nigh as if a mother had been taken from the head of every home.

"In other respects also, besides the household cares and the noisy feastings, the change was great from the monastery to the home; as if a boat drifting down the broad current of some great river where sailed ships of all nations, from amidst the busy sounds of traffic, with men hailing each other eagerly in all languages, bringing news from every land, were suddenly steered up a little narrow tributary stream just deep enough for one shallow skiff, and moored among the rushes of some quiet lonely valley, with not a glimpse into the world beyond.

"Certainly to me the convent was the busy world, and the home the hermit-like retreat.

"Among all the household I was the only one who could read; and I had only two books—an Anglo-Saxon Gospel of St. Luke, and a Latin and Anglo-Saxon psalter, with prayers and meditations at the end of each psalm. Osric, indeed, had begun to learn; but his stay at the abbey school had not been long, and reading never became to him anything but a very laborious effort of mind, for which, at the end of a toilsome day on the farm or at the chase, he had little taste.

"Our estate lay far to the north of Whitby, near the sea, on the river Tyne.

"At first we used every Sunday to walk or ride many miles to attend the service of God in the abbey church at Wearmouth, on the Wear; but as the children grew up around us, it became difficult to take the little ones so far, and it was, therefore, a great delight to me when another monastery began to rise on the Tyne, quite near us, at Tarrow. Osric did not much rejoice in this.

He had no desire that our children should become monks or nuns. The boys he destined for the profession of arms in the service of the king, and the girls for wedded life.

"But I continued to pray to our Lord that if it pleased him he would call at least one of our sons to serve him among the heathen; and from their earliest childhood I told them the stories of Bishop Aidan, of Cuthbert carrying the Gospel into the homes of our own happy land, and of Bishop Wilfred shipwrecked on the shores of Friesland beyond the seas. Our children always listened with eager interest, and often in their infancy the look of reverent awe, which makes the faces of little children like those of angels, would come into their eyes. But as they grew older, the boys seemed to emulate the adventures of the missionary's life far more than its purpose. I sighed sometimes, brave and affectionate as they were, to see them grow up so much more like me than like Deorwyn, so much more like me than like my lessons.

"But one day when I had been musing mournfully about these things, and wishing that God would vouchsafe me some sign, such as the mothers of saints have concerning their children, and thinking that there must be some great fault in me since my prayers were not heard, my husband found me in tears, and would know why.

"'What sign wouldst thou have?' he said.

"'Some have had wondrous dreams of discovering fair heavenly jewels, or have seen a great glory of light round their infants' brows, or have heard voices of angels.'

"'And what were these signs of?' he said.

"'That the babes were especially dear to God, and that he would make them great servants of his.'

"'What sign dost thou need,' he said, 'that the babes are dear to God, when he says so? Dost thou think the little ones the Lord Christ took in his arms and blessed were all grave little precocious monks and nuns? For me,' he continued, 'it is sign enough of good that they were signed with the holy cross in baptism, and to see the glow of health on their faces.'

"'But,' I said, 'the lads are often in so much mischief, and the girls so full of wild glee.'

"'Are not the girls very much like what thou wert as a child, my love?' he said, smiling.

"'Yes,' I said, 'that is the worst of it. They are like me, and not like what I teach them.'

"'Life will teach them soon enough,' he said gravely. 'Better than thee I do not wish the maidens to be or to grow; nor do I desire that the boys should serve God better than Joseph the ealdorman, or David the king.'

"I was afraid Osric might not quite understand. Yet his words comforted me. After that I began to look less for signs of God's especial favour to my children, and to treasure up more all the words of his grace and love in Holy Writ. And seeing there seemed so little chance of our little ones growing up to be saints, I tried to do my best to make them good men and women.

"In which I think God heard and helped me. We must also remember that in the lives of the saints, no doubt, as it is fit and reverent they should, the biographers have left out all but what is good. Otherwise, how is it possible that the commendations of the historian and the self-reproaches of the saint should both be true? which, no doubt, they are.

"The only one of our sons who early showed an ambition to emulate the austerities of the saints was Oswald, our second son, who delighted often to try how much cold, and fatigue, or hardship of various kinds he could endure. One winter, I remember, he nearly died of a cold and cough he caught we knew not how, until one of his brothers confided to me that he had been trying the plan of the monk Drythelm, who, after awaking from some dreadful vision of the torments of the wicked in the other world from frost and fire, would often say his prayers standing in half-frozen water, and when remonstrated with would answer, 'I have felt greater cold than this.'

"However, when I questioned Oswald, he said he was only trying what he could bear, that he might be fit for any kind of life hereafter. Soldiers, he said, endured more. And then he told me stories of the training of boys in an ancient heathen kingdom called Sparta, which, he said, he had heard from Bede, the learned young monk, who was the glory of the monastery at Tarrow. This made it easier for me to forbid such attempts in future. I could, of course, say nothing to dissuade him from following the saints; but those cruel old heathens could plainly be no models for a Christian lad.

"Marvellous was the learning Oswald brought back from the monastery. The school at the Abbess Hilda monastery seemed to me nothing to it; the *mensa pythagorica* (multiplication table); the long sentences he could repeat by rote in Latin; the many-syllabled Greek verbs and nouns, which, if the Greek little girls and boys all learned at their seminaries, it is no wonder they grew up to be the wisest people in the world!

"The zeal of Bede, the young monk, seemed to have inspired our Oswald. He alone of all our boys seemed to look on learning as a delight rather than a task, and would tell me long histories of what he learned at school. He and thou, Hildelith, our youngest born, were always especial friends, and it was sweet to see you together, so close was the love between you from infancy. A delight it was to watch you when in the pauses of your play you sat together, thine earnest eyes looking up full of reverence and awe into thy brother's ardent animated face, as he tried to impart some of his learning to thee.

"Often have I pointed you out to your father, and he would smile, and say,—

"'Are you content with that sign, my Adeleve? There is hope that two of our children may yet appear in the lives of the saints.'

"He was not wrong, Hildelith, we know, at least, as to your brother.

"But disappointment awaited me, and far longer waiting than I was prepared for.

"When Oswald was fifteen, and according to the custom of our people, might choose his way in life, to my dismay he came to your father and asked, not as I had fondly hoped, for permission to enter the monastery of Tarrow, but for a horse and all the equipments of a soldier, and an armed servant on horseback to attend him, that he might ride forth and see the world, and enter the service of any king who seemed to him best worth serving.

"Of that journey and its results thou knowest. I wept many bitter tears as I wove the garments for his outfit, and embroidered the silken bag that he might carry round his neck the dust from the grave of St. Oswald the king; and many more, as I thought of him wandering forth thus alone into the dangerous and treacherous world. But your father bid me be of good cheer, and have patience; an oak would not grow like a mushroom, and if we watched each branch, would often seem to grow the wrong way.

"And Bede, the young monk, told me of Oswald the king, who was a true saint although a layman. Also, he told me a wonderful story of St. Monica, a Roman lady who lived and died not three centuries since, and her son; how for many years he seemed to throw off the faith of Christ utterly, yet at last was brought back to the fold, and became the light of all the Church, even the great Father Augustine!

"But especially I remember all that your father said to me at that time, because so soon afterwards he was brought home with a broken leg from the chase, and was laid on the bed from which he never rose, although one of the best leeches in all the land was a monk of the monastery at Tarrow, and attended him constantly, skilfully binding up the broken limb in tight ligatures.

"Before any surgeon could come, however, when he was brought in stunned, I ventured myself to bleed him as I had learned at the abbey of Whitby. And for this I shall reproach myself as long as I live as one thing that hindered his recovery. For in my fright and distraction I forgot that at that time the moon was waxing instead of waning; at which time, the Archbishop Theodore himself said, it was dangerous to let blood.

"Yet when once I, with bitter tears, told this to your father, he said, 'Surely, if the Lord Christ sees it time to call me, he will see that his summons is delivered, be it by whose hand it may.' That is true, and it comforts me much to think so. But surely the compassionate Lord would never have given such a message to me. No doubt it was the distracting devil who confused my senses.

"Your father's illness was long, and his suffering (except from the treatment of the doctor) not great. Very often the good monks would come to visit him, and held edifying discourses, especially the young monk Bede, who had always wise words to say (either his own or from the innumerable books he knew); and also examples of the lives and deaths of good men to encourage us with from the days of the Gospels to our own, when many can still remember the dying looks and words of Bishop Aidan, and of Cuthbert, and of the Abbess Hilda, Bishop Chad, and other saints.

"His story of the death of Bishop Cuthbert and his friend Herebert went to my heart, partly because I had known the anchorite Herebert on the Derwent Lake in my childhood.

"'Herebert was wont,' the good monk Bede told us one day, 'to visit Bishop Cuthbert on his island in the lake every year, and to receive from him spiritual advice. Hearing that Cuthbert was come to the city of Carlisle, he repaired one year to him according to custom, being desirous of being still more inflamed in heavenly desires through his wholesome admonitions. Whilst they alternately entertained one another with the delights of the celestial life, the bishop among other things said, "Brother Herebert, remember at this time to ask me all the questions you wish to have answered, and say all you design, for we shall see each other no more in this world. For I am sure that the time of my departure is at hand, and that I shall speedily put off this tabernacle of the flesh." Hearing these words, he fell down at his feet, and weeping, said, "I beseech you by our Lord forsake me not, but remember your most faithful companion, and entreat the Supreme Goodness that, as we served him together on earth, we may depart together to see his bliss in heaven." The bishop applied himself to prayer, and having presently intimation in the spirit, that he had obtained what he had asked of the Lord, he said, "Rise, brother, and weep not, but rejoice, for the Heavenly Goodness has granted what we desired." And even so it happened. They saw each other no more in the flesh; but their souls quitted their bodies on the same day, the 20th of March, one from the wooded islet on the Derwent Lake, the other from the rocky island of Farne in the sea; they were immediately again united and translated to heaven by the angels; and Herebert being by a long previous sickness disciplined to holiness as great as that of Cuthbert, on the same day they ascended to the same seat of eternal bliss, there to pass through all the endless stages of the glorious life together, twin brothers in the heavenly world.'

"When the good Bede had finished, and I sat silently weeping by my husband's bedside, he took my hand and said,—

"'Come, let us pray for this, even this.'

"'It would be sweet, indeed,' he said, smoothing my hair, 'but can we ask it?'

"'Not yet, perhaps,' I sobbed, 'not now! but that he might spare us both till the elder ones could care for the younger, and then—'

"'What if one of us should be left to bring all the flock to the other waiting in heaven, and to the Lord the Good Shepherd, who gave his life for all? Would not that also be sweet, my wife?'

"I could not answer, the words seemed like a terrible doom of separation; but as I sit here, an old gray-haired woman, now that so many have gone, and gone, as I trust, home, I could almost think it might be sweet thus to close the eyes of all, and then follow them, if God willed it so, to Christ and to him.

"One thing perplexed me in the holy monk Bede, as in many of the monks at Tarrow. Much as he honoured our Father Aidan as a true servant of God, he thought him and the Scotch monks in very great darkness about Easter and the tonsure, only indeed to be excused by their ignorance. One day, however, when I, who could not endure to hear a word of blame on those holy men, the teachers of our sainted mother the Abbess Hilda, had spoken to him of their devoted labours and self-denying holiness, and of the love all the people bore them, he said,—

"'These things I much love and admire in Bishop Aidan. His love, his continence and humility; his mind superior to anger and avarice, to pride and vain glory; his industry in keeping and teaching the divine commandments; his diligence in reading and watching; his authority as a priest in reproving the haughty and powerful; his tenderness in comforting the afflicted, and in relieving and defending the poor; his willingness to perform to the utmost all he found in the apostolical or prophetical Scriptures, because I doubt not they were pleasing to God; but I do not praise or approve his not observing Easter at the proper time. Yet this I approve in him, that in the celebration of his Easter, the object which he had in view in all he said, did, or preached was the same as ours, that is, the redemption of mankind through the passion, resurrection, and ascension into heaven of the man Christ Jesus, who is the mediator between God and man.'

"Nobler praise than this even the Abbess Hilda could

not have desired for Father Aidan, wherefore I never again debated these points with the holy monk Bede, who in all things was so much wiser and better than I.

"But dearer to your father than even his words was my reading to him in the Gospel of St. Luke, or in the Anglo-Saxon Psalter, or my repeating hymns and prayers which I had learned. Especially he loved the verses of this Saxon hymn,—

'O Lord beloved!
O God, my Judge!
Hear me!
I know that my soul
Is wounded with sins.
Heal thou it,
Lord of Heaven!
For thou easily canst,
Physician of us all.
O Light of light!
O joy of life,
Thou art the Saviour, God!
Nor can we ever say
Nor indeed know
How noble thou art,
Eternal Lord!
Nor through the hosts of angels
Up in heaven,
In their assembled wisdom
Should begin to say it,
Might they ever tell
How great thou art,
Lord of angels,
King of all kings,
Creator of all worlds,
The living Christ.
Thou art the Prince
That of former days
The joy of all women,
Wast born at Bethlehem
A glory to all
The children of men,
To them that believe
On the living God.
I confess thee,
I believe on thee,
Beloved Saviour!
Thou art the Mighty One,
The Eternal King
Of all creatures
And I am
One of little worth,
A depraved man,
Who is sinning here
Well-nigh night and day.
I do as I would not,
Sometimes in actions,
Sometimes in words,
Sometimes in thought,
Very guilty
Oft and repeatedly.
But I beseech thee,
Human born,
Mighty Lord,
Pity me,
With the Holy Spirit
And the Almighty Father,
That I may do thy will.'

"These words came back to me always as if spoken by your father's voice, so dear they were to him. And also the prayers in the Psalter,—

"'O Lord our Redeemer! O God of truth! who hast redeemed mankind, sold to sin, not by silver and gold, but by the blood of thy precious Son, be our protector, and look down on our low estate, and because great is the multitude of thy kindnesses, O raise our desires always to partake them, and excite our minds to explore them.'

"And—'O Lord, who hast been our refuge before the mountains were brought forth; Author of time, yet without any limit of time thyself; in thy nature there is no past, to thee the future is never new. May no pride creep into our thoughts to avert from us the eyes of thy mercy.'

"There were also hymns to the Virgin; but for these he did not care so much. He thought such elaborate devotions must be more for the monks. Whatever others might do who had more time, he thought he should never have time enough to praise the living Lord who died to redeem us, and to beseech his mercy for his many sins.

"In that mind he passed those last precious days of weakness, and in that mind his spirit departed, as a sinful man calling with his last breath on the Saviour.

"No mysterious, unwonted light came into the chamber where he died; but great peace came into my heart as I looked on him, and prayed God to give me grace to lead all our little flock, as he had said, to join him again in heaven.

"Afterwards other thoughts came, dark and bitter hours, when I thought of the dreadful visions some have had of little sins being visited with frost, and fire, and torment in the other world; of the devils who, the monks say, wait to accuse us; of the deathless serpents who whet their bloody teeth to pierce guilty souls; of dwellings most bright and fair, which they see from afar, but may not enter; of the angelic choirs whose radiance they hear, while the mocking devils say, 'There you may never dwell,' and the wretched soul exclaims, 'Wo is me, that I ever saw the light of the human world!'

"Especially did the vision of Drythelm distress me, as it had been related by the holy Bede.

"Drythelm, as thou mayest have heard, was a thane, and master of a family, who lived at Cuningham, beyond the Cheviot Hills,—a layman, but one who led a religious life, with all that belonged to him. This thane fell sick, and his distemper daily increasing, 'at the beginning of one night,' said the good monk Bede, 'he died. But, in the morning early, suddenly coming to life again, all those who sat weeping around the body fled away in a great fright, except only his wife, who loved him best, and, though, in a great trembling, remained with him. He comforting, said, "Fear not, for I am now truly risen from death, and permitted to live again among men; however, I am not to live hereafter as I was wont, but in a very different manner." Then, rising from his bed, he repaired to the oratory of the little town, and continued in prayer till day; immediately divided his substance into three parts,—one whereof he gave to his wife, another to his children, and the third he divided among the poor. Not long after he repaired to the monastery of Melrose, which is almost enclosed by the winding of the river Tweed; and having been shaven as a monk, dwelt there, in a cell alone, apart from the brethren, till the day of his death, in extraordinary contrition of mind and body, saying prayers and psalms through the winter all but immersed in the river, the cakes of ice floating around him. And when any wondered how he could endure such cold and such austerities, he would say, "I have seen greater cold and greater suffering than this."

"'He would not relate what he saw to slothful or negligent persons, but only to such as would make use of his words to advance in piety.

"'At first, he said, one with a shining countenance and bright raiment led him silently to the northeast (between the east, where is the seat of Christ, and the north, where is Satan's seat). They came to a great valley, on one side full of dreadful flames, on the other no less horrid for violent hail, and cold, and snow, where multitudes of deformed human spirits were continually leaping in intolerable agony from the ice to the fire. But this was not hell. At the end of this valley on a sudden the place began to grow dusk and dark, till nothing could be seen save the shining raiment of the guide. As they passed, great globes of flame shot up, as if from a black pit, and fell back into it again; and these were full of tortured human souls. Then behind him rose the sound of hideous lamentation, mixed with insulting laughter of fiends; and as the noise drew nearer, he saw the howling and wailing souls of men dragged into the darkness. And as they passed, he discovered among them the form of a shaven monk, of a layman, and of a woman, showing that none may escape. Ever louder grew the wailing of men and the laughter of devils, until the fiends sought to seize him with burning tongs. But they durst not; and when the bright guide reappeared they all fled.

"Then turning towards the southeast, he was led into an atmosphere of clear light; and before them arose a vast wall, without door, window, or opening. Soon, he knew not how, they were at the top of it and saw within a great and pleasant field, full of fragrant flowers, and irradiated by light beyond the brightness of midday. In that field were countless assemblies of men in white, young and cheerful, and many companies seated together rejoicing. But this was not yet the kingdom of heaven for beyond it shone a fairer light, and he heard sweet voices singing, and perceived a surpassing fragrance, compared with which even the light, and sounds, and odours of that first fair field seemed poor and mean. And the guide told him that the valley of ice and fire was the place where souls are tried and punished who delayed to confess and amend their crimes until their death-bed; yet, because they confessed and repented, at last shall at the day of judgment be received into the kingdom of heaven. The fiery pit was the mouth of the eternal hell. The flowery field, where were so many in white, ever youthful and joyful, is the place where sojourn the souls of those who have died in good works, yet not so perfect as to be admitted at once into the glorious kingdom of heaven, whose rays so far surpassed it. Yet shall all at last, except those in the hopeless hell, at the day of judgment see Christ, and be admitted to the joys of his kingdom.

"'This,' said Bede, 'was the vision of Drythelm the thane.' And many a sleepless night have I passed thinking of these terrors, and of the sinfulness of the best among us. For which of us can know, if this be true, whether our souls may not be plunged, from the loving, parting looks of weeping friends, into that homeless, inhuman ice and fire?

"Indeed, all that vision seems dark and drear to me;

for what are mid-day light, and fragrant odours, and flowery fields to me?—or what dreariness would there be in darkness, or what insupportable in pain, if only till the judgment day my hand might touch the hands of my beloved, and if only, from time to time, a word might come to us, dropping on us softly through the silence, from the blessed Lord himself, such as he spoke on earth, when he said to the multitudes, 'Come unto me ye that are weary;' to the sinner weeping at his feet, 'Thy sins are forgiven;' or to the dying thief, 'To-day thou shalt be with me in Paradise?'

"But Drythelm, it seems, neither saw the Lord Christ, nor any that he knew, in that dreary other world!

"Have things changed then in the other world since the poor beggar was carried from the dogs and the pitiless rich man's gate to Abraham's bosom, or since the penitent thief, who had no time to do penance, and none to pay for masses to be said, went straight from the cross to Paradise?

"Since then, indeed, the compassionate healer of men, the Lord who died for us, has gone into that world, and lives there. Can His welcome be less pitiful than Abraham's?

"Through all my terrors sometimes those dying words of the Lord, so precious to my dying husband, come to my heart like my mother's voice when the storms were howling over our cradles amidst the mountains; all the rest—visions, prophecies, dreadful threatenings seem to me but inarticulate howls and wails, and those words only living, human, and eternally true.

"Slowly they fall on my heart, and my heart responds '*To-day,*' and my heart answers, '*To-day!*'—not after countless ages, but *to-day*, straight from the farewells of our beloved to thy welcome! '*shalt thou be with me in Paradise.*' And I can only weep and say, '*With thee,* pitiful Lord, with *thee!*' Then I will not think any more of the fiery valley or the fragrant fields, but of Thee, only of Thee. That promise is enough for me and mine. 'Hildelith, my child,' said my mother, as she finished, 'thou hast been a nun from childhood, and art better, and knowest more than I, can I be wrong?'"

V.

SAXON MINSTERS AND MISSIONS.

THE WORDS OF OSWALD, THE SON OF OSRIC AND ADELEVE,

WHICH HE SPAKE TO ME, HIS SISTER HILDELITH.

V.

SAXON MINSTERS AND MISSIONS.

THE WORDS OF OSWALD, THE SON OF OSRIC AND ADELEVE, WHICH HE SPOKE TO ME, HIS SISTER HILDELITH.

"THE first great event which rises into clearness from the sunny haze of childish memories was the death of the Abbess Hilda, probably because it was the first sorrowful event which shadowed our happy home, falling not like the shadow of some especial rock across our especial path, but like the darkness of an eclipse on the joy of all the land. Well I remember my mother leading me, then a boy not five years old, by the hand, after the bier, weeping as she went. Our mother, whom I had never seen weep, who was only known to me as my angel of consolation in all my childish griefs! And well also I remember the dead silence whilst the coffin was being lowered into the grave, followed by the great burst of unrestrained weeping from all the multitude assembled, when the grave was raised to the level of the common earth around, and the last trace of the 'Mother of the people' was buried out of our sight. All that dark day stands out clear and distinct from the sunny days before and after, even to the last hour, when we children stood lisping our vesper hymn, as was our wont, around our mother, and she told us always to remember that day, and to learn from it how the good were honoured, who loved God and all the people, as the Abbess Hilda did. And she told us also that at that hour, while we had been singing our hymn, the Abbess Hilda had been joining in the songs of the happy angels, in the palace of the Lord Christ, which was to be her home.

"My next distinct recollection is of being taken to the green island on the Derwent Lake, to see the holy anchorite Herebert, who dwelt there—a white-haired, grave, old man, who welcomed us on the little green glade among the trees, and laid his hands on our heads and blessed us. The words I cannot recall, only the gentle tone, and the trembling pressure of his withered old hand (so different from my mother's), and the tears in the grave, kind eyes. For he had blessed our mother also in her childhood.

"And not long after this we were told his spirit had gone, on the very same day as his friend Bishop Cuthbert's, because he asked God that they might enter heaven together.

"All around us, north and south, and west, the land was rich in hallowed places, sacred not with the dim light of ages past, but with the sanctity of holy lives, lived and ended amongst us within the memory of man, inspiring us also to aim at posts of honour in the army of our Lord, since the roll of his saints was not yet closed.

"The Holy Island of Lindisfarne, whence missionaries had gone throughout our country, and made it from a heathen into a Christian land; the lonely rock of Farne, whence prayers had gone up to God from the heart and voices of Aidan, Ethelwold, and Cuthbert, warding off flames from the besieged city, and tempests from imperilled mariners; the Abbey of Hilda, the royal maiden; the post of the little wooden church on which Bishop Aidan was leaning when he died in the tent outside; the royal country seats where St. Oswald the king sat at Bishop Aidan's feet, interpreting the words of life to his people; the field where he knelt with his army before the battle at the foot of the wooden cross, and conquered; the field where he died in fight for his people and his faith with the heathen Penda; these were the holy places of our childhood, and the men and women our mother taught us to revere and to follow.

"Thus the common moorland, hills, green valleys, and seas, and lakes around us, with their islands and shores, were a kind of Holy Land to us; and our saints were not merely glorified, far off, heavenly beings, to be religiously venerated, but human beings, whose voices our kindred had heard, whose hands had touched us, and in whose steps, not yet effaced from the very paths around us, we might humbly tread.

"In the very Monastery of Jarrow, whose school we attended, was there not indeed one, scarcely older than myself, who trod close in those very saintly steps? making their traces deeper for others to see and follow; even the good and learned Bede, the devout and studious and truthful, who pursued learning with the ardour which other men devote to war or ambition. He had scarcely known any other home than the monasteries of Wearmouth and Jarrow, and he scarcely desired to know any other world. Given in to the care of the monks at the age of seven, there he studied, and wrote, and prayed, and meditated, and taught, for sixty years, serving God in true humility by making known to men the services of others.

"He knew Latin, and Greek, and Hebrew, was a proficient in sacred music, and learned in theology, but most of all in the sacred Scriptures. Did he not die in the very act of unsealing these life-giving truths to his people through the medium of our Saxon tongue?

"He also believed firmly in the continued existence of the Holy Catholic Church, that when we read in the Holy Bible the lives of the apostles and martyrs, we read not of the heroes of a far-off golden age, divided by sharp boundaries from our own, but of men and women subject to like passions, and upheld by the same living God as ourselves. He felt that while he was studying the Church history of other days, the Church history of his own was being written in heaven. Thus he accepted it as his more especial vocation to transmit the chain of saintly history to the generations to come; and unwearied were the pains he took to ascertain from witnesses every fact he could of the lives and deaths of the good men whose biographies he afterwards wrote.

"His was not, however, the life I desired for myself. No such pale and still reflection of the life of others was my ambition.

"I knew that my mother had great hope of me that I should grow up to be a saint; and I knew well that the saints she held before us as our guides and patterns had all devoted themselves to God in the monastic or eremitical life; all, with the exception of St. Oswald the king, and my father, whom my mother held by some rare exceptional grace to be equal to any saint that ever tormented himself, or was tormented.

"Her hope of me was founded on my ardent desire for knowledge, which made books as one means of acquiring it my delight, and on the interest with which I always listened to her narratives of the missions of holy men among the heathen, whether she spoke of the Scottish monks of Iona and Lindisfarne, or of the Irish and Saxon monks, who in our own time were carrying back the Christian faith to the original homes of our heathen ancestors in old Saxony. But both these feelings had another source in me. My devotion to study was, I think, rather a spirit of intellectual adventure than any vocation for a contemplative life. It was a phase of that passion for wandering which, as she often told me, is an inborn instinct of our race. My mind was voyaging through grammars and histories into far-off times and lands, until the time for action should begin. Thus, also, in the acts of the missionary saints, what interested me was the peril, the change, the mysterious forests into which they plunged, the strange people they encountered, rather than the religion they taught. Interwoven with all, no doubt, was the glory of the ennobling end for which they ran these risks; yet to me the charm lay rather in the risks than in the end.

"I knew what my mother was hoping from me, and I was not without a vague intention of one day finding myself engaged in such a work, but, nevertheless, I felt myself impelled to thwart her plans. It was not altogether the spirit of perversity which led me. I loved and honoured her fervently, and would have done almost anything to save her pain or give her pleasure. And yet in this dearest purpose of her heart I could not yield my will to hers. I could not take her desire for my vocation. I could not enter on a religious life at the impulse of another will. Often I had intended to speak to her of this, but never could make up my mind, knowing what a world of bright visions in her heart it would destroy. So it happened that at last I told her of my purpose in the most abrupt manner, asking her to request of my father equipment for me to go forth and seek my fortune in the world.

"I felt too much for her to dare to show what I felt. I knew she thought I was tempted if not possessed by evil spirits, and was merely going forth idly to drink my fill of the vain and bitter world. I felt I was but obeying an instinct which had grown from her nature into mine—the instinct of our Saxon race, and, above all, of its royal house of Odin, to press ever further, outward and onward into the unknown world.

"I remember well her asking me to read to her the parable of the Prodigal Son the evening before I left, and feeling the parallel she was silently drawing, as the tears flowed down her face. But that strange dumbness which so often comes over our people when our dearest feelings are wounded and our deepest heart is touched, came over me. I could neither justify myself, nor comfort her, nor shed one tear, but sat polishing my armour, while she was weeping over me as the prodigal.

"Yet I knew she had parted with some considerable portion of her wedding 'morning gift' to make my equipment better; and she knew there was none in the world so dear to me as she was.

"And so we parted; we two who loved each other so tenderly, and were so much alike; and because we so loved and so resembled each other, were wounding each other so sorely.

"My father understood us both, and as I rose early

in the morning, that I might not have a second parting, he was in the stable before I had saddled my horse, and said,—

"'God bless thee, boy. Thou wilt not forget thy mother's words; her voice will come back to thee morning and evening. No bird can learn to fly in the nest.'

"Then the tears came irrepressibly, and I, who had felt so strong in manly purpose, yearned like a child for my mother's embrace.

"But I could only say,—

"'Father, thou knowest I am not going to be like the ungrateful son in the parable. Tell her so.'

"He smiled, and brushing his hand over his eyes, said,—

"'Nay, nay, thou art no prodigal. If thou art needed and called back to the old house, thou wilt not be slow to come.'

"Well I remember these words, for they were the last I ever heard him speak.

"Then he gave me his hand; and I sprung into the saddle and rode away. But thou, little Hildelith, hadst been watching me from the window, and wert waiting for me by the old apple-tree in the orchard where I used to teach thee to read.

"Thy poor little face was pale and grave as any woman's, and thou hadst much too awful a sense of thy mission to be weeping; for, laying one little trembling hand upon the horse's neck, and the other on my arm, thou stretchedst up towards me and didst whisper,—

"'Oswald! brother Oswald! thou art not going into the far country, away from God, among the wicked people, to feed on husks, and to forget us all?'

"It was some time before I could reassure thee, and persuade thee that I was not going away from God; and when that fear passed from thee, all the tenderness of our love came over us both, and it was hard to part, until at length I said to thee,—

"'Thou must be our mother's stay and comfort, and watch her looks and movements, and do everything to cheer her until my return. For our elder brothers will be at the chase or in the field, and will have houses of their own; and our elder sisters will soon be married; and thou wilt be the joy of our parents till I return. And then,' I said, half in jest and half in purpose, 'when thou art a grown-up maiden, and I a staid, grave man, we will go together among the heathens in the wild German forests, and teach them to be good.'

"So I went out into the world.

"There is little need to say much of what I saw there. The hills and valleys, and the men and women, were much more like those of our home than I had expected. In the distance, always soft blue hills and purple-shaded valleys; or at morning and evening a glow of gold, and rose, and violet, over city, hill, and plain, and river. At our feet, when the distance is reached, brown earth, green blades of grass, gray rocks, cities, and homesteads like those we left yesterday.

"Not that I mean that my life was a continual breaking up of illusive dreams. Is not every blade of grass as delicately varied in tint as distant hills at sunrise? Is not every mountain flower illuminated with its gold and crimson as richly as the evening clouds? And has not every field and every flower its own fragrance, never known except to those that know and love them? Love of endless change,—the simplest life at home, the simplest scenes around our country homes can gratify it! Not a day, not a face, not a field, not a flower, not a perfume is like another. But we need to wander to learn this. At least I did. And we need to suffer, that we may learn how the passion for wandering onward, and the love of home, are both satisfied only in one pilgrimage and one home.

"Everywhere I found the names of the Scottish fathers of our Church in honour; although scarcely one of them survived, and everywhere the Roman customs, as regarded Easter and the tonsure, prevailed. At Lichfield I visited the very monastery where the holy Bishop Chad, of whom my mother used to tell us, prayed and preached, and at length heard the heavenly music summoning him to go the way he came.

"Throughout the kingdoms of the East and South Angles, of the Mercians, and in Lindsey (Lincoln), were churches founded by the unwearied labours of the holy men of Iona and Lindisfarne, and also in Wessex. Towards the south the streams began to flow the other way. In Kent the traditions had a western instead of a northern source. There I saw the cathedral church of Canterbury, and the abbey consecrated by precious relics from Rome, and by the memory and relics of Augustine, the first missionary whom the great Pope Gregory had sent to make the Angles into angels. There was the silver cross which had been borne before Bishop Augustine. The Kentish monks were very proud of tracing the descent of their Church to the Church of the imperial city and of the apostles. And although my heart reverently clung to the sacred names of our childhood, to the memory of Iona, and Aidan, and Hilda the abbess, there was something that seemed great and glorious in thus having our country linked to the city which is the heart of Europe; which was the metropolis of the Empire of the World, and is now, as it were, the metropolis of the Church. It seemed like coming forth from a still valley among the hills into the plains, where are the cities and the great rivers linking all lands to each other with their silver chains.

"At London I saw the bones of Sebbi, the pious king who had died a monk, laid in the great church of St. Paul's, on the Thames, built over the old Roman Temple of Diana; while, some way up the stream, still stood, on the marshy island, the ruins of the Temple of Apollo.*

"Around some of the cities the Roman walls still stood, although they had been destroyed and burnt to ashes again and again, in the continual wars between the kings of the Saxon kingdoms.

"At the time I travelled through the land there was no great war; but occasionally I came in with a band of armed men bent on avenging some private wrong. The kings did what they could to restrain these private feuds, and the bishops and priests did more. But law was slow, and the blood of our people is hot, and the more powerful thanes and earls often preferred taking the law into their own hands.

"But altogether the land was peaceful. Everywhere in the fairest valleys were rising monasteries, with their little villages of humble dwellings clustering round them. The dwellings of the nobles were not usually of stone or fortified, and therefore, when any part of the country was unsettled, the women and children were frequently placed under the care of the nuns, for a double protection of stone walls and religious sanctuary.

* On the site of Westminster Abbey.

"It was on her flight to such a refuge that I met the maiden Etheldreda, with her mother, and was able, with my servant to succour and defend them, and bring them to the convent in peace.

"One spring morning in the forest near Glastonbury we rode together, the maiden Etheldreda and I; and I held back the boughs from brushing against her fair face; and as she passed through the wood on her white palfrey, everything around her seemed to change and shine; and the birds sang no more like birds, but like fairy songsters singing bridal songs at a wedding; and the sunbeams were no more common sunbeams, but messengers direct from heaven, that touched with gold her waving hair and found a home in her eyes.

"The feud was healed. The maiden Etheldreda and her mother left the convent, and rejoined the court of Ina, king of Wessex. And with Ina I took service, and Etheldreda and I were married before the leaves of that spring had faded into autumn.

"And my mother thought I had forsaken forever the purpose to which she had longed to dedicate my life.

"Three years God gave us to live together. I saw my fairy queen of love and beauty grow into the gentle wife, the unutterable, daily joy of my heart, and the wise lady and ruler of my household, whose gentle commands no one ever thought of disobeying. For these years she moved about the house with her 'three keys of household rule, of the storeroom, the linen chest, and the money box.' And beauty and poetry came into every simple household event with her presence and her touch.

"And at last I saw her with her babe, when she said she thought there could be no other joy left for her to know, except it was the joy of entering into heaven and looking for the first time on the face of Christ. For she was as devout as a nun.

"And then the whole world of happiness vanished like a vision from my life.

"Mother and infant were laid in the abbey church, where we had been wont to listen morning and evening to hymn and prayer.

"They said the joy was too much for her, and so she was taken to the greater joy beyond; and the babe followed her, sleeping silently away with a smile on its face, as if it had been awakened to heaven by its mother's kiss. And I was left alone, without home or wife or child or purpose or wish in life.

"Weary as I was of the world, I had not a thought at that time of entering a monastery. The monastic life had never had any attraction for me as a refuge, and I had no longer energy to think of the missionary work, which was the only form in which I had ever felt it possible for me.

"Therefore I remained at the court of the good King Ina until he sent me on a mission to the Abbey of Exeter.

"At that time Winfried—afterwards the great Archbishop Boniface—was there as an humble monk. He had the greatest veneration for the learning and piety of our old friend, the monk Bede of Jarrow. And many a question he asked me about him, until we became friends; and he began to unfold to me his own projects for the conversion of our heathen kindred in the ancient forests of old Saxony. I was a few years older than he was, but the zeal in his young heart seemed to enkindle something of the old glow in mine. In him also the instinct of our race was strong. He was impelled to his missionary labours, as he himself said, 'by the love of travelling and the fear of Christ;' by which he meant, doubtless, the fear of grieving Him who had laid on him the debt of preaching the Gospel to the heathen.*

"The love of wandering had lost some of its old force in me, whose vision of delight lay no more in the future, but inwrapt in the pall of the irrevocable past. Nor was the sense of duty towards the heathen as yet strong in me as in Boniface. Yet I returned from his monastery to the court with some kindlings of a higher purpose, and some faint sense that since God yet kept me in life, he would yet make it worth living.

"I could not quite share the enthusiastic devotion of Boniface to the Church of Rome, but some words of his sank into my heart. 'Cast all which hinders thee away,' he said, 'and direct thy whole study to the Holy Scriptures, and seek there that divine wisdom which is more precious than gold; for what does it become youth more to seek, what can old age more profitably possess, than the knowledge of the Holy Scriptures, which guided our souls, without risk of shipwreck, through the storm to the shores of the blessed paradise, to the eternal and heavenly joys of the angels?'

"Therefore, on my return to King Ina's court, in the intervals of my work in administering the wise laws which he had collected from the customs of our fathers, and had improved by the wisdom of the wise men of our times, and was now enforcing throughout the land, I used much to frequent the monasteries and churches, and especially to lose no opportunity of hearing or reading the Holy Scriptures of the apostles and evangelists.

"By this means, and by God's grace, the words of

* Neander's Memorials of Christian Life.

Christ the Lord took root in my mind, and his love took root in my heart. I learned to mourn for my sins, I learned to adore Him who died that we might be forgiven our guilt and healed of our sins. I began to feel I had a message to take to the heathen, to those Saxon heathen who, as Boniface said, are our 'own flesh and bone,'—a message of peace, and love, and joy, which it was worth while to stay on earth to carry far and wide.

"At times, however, my heart was weighed down by the fear that I had indeed neglected my vocation in choosing the court instead of the cloister, and that death had fallen on my beloved for my sins. To relieve my conscience on this point, I laid my grief open, according to the custom of our fathers, before a discreet and learned priest, before Lent. 'Confession to God,' says a holy bishop, 'blots out sins; and that which is made to man teaches how they may be blotted out.' The priest deemed no public penance needful, but enjoined on me the secret wearing of a hair-cloth shirt, and throughout Lent an especial attendance on the penitential services.

"That year, therefore, I watched with peculiar interest the penitents who commenced their public penance on Ash Wednesday. Barefooted, and covered with sackcloth, they prostrated themselves at the door of the cathedral. Some of the clergy received them there, enjoined their respective penances, and led them into the house of God, chanting as they went the seven penitential psalms. Within the sacred walls the bishop laid his hands on them, sprinkled them with ashes and lustral water, covered them with hair-cloth, and then commanded them to depart from a place dedicated to God's especial honour and service, and polluted by their presence.

"Rich and poor were there together, noble and thrall,

but, humbled and reproved, all went away together, with heads bent down, many of them weeping.

"In heart I went with them, following them silently from the church.

"That Lent was a time of solemn secret repentance and preparation to me, although man's eye saw not my penance, my sins having been against God rather than men. On Holy Thursday, the eve of the solemn crucifixion day, I went once more to the cathedral gates, and stood near the penitents. Once more they were required to suffer the humiliation of confessing those unholy deeds which had brought scandal on the worthy name by which they were called.

"This being done, the bishop solemnly prayed over them for the gracious forgiveness of the Heavenly Father, and re-admitted them into communion.

"Great was the sweetness on the following Easter of receiving 'the sacramental image—the pledge of eternal life,' as St. Gregory, founder of our southern English Church, terms those holy mysteries. Everything was so deepened in my heart that it seemed to me like my first true communion. The teaching of the holy Bede came especially to my mind at that time, how he compared the Eucharist to the passover: 'Our Lord having substituted for the flesh and blood of a lamb the sacrament of his own body and blood.'

"Heartily my heart went out in the post-communion prayer—

"'Grant that we may behold face to face, and may enjoy truly and really in heaven, Him whom here we see enigmatically; and, under another species, Him on whom we feed sacramentally.'

"And with joy afterwards I listened to the paschal homily—

"'Much,' said the preacher, 'is between the body Christ suffered in and the body that is hallowed to housel.* The body truly that Christ suffered in was born of the flesh of Mary, with blood and bone, with skin and with sinews, and human limbs, with a reasonable, living soul; and his ghostly body, which we call the housel, is gathered of many ears of corn, without blood and bone, without limb, without soul; and therefore nothing is to be understood therein bodily, but all is ghostly to be understood. And yet that lively bread is not bodily so notwithstanding,—not the self-same body that Christ suffered in; nor that holy wine is the Saviour's blood which was shed for us, in bodily thing, but in ghostly understanding. Both be truly, that wine His blood, and that bread His body; and was the heavenly bread which we call manna, that fed forty years in the wilderness God's people; and the clear water which ran from the stone was then His blood, as Paul wrote, All our fathers drank of that ghostly stone, and that stone was Christ. They all ate the same ghostly meat, and drank the same ghostly drink. And he said, not bodily, but ghostly. And Christ was not yet born, nor his blood shed, when the people of Israel ate of that meat and drank of that stone. It was the same mystery in the old law, and they did ghostly signify that ghostly housel of our Saviour's body which we consecrate now.'†

"Thus the paschal feast was to me as the passover eaten with bitter herbs, with loins girt for pilgrimage through the wilderness; as the manna and the living

---

* The consecrated bread.

† These words are from Epistles and Homilies of Archbishop Elfric of Canterbury, from A. D. 990 to 1000, considered an authoritative representation of the doctrine of the Anglo-Saxon Church on the subject of the Holy Communion.—*Vide Soames' Bampton Lectures.*

water from the rock which flowed for the people of old. For Christ, the living Lord, the bread of life, is ever the bread of God to all who trust him. And was not I too going on an unknown journey?

"King Ina saw me looking worn and sad, and knew not the healing touch that was on me, probing to the sins which were at the root of my sorrows, and turning my sorrows into bitter draughts of strength and life; and he and devout men of his court counselled me to make a pilgrimage to Rome, as he himself did in his old age. But I had no mind towards it. The hearts of many of the religious men and women around me, when weighed down with care or sorrow, or weariness of life, turned instinctively to Rome, the city of the Holy Father, successor of St. Peter, as a spiritual home, the holy city and the father's house of Christendom—type of the holy city and the Father's house above; and not only type, but threshold. With me it was not so. The sanctuary of my childish reverence had been rather Iona than Rome; the lonely island of the northern seas—not the metropolis of the ancient empire. Besides, I felt my work lay not behind, but before me. What I required was, not a sacred refuge wherein to repose after the day's work was done, but a field wherein to work during the long day of life that remained to me. Not on the quiet graves of apostles, but on the battle-field among the heathen, beyond the boundaries of Christendom, would there be any rest for a heart whose possible earthly future was so long, and whose earthly hopes had blossomed and faded so early, and were buried for ever in the past.

"Not far from Glastonbury an old Roman bridge crossed a river, and over it the country people used to pass in great numbers on market or on festivals. There, after the example of the learned Aldhelm, Bishop of Sherborne, I placed myself one Easter morning with the harp to which I had learned in youth to chant the sacred songs of Cædmon, the Saxon version of the Creed, and the Te Deum. Many paused to listen, and when the song ceased, the more thoughtful would sometimes linger to ask the meaning of some of the words, to converse and to listen as I repeated to them portions of the Saxon Gospels which I knew by heart. In this way I became familiar with the difficulties and sorrows of the common people; and they became familiar with me, and told me of their cares and griefs, so that of the balm of sacred consolation which had been poured into my wounds, I might often drop comfort into theirs. That seemed to me a better preparation for preaching among the old Saxon heathen, than a pilgrimage to Rome.

"All this time, doubtless, thou, Hildelith, my sister, and my mother, may have thought I had forgotten utterly my father's house. But it was not so. More than once I had sought permission of King Ina to leave his court; but he had entreated me to stay yet a while, until other thanes could be instructed in the new laws which he was so anxious to have faithfully administered among the people. Especially he was very earnest that justice should be done to the slaves of the soil, and that the wretched heathen pirates should be prevented from buying or selling kidnapped men, or women, or children, Saxon or British, at the ancient slave market at Bristol, on the Severn. Many a journey I made thither to stop this unholy traffic. There was a wide difference between the slaves of the soil on our estates—each tenanting his own cottage, and tilling his own ground, on payment of a certain sum to his lord, although they are not free to wander whither they will, or to change masters—and this kidnapping of any, free or bond, from their homes, and selling them into hopeless bondage in foreign lands.

"Many questions had also to be settled between the Britons and Saxons; and many a rich man went angrily away from the judgment-seat because he had been compelled to pay a fine for making his slaves work on Sunday, the Lord's Day, reckoned free for all alike.

"Few of the nobles could read, and not all had patience to investigate the truth, as a judge is bound to do, without fear or favour between man and man. Therefore I did not dare hastily to abandon my post.

"At length, however, came the tidings of our father's death, and of our elder brother's absence at the Northumbrian court. Wherefore I hesitated no longer, but returned to the old home.

"To thee and to my mother it seemed unmixed joy thus to meet once more. It was taking up the dear old life again. But between that past and this present a whole world of love and hope had been promised to me, and given and withdrawn. And for all my buried world I had nothing to show but two locks of fair hair—a long flaxen tress, and a tiny golden curl. It was then Hildelith, that thou first becamest to me all thou hast been ever since; taking my dead to thy heart, thou wouldst never weary of listening as I spoke of them; and as thou listenedst, in the light of thy tearful eyes, and at thy words of faith and heavenly hope, the dead seemed to live again, and once more paradise grew up for me in the future, when I hope to meet all our beloved 'with Him.'

"With my mother we spoke more of the future work

among the heathen Saxons, which more and more became the definite purpose of us three. I am not sure whether our mother ever looked on Wessex as better than the prodigal's far country, of which King Ina was the citizen who had fed me on husks; or my absence altogether as other than a temporary seduction from the way in which I had been called to walk. Had she known my wife, and held our babe in her motherly arms, it would have been different. As it was, the whole period, I believe, seemed to her a scheme of diabolical seduction; and the utmost she ever said in extenuation was, that doubtless the Almighty would make even our wanderings the means of training us for our work, and could change Nebuchadnezzar furnaces into fires to free the dross from the gold.

"It was not long before we decided to retire into monasteries—you and our mother into that of Whitby, I into that of Jarrow, to which the great learning and fame of the monk Bede was now attracting scholars from all parts of England, and also from Ireland and from the continent of Europe. He had refused to be made abbot of this monastery, deeming that the work God had given him to do would be 'hindered by the cares of such a family.' The example of his steadfast diligence, his humble submission to the same duties as the most obscure monks, his terror of infirmity and sin, his daily dependence on the grace of God, and his delight in the Holy Scriptures, were a light to the whole monastery, and a hallowing recollection to bear with me wherever I went.

"It was not, however, for the pursuit of learning I had entered the monastery, nor was the monastic discipline to me anything but a means. The sleep broken by vigils of prayer and praise, the plain fare, the rigidly-observed fasts, the unquestioning obedience, and the minute order of the Benedictine rule now established there, were, I trusted, preparations for the life of hardship and privation before me.

"The abbot recognized my purpose, and in every way favoured it. Nor was I alone in my vocation. Many others of the monks shared it with me, incited by the reports which reached us from time to time of the labours of Willibrord in Friesland, and of the martyrdom of the two brave Saxon priests, the black and the white Hewald, while preaching to the heathen on the Rhine.

"These last were especially honoured and commemorated amongst us. They had gone to preach the faith among the ancient Saxons and the Hessians. Both were devout and true-hearted men, but the black Hewald was the more learned in the Scriptures. They had dwelt some time among the barbarous people, telling them of the Redeemer, and daily showing forth his death in the offering of the Holy Eucharist, and night and day praising God in psalms and hymns, when suddenly a panic seized the heathens, that some mysterious spells lurking in the words of the strangers (such as they attribute to their magical letters or runes) would force them from their old religion whether they would or no; and, to break the spell, they slew the white Hewald with the sword, and savagely tore the black Hewald limb from limb, and threw him into the river Rhine.

"Such histories did not deter the bold spirits of our younger monks from desiring a similar life. That dark unknown land, still covered with the ancient forests, with temples in their black depths sacred to gods scarcely dead amongst us yet as names of terror, whence our forefathers had issued not a hundred years ago; with its wild beasts and wilder men, yet men of our very flesh and bone, who might rise into scholars such as our Bede, and saints such as our Oswald; those wild nations in their untamed youth, those wild forests in their incalculable age, had stronger attractions for young men of our race, whatever perils lay amongst them, than a life of rigid rule and monotonous quiet in a Benedictine monastery.

"But when time and circumstances had tried the temper of those who volunteered for the service, the abbot decided on only two as equal to the work, Paul the chanter, and Siegbert, the mason and carpenter—both tonsured priests, yet skilled in their various arts.

"We three being at length set apart to this mission, spent the few months remaining to us in acquiring all the knowledge and manual skill which we thought might be useful to us; and in the Abbey of Jarrow there were mechanics instructed by the best Italian workmen in every art, from delicate illuminations in colours and gold, and jewel work, for the adorning of sacred books, to the roughest work in the field. More especially we had amongst us adepts in every portion of the builder's work, from the mason's and the glassmaker's to the fine carver in wood and stone.

"The abbot did not suffer us to weaken our strength by immoderate fasting, nor did I myself affect any unusual austerities. My bodily strength was God's, would be needed in work, and must not be wasted. My ambition was, not to be renowned as a saint among men, but to bring sinful men on earth to Christ my Lord, and, if it might be, to train them by his grace to be his servants and saints in heaven. I have ever thought it would be better, when I appear before him, to see him welcome one, and another, and another, who, but for my poor labours, might never have seen his gracious face at all, than to hear him even assign the highest reward of saintly austerity and devotion to me alone.

"At length the last Sunday in England came. The ship which was to carry us to Europe lay at anchor in the Tyne, just below the monastery. And for the last time we joined in the chants of the choir at Jarrow, and heard faithful words of exhortation from the priest Bede, who was preaching on that day. For the last time I looked on those paintings on the walls of the church, which the good abbot, Benedict Biscop, had brought from Rome, and which had so often helped me to understand the work of our Saviour, and also my own. I gave one lingering look at the form of the lad Isaac meekly carrying the wood of sacrifice behind his father Abraham, not knowing who was to be the lamb for burnt sacrifice. I seemed to hear the old man say, with trembling voice, those simple words of truth, so deep and eternal in their significance, 'My son, *God will provide himself a lamb.*' And then my eyes turned to the corresponding picture of the form more marred than any man's stooping beneath the weight of the cross. My heart adoringly responded to the patriarch's prophecy, 'Behold the Lamb of God, which taketh away the sin of the world.'

"And then, from those lips once parched with thirst for me on that very cross, I seemed to receive the rule of the daily cross to be borne after him, and prayed that henceforth indeed he would lay the daily yoke on me, and make my work no longer mine, but His.

"On the morrow we started.

"My mother was there, Hildelith, with thee, as we stood on the shore waiting for the boat to take us to the larger vessel.

"I knew I was fulfilling the most fervent desire of her heart, which had become my own; and no benediction could have sent me on my way with such hope and peace in my heart as the simple words in which she commended me to God, and bade me send for her and thee, if ever I found work to be done among the heathen in which women might help.

"Our provision for the way was small—a net for fishing in the rivers which flow through the forests, a few carpenter's and mason's tools, Aldhelm and Guthlac's Anglo-Saxon Psalter, a Hymnal and a copy of the Holy Gospels in Latin, with Archbishop Theodore's Penitential. For food and raiment we trusted to God, to the labour of our own hands, and to the charity of our fellow-Christians.

"At sea already we had some encouragement; for the sailors, hearing us chant the hymns to Christ morning and evening, and at the sacred hours, used to gather around us, and afterwards would listen earnestly as we spoke of Him who of old walked on the sea, and made the storm a calm for those who trusted in him.

"Our ship was bound for the coast of France, and there we had expected to find churches such as we left in England, and a welcome. But the land was overrun with contending hosts, the monasteries were laid waste, and many of the peaceful people had taken refuge in the forests, to escape the bands of marauders which roamed hither and thither in the train of the various contending princes of the Frankish and Burgundian races.

"We had intended to make a pilgrimage to Rome

before commencing our work among the heathen; but the country between the Alps and the Pyrenees was at that time so possessed by hordes of swarthy barbarians from the East, the followers of Mohammed the false prophet, that we judged it best not to delay our progress by attempting the journey, but to strike at once to the northwest, across the Vosges mountains into Swabia and Saxony.

"On our way through the Vosges, by the Lake of Constance, we came on many monasteries founded by Irish and Scotch monks, the kindred of our father Aidan. We spent many reviving days at Luxeuil, the abbey built by the holy Columba. There we heard how, not a hundred years before, coming from Ireland, passing by the coasts of England, then wholly given to idolatry, Columba and his brethren went into the wilderness to lead a pilgrim life, and, if it might be, to win the heathen around to Christ. They wandered long, until they came to a valley where the grass was growing and the young trees were springing out of the ruins of an ancient Roman city; and there, out of the walls of Roman temples and the pavements of Roman baths and palaces, they reared this Abbey of Luxeuil. They showed us also a cave in the forest where the abbot Columba used to retire with his Psalter to read and pray, and told us how the very bears and wolves used to respect the holy man, and how the heathen listened and believed. They also transcribed for me this prayer of Columba, which I ever bear about with me: 'O Lord, give me, I beseech thee, in the name of Jesus Christ thy Son, my God, that love which never faileth, that my light may be kindled and never quenched; that it may burn in me, and give light to others. And thou, O Christ, our dearest Saviour, do thou thyself constantly kindle our lamps, that they may shine evermore in thy temple, that they may receive unquenchable light from thee, the unquenchable Light; that our darkness may be enlightened, while the darkness of the world flies from us. My Jesus, I beseech thee, give thy light to my lamp, that in its light may be manifested to me that Holy of Holies in which thou, the eternal Priest, dost dwell; that I may continually contemplate thee only, long for thee, gaze on thee, and yearn for thee in love. O Saviour, full of love, show thyself to us that knock, that we may perceive and love thee alone, think of thee day and night; that thy love which many waters cannot quench may possess our whole souls, and never more be quenched by the waters of the earth.'

"From Luxeuil we wandered further to the Abbey of St. Gall, by the lake, where one night its first founders are said to have heard the spirit of the mountains calling on the spirit of the waters to unite against those daring men who came to subdue their solitudes in a mighty Name which they were constrained to recognize.

"Day after day we wandered on, through regions desolated by the marches and conflicts of tribe after tribe of northern heathens, and rested at night in some solitary abbey founded by pilgrim Irish monks on the sites of ruined Roman cities.

"But our way lay yet beyond, to regions never penetrated by civilized men—to heathens who had never owned the Roman sway.

"At length we came to a forest in the Thuringian land, through which we had often to cut our way with axe and hammer, and traced the course of a stream through the thick trees until it grew deep and wide enough to bear us on its waters. Then we built a rough raft of pine stems, and embarking on it with our few treasures—our tools, our nets, and our four books—committed ourselves to God, and implored him to point out the place of our rest.

"Night and day we chanted the psalms and hymns at the sacred hours. By day a thousand busy creatures were stirring in the woods besides ourselves; and in many a green glade we fancied the innocent, harmless beasts welcomed us—the green lizards among the water, the squirrels peering at us from the trees, the birds twittering their happy morning songs. But at night the very sound of our own voices had something weird and awful in it, and very weird and wild were the echoes from the dark and silent woods. Many a time we felt they were more than echoes. Mocking laughter or wild wails answered us, dying away in the unknown depths of the wilderness; and then our spirits would have failed, had not faith prevailed, for we knew the evil sprites were aroused, and were defying us to battle—we, so weak in ourselves, yet so strong in our Lord.

"At length one evening we came to a green valley in the midst of the wood, sloping up to a grassy knoll, round which wound the stream. On landing we found it was a clearing made by the hand of man, for felled trunks lay buried here and there among the tangled brambles and long grass.

"We thought this might be our appointed rest, and kneeling down, we prayed that He who guided Abraham the Hebrew would guide us now.

"Then, throwing our net into the stream, Siegbert and I drew it up full of fish. We had lighted a fire, to broil the fish and scare away the wolves, when Paul the chanter, who had been exploring the forest, came hastily towards us and said, with a voice trembling with agitation, 'Touch not a morsel here. The place is enchanted. In a recess of the forest on the other side of this hill is a heathen temple, and within it is an altar of unshapen stones, blackened with recent fires, and strewn with bones; the bones of men,' he added, throwing down what seemed the skeleton of a human hand. 'But more than that, as I was turning away, a creature that seemed neither man nor brute, with hands like claws, and long tangled hair, glared at me with wild eyes from among the trees, and then disappeared, with an unearthly yell, into the forests. Let us embark at once, and hasten from this accursed spot.'

"But it came into my heart to say,

"'From this curse the Lord came to redeem us and the world. On the very seat of Satan why may we not erect the throne of Christ the Lord?' Siegbert thought with me. And after passing the night in prayer and chanting, on the morrow we drew our boat to the shore, and setting up a rude cross in the very midst of the heathen temple, cleansed it of the bones and ashes, and consecrated it as a temple to Almighty God, dedicating it to St. Peter and St. Paul. I had also another hope. To this temple the heathen were sure to resort again, and here might be the beginning or the end of our work; here we might plant a church by the power of the Gospel, or lay the foundations for others to build, as such foundations must often be laid, in the blood of martyrdom.

"Having claimed the temple for God, we did not dare to use its materials for our own purposes, dreading at once the displeasure of the saints to whom we had dedicated it, and the assaults of the evil spirits to whom it had belonged before.

"We therefore erected a hut at some little distance

from it, and began our tilling of the ground on the other side of the little knoll. For our stock of provisions was all but exhausted, and it was not too late in the summer for us to hope for a crop from the seeds of wheat and corn we had brought with us.

"For some days we saw nothing of the strange being who had so appalled Paul the chanter. But at length, one evening as we were singing our vesper hymn, I espied a human figure crouching among the bushes. I said nothing until the hymn was finished, and then approached it; but the poor creature was more terrified at us than Paul had been at him, and it was long before we could persuade him to venture near us, when, to our relief, we found it was no misshapen dwarf, or satyr, or demon of the woods, but a poor wild boy who seemed to have escaped into the forest at some of the terrible human sacrifices of the heathen, and to have grown up among the beasts. We clothed him from such of our own garments as we could spare, and by degrees taught him to speak and to understand us, so that this wild man of the woods became our faithful servant. His mind, indeed, was weak and easily bewildered, and we could never get him to understand any difficult theology. But in that he came to love the name of God the Father who made us, and of Christ the Lord who redeemed us, and to understand what it was to pray, we deemed him at last worthy to be baptized, which we did, by the name of John, in the stream, thus consecrating at once the wild waters and the wilder man. Our little field bore a fair crop, so that we had wherewithal to store our granary against the winter.

"The winter was severe. The stream was frozen, and the marshy ground near it. The snow lay thick through the forest, and drifted so as almost to bury our little hut, and no heathen came near us. And, moreover, Paul the chanter, who was of a feeble constitution, was laid up with aguish fever. I began to have misgivings as to whether we had chosen right, and lest we should sink into mere settlers in the wilderness.

"Many a night I wrestled alone with God in prayer, when one mid-winter day the boy John came rushing into the hut, where I was watching by the sick-bed of Paul, and exclaimed,—

"'Fly for life; they are coming to murder us all.'

"The shock aroused our sick brother from the stupor in which he was lying, and wrapping his garments about him, he sat up in his bed pale and trembling. But this was the moment for which I had been praying for weeks.

"We resolved to await the heathen by the cross in their temple, offering up the Holy Eucharist, and chanting the praises of the Lord.

"Before the sun had risen above the trees they came. When first they saw us standing by their altar in our white priestly robes, they paused and drew back. We continued chanting, when one of them, bolder than the rest, angrily threw his spear at us. It pierced the right arm of the cross, which we felt to be a sign from heaven. Therefore, advancing towards them with the cross in my hand, I spoke to them, calling on them in the name of Christ to forsake their cruel idols and worship Him.

"To my joy they understood the words I spoke; and in a dialect sufficiently like our own for me to understand, one of them came forward and said,—

"'Who are ye that invade our forests, and speak to us of strange gods?'

"'We are the servants of the God whose sign is our

defense,' I said, pointing to the spear lying at the foot of the cross, from which it had rebounded. 'See, your weapons are powerless against ours.'

"At that moment two women escaped from the men who had brought them hither to sacrifice, and rushing forward, threw themselves at the foot of the cross, exclaiming, 'Save us, O Lord Christ, and ye his servants.' One of the women remained with her arms clasped around the cross, but the other, rising to her full height, clasped her hands, and looking up to heaven said,—

"'O Christ, thou art mighty to save;' then turning to the bewildered heathen she said,—

"'See, you brought us hither to slay us, and the God whom we serve has sent his servants before us to save us and you.'

"As she stood thus, her long robe floating around her majestic form, and her fair hair shining about her, she looked like an angel, and the heathen Saxons, among whom there is much religious reverence for holy and devout women, exclaimed,—

"'She is a Vala, a prophetess! Let us listen to her words.'

"The captive woman bid them hearken to us, who, she said, were sent of God to teach them. Then I gave to them the great message from God concerning his Son, enforcing it as well as I could by contrast with their own selfish and revengeful gods. I tried to make them understand who the Lord Christ is, and what he has done and suffered for us; how, even as we spoke, he listened, and was waiting to receive us.

"When they sought proofs of His power, I pointed them to the fallen and broken images of their gods, powerless to defend their own temples from the invasion of us the feeble servants of the Almighty. I told them also of the cities and fertile fields which everywhere replaced the wilderness where the name of Christ prevailed. All day they listened, and through the night, as we retired to our hut, in the interval of our chanted psalms, we heard them debating our words with each other as they sat around their camp fires. The next morning their chief came to us, and said,—

"'The words you speak are good, the things you promise are fair. Nor are they altogether strange to us. We have heard of this great Name of which you speak, that it is strong in the battle-field, and against fire and flood; and we would hear more.'

"After some more discourse they departed, leaving with us the two Christian captive women, for whom we built a hut on a meadow on the opposite side of the stream, hoping it would prove the germ of a nunnery, and that ere long I might send for thee, Hildelith, and my mother.

"Before many days, the heathen returned with their women and children; and, after due instruction, we baptized them in the little river. Never had the forest seen such a festival before, and never had our hearts known such gladness.

"Soon a village sprang up around the little wooden church which we built on the site of the heathen temple, and around the village the trees were felled; on the slopes of the little hill we taught them to make vineyards, and cornfields sprang up in the clearings of the forests; while around our huts we planted gardens of herbs, mallows, thyme, and other flowers such as bees love, from which we gathered stores of honey, and distilled also many a healing balm for sickness and wounds. Bread and wine were provided for the Eucharist from the vines and corn, fruits of the labours of Christian hands; and Christian hearts were there to honour and to share the blessing.

"Their progress in holiness was, however, slower than we could wish. Often our quiet was broken by sounds of angry strife, and with all our care we could not always stop the contest before blood had been shed; nor could we always prevent that blood being cruelly avenged by the kindred of the dead.

"In these matters I found my experience in administering the laws of King Ina very serviceable. I endeavoured to modify their often savage customs by the good king's Saxon code. If I could gain their attention, they would generally obey.

"Our greatest disappointment, however, was after Siegbert, the carpenter monk, and I had made a missionary journey further into the forest, on which we had been delayed some weeks. It was in spring; the long-continued rains had been unfavourable to the sowing of the crops; there had been great mortality among the swine that were pastured in the forest, and also much dangerous sickness among the people.

"As we came back towards dusk, to our great grief we found a number of our baptized Christians performing a religious dance around a sacred oak which had been left standing on the summit of the hill whereon the village was built. They were directed by a weird old woman who had been a priestess and prophetess among them, and who was muttering monotonous incantations as they moved in a circle round the tree.

"The circle was breaking up as we approached, and we reached the hut, where Paul the chanter was awaiting us, without any one knowing we had arrived.

"He told us a sad tale:—how as the pestilence increased the faith of the people seemed to waver, and the church was less and less attended, until at length the murmurs of discontent arose to a storm, and this aged prophetess, whom at first they had consulted secretly, persuaded many of them that we were murdered, that the gods of their tribe were avenging their insulted majesty, and that the only hope lay in returning to the old worship.

"All night I spent alone on the floor of the church in tears and prayer. It was the story of the absent Moses and the idolatrous Israelites once more. The same, and yet, I thought, perhaps how different in God's sight! I was, indeed, no Moses. Might not I myself have been the cause of this sin of the people, by too hastily receiving them into the fold of the Church; and, perhaps, by too much picturing earthly blessings as the reward of piety? The fruit of piety and a good life they surely are; but had I warned these children enough of the chastenings with which God sees it needful to discipline his beloved?

"Before the morrow I had resolved what to do. The sacred tree, which I had spared for its noble beauty as a shade for the people to gather beneath in summer, was too much linked with unhallowed memories to live. Temptation whispered to the people in every rustle of its myriad leaves, and it must fall.

"Our re-appearance among them already in some manner counteracted the influence of the prophetess by disproving her predictions. Many at once welcomed us with tears of joy, and confessed how their faith had all but failed; but others scarcely returned our greetings at all.

"No time was to be lost. I took an axe in my hand, and approaching the oak, sacred as it had been to Thor the Thunderer, began to fell it.* Some of the faithful people formed a circle round me; but the majority of the tribe, slowly gathering, uttered murmurs which rose to angry cries as the strokes of the axe fell on their ears, till the boldest broke through our faithful disciples, and one powerful man seized my arm.

"Disengaging myself from him, I held the axe aloft, and said,—

"'Who am I, a feeble man to fight with him ye call the Thunderer, if he is indeed so mighty? Clear the field, and let there be a fair fight. If Thor is to be trusted, he will defend his own.' The crowd fell back in an instant; then, grasping the axe in my hands, I exclaimed aloud,— 'O Christ our Lord, show thy strength in the weakness of thy servant, and save this thy people from their sins.'

"The next strokes fell through the silence of the expectant crowd. Again, however, the angry murmur began to rise, when the axe penetrated to a larger hollow in the tree, and part of it began to totter. At this sight the murmurs deepened, but they were answered by the triumphant shouts of the faithful. A breathless silence followed, and at length a portion of the mighty trunk, which had already been doomed by time, fell crashing to the ground, scattering the crowd right and left. When they re-assembled and found that no one was injured, and that I was still cutting the remainder with my axe, some of the men who had welcomed us back took courage and joined in the work, until the whole of the giant trunk lay prostrate, its branches stretching their helpless monster arms far down the hill.

"A shout of triumph burst from the faithful. Afterwards a low chant was heard from the voice of Paul the

* An incident in the life of Boniface.—*Neander*.

chanter, which was caught up by voice after voice until nearly the whole throng joined in the Saxon Te Deum, acknowledging Christ to be indeed God and Lord.

"Then I began the Saxon Creed, which the people repeated reverently after me. And afterwards I asked them if they had indeed forgotten the message of divine love we had brought them, the precious blood shed to redeem them, the glorious Lord to whose service they had sworn themselves for ever? I asked them who it was who, having first given them Himself, had given them all the good things they possessed, with the promise of endless joy in heaven, if they would obey Him? I asked them what they would think of a child who, after being tenderly cared for by father and mother, and provided with everything he desired or needed, should lift his hand against his father or his mother because they refused him once something his sick fancy lusted for? The love of God, I said, was at once a father's and a mother's. I told them that I reproached myself that I had not told them more of the discipline with which he chastens those whom he loves. 'But God,' I said, 'himself has taken the teaching from my unworthy lips by His afflictions, and, showing you the weakness of your faith, calls you to repent and turn to Him, and seek His pardon and a tenfold measure of the grace you need.' Then repeating to them the vow they had made in Saxon at their baptism, many of them said it after me with voices broken with sobs. And afterwards we all knelt beside the prostrate oak, while the people, weeping like penitent children, said after me the Lord's Prayer.

"I thought it right afterwards to impose many penances on them. And after this I felt greatly the need of faithful and instructed Christian women to teach the mothers and little ones. The Christian captives had been restored to their kindred, and therefore, Hildelith, as thou knowest, I thought it time to send for my mother and for thee."

THE WORDS OF HILDELITH.

THESE words of Oswald, my brother, I have written. I have few of my own to add.

"Many years after Oswald left us on the banks of the Tyne we looked for tidings of him, and at last they came. He sent a messenger to bid us follow him into the far-off Saxon forests, and gladly we went.

"It was a joyful day, when, after many perilous wanderings through Friesland (where Willibrord, our countryman, had been labouring so long, and yet many of the people remained heathen,) and the land of the Rhine; after seeing the spot where the bodies of our countrymen, the martyred Hewalds, had been thrown into the river, now marked by the blackened ruins of the village where their murderers had lived; after wandering among many heathen tribes beyond, we at length reached the Christian settlement, deep in the Thuringian forest, where my brother had built cells for himself and for us.

"The simple people showed us no little kindness, welcoming and honouring us like beings from a better world, so wonderful did the few arts we possessed seem in their eyes. There we spent many happy years, teaching the women how to order their homes, and the young maidens to spin and sew, and chant the Christian hymns, and some of them to read in their native tongue, which was closely allied to our own; as Oswald had taught the men to till the ground and clear the forest.

"From time to time wonderful tidings reached us of the success of the preaching of our countryman, the great Archbishop Boniface, known to Oswald of old as Winfried of Crediton. Tribe after tribe received Christian baptism from him and his monks, thousands and ten of thousands were added to the Church. Bishopric after bishopric was founded where all had been heathenism. Abbeys and towns of civilized men arose where all had been forest and wilderness; until our Christian village, which had been an outpost in the furthest haunts of the missionary field, became surrounded by many Christian tribes. And not far from us arose the abbey and the city of Erfurt, the seat of the bishopric of Thuringia.

"Some, indeed, of the earlier missionaries, Irish and Scottish, scattered here and there in lonely places, thought Archbishop Boniface too ambitious and desirous of subjecting all to himself; and some contended against the strict subordination which he enforced to the See of Rome, and also against the celibacy which he insisted on, not only for the monks, but for the secular priests. To us Northumbrian Saxons, who had derived our Christianity from Iona, the claims of Rome to universal sovereignty seemed scarcely like the humility enjoined by our Lord and manifested by Bishop Aidan and his disciples; but Oswald thought it better not to contend. He said he knew not how far it might be God's will to train the nations into order, and to unite them into one visible Christendom, by appointing one visible head; he thought time only could prove, by proving if Rome was indeed to be the holy place, inhabited by holy men, which should be a spring of holy influences to the world.

"At all events he felt his work was elsewhere. One day he came to us with the calm determination on his face which we knew it was in vain to oppose, and told us this village had become too much of a home for one who had vowed himself to live as a pilgrim and a stranger, and to carry the standard of the King on and on into the unconquered wilderness.

"Seven days the whole community set apart for fasting and prayer, and then a new abbot was appointed; and Oswald with three of the brethren, departed into the forests to the north and west. Such partings were hard. The peril was so certain, and the chance of ever seeing or hearing of one another more so uncertain. But our mother said,—

"'I have prayed God night and day my children might be his servants, and it is not for me to choose the service.' Months and years passed away. Tidings came to us from the south, and west, and east: letters and holy meditations from Bede, the learned monk at Jarrow; commands from Rome; tidings of the defeat of the Saracens by the Frankish general Charles Martel near Tours, stemming the great tide of infidel invasion from overflowing Christendom. But no tidings from that dark and heathen north where our Oswald was wandering! No tidings at all through all those years; until two strangers came one evening to the abbey gate leading a crippled, blind old man.

"And that was Oswald!

"Soon afterwards we were required to return to England with some young converts, who were to receive instruction of the holy Bede at Jarrow. And here we have dwelt ever since.

"Sight and strength gone! and these two converts gained! And, as far as we could see, that was all the fruit of those long years of suffering and toil. His companions had been murdered, and he himself blinded by the heathen. As far as we could see! But who expects to see foundations? and what church is securely founded without the bodies of martyrs being laid beneath it?

"Without martyrs, whose names are hidden, there would be no archbishops; and perchance, hereafter, we shall find our Oswald's crown not among the meanest.

"But our Lord will judge rightly; and perchance in heaven I shall be so much better than I am that it will please me as much to see Boniface have the higher place as Oswald. To him I well believe it would be the same now. But he is better and nobler than any one I ever knew. I used to love to see the glow of joy that came over his face when he heard of the triumphs of the cross through Germany; how bishopric after bishopric was founded in Hesse, and Friesland, and Bavaria, and Thuringia, and even in Russia; and everywhere the name of the English Boniface was lauded as the apostle of all the land.

"Only once I heard him utter a word approaching a murmur, and that was when we heard how, after that life of noble and successful effort in Germany, Boniface in his old age had left his prosperous mission and his archiepiscopal honours to return to the heathen Frisons among whom his missionary work had begun, and many of whom still remained heathen, and there had joyfully met the martyr's death. When he heard this, Oswald lifted up his sightless eyes to heaven, and said,—

"'If Thou hadst only suffered me to die for Thee, me who can serve Thee so little here! If my crippled life could have been taken instead of his!'

"But soon after the children of the choir came to receive instruction as usual from him. And among them were two boys from Thuringia. I sat by him as he taught (as was permitted me), to point out the notes, and as he laid his hand softly on the heads of those German lads, he smiled and said,—

"'Soon you will return to your people, and in Thuringia the praises of Christ my Lord will be sung a little better for the lessons of old blind Oswald. My Master has need of me on earth yet.' And as I led him back to the monastery we passed Bede, whose learning is the light of England and the admiration of Europe, quietly digging in the herb garden, like any other monk; and I felt comforted for my brother, remembering that obedience is the only service men or angels can render God, and the lowliest obedience is the highest service.

"The example of Bede did not shine before us on earth long after this. The letter of his pupil Cuthbert to his school-fellow Cuthwin, made known to all who honoured him how the venerable Bede died, and what the Church has lost in him. Part of it I copy:

"'He, our father and master, was much troubled with shortness of breath, yet without pain, before the day of our Lord's resurrection, that is, about a fortnight; and thus he afterwards passed his life, cheerful and rejoicing, giving thanks to Almighty God every day and night, nay, every hour, till the day of our Lord's ascension, that is, the seventh before the kalends of June (May 24th), and daily read lessons to us his disciples, and whatever remained of the day he spent in singing psalms. He also passed all the night awake in joy and thanksgiving, unless a short sleep prevented it; in which case he no sooner woke than he presently repeated his wonted exercises, and ceased not to give thanks to God with uplifted hands. I declare with truth that I have never seen with my eyes, nor heard with my ears, any man so earnest in giving thanks to the living God.

"'O truly happy man! He chanted the sentence of St. Paul the apostle, "It is a dreadful thing to fall into the hands of the living God," and much more out of Holy Writ; wherein also he admonished us to think of our last hour, and to shake off the sleep of the soul. And being learned in our poetry, he said some things also in our tongue concerning the departure of the soul. He also sang antiphons according to our custom and his own, one of which was, "O glorious king, Lord of all power, who triumphing this day didst ascend above all the heavens, do not forsake us orphans, but send down on us the spirit of truth which was promised to us by the Father. Halleluiah!"

"'And when he came to that word, "Forsake us not," he burst into tears and wept much, and an hour afterwards he began to repeat what he had commenced, and we hearing it mourned with him. By turns we read, and by turns we wept; nay, we wept always while we read. In such joy we passed the days of Lent till the aforesaid day, and he rejoiced much and gave God thanks because he had been counted worthy to be so weakened. He often repeated that "God scourgeth every son whom he receiveth;" as also this sentence from St. Ambrose,—"I have not lived so as to be ashamed to live among you; nor do I fear to die, because we have a gracious God." During these days he laboured to compose two works well worthy to be remembered, besides the lessons we had from him, and the singing of psalms,—namely, he translated the Gospel of St. John as far as the words, "But what are these among so many?" (St. John vi. 9,) into our own tongue, for the benefit of the church; also some collections out of the Notes of Bishop Isidore, saying, "I will not have my pupils read a falsehood, nor labour therein without profit after my death." When the Tuesday before the Ascension of our Lord came, he began to suffer still more in his breath, and a small swelling appeared in his feet; but he passed all that day, and dictated cheerfully, saying now and then, among other things, "Go on quickly; I know not how long I shall hold out, and whether my Maker will not soon take me away." But to us he seemed very well to know the time of his departure, and so he spent the night awake in thanksgiving; and when the morning appeared—that is, Wednesday—he ordered us to write with all speed what he had begun; and this done, we walked till the third hour with the relics of saints, according to the custom of that day. There was one of us with him, who said to him, "Dear master, there is still one chapter wanting. Do you think it troublesome to be asked any more questions?" He answered, "It is no trouble. Take your pen, make ready, and write fast;" which he did. But at the ninth hour he said to me, "I have some articles of value in my chest, such as pepper, napkins, and incense. Run quickly and bring the priests of our monastery to me, that I may distribute among them the gifts which God has bestowed on me. The rich in this world are bent on giving gold and silver and other precious things; but I, in love, would joyfully give my brothers what God has given unto me." He spoke to every one of them, admonishing and entreating them that they would carefully say masses and prayers for him, which they readily promised; but they all mourned and wept, chiefly because he said that "in this world they should see his face no more." They rejoiced for that he said "It is time that I return to Him who has formed me out of nothing. I have lived long. My merciful Judge well foresaw my life for me. The time of my dissolution draweth nigh ; for I desire to depart, and to be with Christ." Having said much more, he passed the day joyfully till the evening, when the boy above mentioned said, "Dear master, there is yet one sentence not written." He answered, "Write quickly." Soon after, the boy said, "The sentence is now written." He replied, "It is well. You have said the truth. It is ended. Take my head in your hands, for it is a great satisfaction to me to sit facing my holy place where I was wont to pray, that, thus sitting, I may call on my Father." And thus, on the pavement of his little cell, singing, "Glory be to the Father, and to the Son, and to the Holy Ghost," when he had named the Holy Ghost, he breathed his last, and so departed to the heavenly kingdom. All who were present at the death of the blessed father said that they had never seen any other person expire with so much devotion and in so tranquil a frame of mind ; for, as you have heard, as long as the soul animated the body, he never ceased, with uplifted hands, to give thanks to the true and living God.

"'His remains are laid under the south porch of the church where he used to celebrate the Holy Eucharist, to chant, and to preach.

"'Through England, in every school and monastery, our English youth benefit by his patient labours, his translations of the Holy Scriptures, his hymns and homilies, and his selections from the writings of good and wise men of old.'

"Thus throughout the lands and throughout the ages

the names of Boniface, the great English missionary and martyr, and Bede, the great English teacher, will be honoured as long as the Church or the world shall last; whilst a thousand names of missionaries perhaps as faithful, martyrs as devoted, scholars as patient, perish from the memory of men.

"But to me there is no longer anything sad in the thought, even with regard to Oswald. God gives him those special joys which are linked to each especial sorrow, and to it alone. We all delight in the wondrous music he brings out of the great church organ; but to him I know it unseals visions of glory and beauty hidden from us, and I think he hears tones in its melodies which recall to him dear voices we never heard, but trust to hear one day in an immortal song of lofty praise. To him those golden pipes are a 'tower of sweet sound,' a ravishing treasury of delight, the very steps leading to the gates of the Golden City of light on high.

"And to me it is a great joy to think that the name of every faithful servant of Christ whom men honour in every age is but one of a roll of countless such names which men know not, but which God has written down in his Book of Life, to shine in the light of His smile now and hereafter, to be uttered by His lips, and to thrill the heart of the whole Church with the memory of long-forgotten works of love. For in the Christian race all patient runners win, and in the Christian battle all who endure to the end are victors. And it seems to me a glorious thing to be the smallest wave in the tide of blessing which has flowed back on heathen Germany, the ancient fatherland of our fathers, through the labours of Christian men and women from this Saxon England, which is the country of us, their children."

VI.

ALFRED THE TRUTH-TELLER.

SCENES FROM THE LIFETIME OF
ENGLAND'S DARLING.

VI.

ALFRED THE TRUTH-TELLER.

I.

ONE evening in the summer of 852 several of the monks of the ancient Abbey of Lindisfarne were gathered in the abbey burial-ground on Holy Island, eagerly listening to Bertric, a young thane who had just arrived among them from the south of England, and was telling them his story of bloodshed and wrong.

"We were living in peace," he said, "on my father's lands, on the range of hills which rise on the north of the Thames. The Danish-men had been defeated a short time before at Wembury in Devonshire, and also by king Athelstan and Elchere the ealdorman in a battle fought on ship-board where a great number of the enemy were slain, and nine of their ships were taken. It was true that for the first time the heathen men had stayed through the winter in our country, on the Isle of Thanet. But many among us drew hope from this. Had not our forefathers, the elders said, once been themselves wild heathen sea rovers such as these? and if these wild men could be brought to dwell with their wives and children in some corners of the land, might they not be dealt with at last like human beings, instead of mere beasts of prey swooping on their plunder and then flying off with it? Might not some portion of the country be cheaply sacrificed to save the rest from plunder? So said some of the older and more peaceable men. Meanwhile the more familiar sight of the dreaded marauders seemed to rob them of half their terrors; and armies were rapidly collecting among the Mercians and West Saxons to defend the coasts. Thus we dwelt securely on the hill-side by the Thames. My father's house was on the site of what was said to be an old Roman camp, commanding a wide view over forest and meadow, and slopes of hills clothed with cornfields and vineyards, to the banks of the river where the city of London rose around the church-tower of St. Paul's. It was a range of wooden buildings guarded by a moat which had encircled the old camp. We were a family of six little children. I was the eldest, and my eldest sister Hilda was a nun in an abbey at Canterbury.

"One evening my father and I had been watering the cattle in one of the range of forest-pools which lay in the valley below our house, and were driving them up to the hill to house them in the sheds within the moat, when, on reaching the summit of the hill, we saw a number of masts advancing up the valley of the Thames. As we looked, more and more came into sight, until we could count them by hundreds. At the door of the house my mother met us with terror in her face. 'Have you seen them?' she said. My father only bowed his head, and then we went to the highest point and watched them in silence. It was a moving forest of masts which seemed countless.

"As we looked, a thrall came galloping up the hill toward us.

"'The heathen men are upon us!' he said, breathlessly. 'They pause nowhere, but are making straight for London to sack the city. There are three hundred and fifty ships full of armed men.'

"All the men about the farm were set to work at once to strengthen the stockade around the moat as best we could. My father hoped it might enable us to withstand an attack from any stray band of plunderers. And having done this, he called the household to prayer. We repeated after him the Our Father, and such Saxon collects as he knew, and then we went out to listen if any sound of the enemy could be heard. Alas! we heard too much. Through the night air came first the solemn tolling of the bells of St. Paul's, and then the clashing of the alarm-peal, sounded in the vain hope of arousing some Saxon force within reach. It was in vain. Flames began to rise through the darkness, until the valley, and hills, and sky glowed with one terrible glare. And then the bells were silent. The flames leaped high above the church tower, and through the silence the south wind bore us the death-wail of the stormed and sacked city.

"The next day fugitives reached us with details of the massacre, and with the further tidings that when the work of plunder and slaughter was accomplished in London it was rumoured that the enemy would march straight on Canterbury and do the same work of destruction there.

"It was decided that I should go at once with a band

of faithful men, well armed, to bring my sister Hilda home from Canterbury, while my father remained to protect the house. Merciless as the Danish-men are to all, against monks and nuns they deal out a double measure of ferocity, and none of us could rest until we knew Hilda rescued from the threatened abbey.

"I went (Heaven knows) as quickly as I could, taking not an hour's rest that could be spared; but I had to make a considerable circuit, on reaching Canterbury, to avoid the Danish forces which were already moving. And when at last the ancient sacred city of our Church came in sight, it was too plain our journey had been in vain. From the blackened ruins of the city, as we silently approached it, came the yells of the heathen and the hopeless cries of the suffering and the dying. The enemy was in full possession. And too soon the crowds of fugitives whom we met flying from the slaughter, told us the fate of the abbey where my sister had been. The sacred buildings lay a heap of smouldering ruins, and for such of the inmates as survived the fire there remained no earthly refuge.

"One old monk only, who had escaped, gave me the faintest hope. He said that a few days before, some of the sisters had been removed to an abbey belonging to the same congregation in the north of England. With this dim outlet from despair as all the result of our journey, we hastened back to defend those who were left at home. We arrived to find no home to defend, and none to tell how it perished, save one old man whom the Danes had blinded and then left in mockery to die. One consolation only he gave me. My mother and the little ones had fallen beneath the Danish arrows before the house was taken: and the charred and blood-stained ruins of my father's homestead were at least the grave of those who had died an honourable death.

"The vineyards and cornfields on the southern slopes towards the Thames were blackened with fire and trodden down by the cattle which the enemy had driven off. The dearest object now left to me on earth, was that faint hope of recovering my sister Hilda, and with this purpose I have come northward through Mercia along the shores of East Anglia and Northumbria even to this island. Everywhere I have found the traces of the heathen men in ruined and desolate cities, heaps of dust and ashes marking the sites of abbeys and the graves of the monks. But of the nuns of Canterbury I have found no trace, and here, alas! ye tell me the same tale."

A compassionate silence followed Bertric's narrative, and then he resumed:

"Some special grace must have guarded this island brotherhood, that ye should be thus spared, dwelling as ye do in the very jaws of danger, on the borders of the sea-king's kingdom."

"Our congregation has not always thus been spared, my son," said an aged monk. "Sixty years ago, while all the rest of the land was tranquil, fearing nothing, the storm burst on our island first of all. One early dawn in 792, we wondered to see a number of strange sails on the eastern horizon. From what shores they came we knew not, nor with what purpose. Not forty years before, Boniface, after spreading the light of the faith from this happy land throughout Old Saxony, had been slain among the heathens of Friesland but since then we had learned that the faith for which he died had been still triumphing, and that the renowned emperor Charlemagne had subdued the heathen nations to his Christian sceptre. We watched the approach of this strange fleet, therefore, with curiosity, but without fear, and wondered to see the raven-standard unfurled, and to hear the fierce shouts of the seamen as they leapt armed on the shore. But before the next dawn the church of Bishop Aidan was burnt to the ground, the dwellings were destroyed, and all the brethren, save myself and a few who fled for life across the shallows to the mainland, lay dead and dying among the ruins. From that day to this the land has had no rest; and most of all, the fury of these robbers seems turned against the houses of God."

"That I saw everywhere," said Bertric. "Why should this be?"

"No doubt," said the aged monk, "it is because the devil hates most the servants of Christ. But I have heard also that the heathen sometimes, as they tortured the priests and monks, mocked them with the name of Charlemagne, and bid them lay their cause before the great emperor, who massacred thousands of their heathen kindred in Old Saxony. They do say that multitudes of the heathen Saxons were slain by the emperor's soldiers, and that others were given the choice of baptism or death. Some of these Danes are fugitives, they say, from that slaughter, and come to us not merely as plunderers, but as avengers of blood. And their chief vengeance, therefore, is against the monks."

"But why avenge the blood shed by Charlemagne on us?" asked Bertric. "Why should we suffer for the sins of the Franks?"

"Nay, my son," said the old monk, "we who suffer have also sinned."

"True," said one and another of the brethren, "the

sins of the land have indeed called for vengeance. In what province have not kings and nobles seized the revenues and lands of the abbeys?" And instance after instance of such spoliation was given.

"The world seems governed in a strange way," said Bertric, bitterly. "Charlemagne slaughters the heathen Saxons, and the heathen Danes wreak vengeance on us who never heard of these massacres. Kings and nobles rob the monks; and as a punishment the same monks are further robbed and murdered by the heathen."

"Brethren," said the old monk, "let us justify God and humble ourselves. It was not in the days of the holy Aiden, nor of those of Bede and Boniface, or of the good Archbishops Egbert and Albert of York, that these troubles came. Have there been no sins in the abbeys to draw down the vengeance of Heaven? If we made the vows of poverty and chastity a cloak for ease and sloth and sin, is it any wonder that God should bring us back to our vows, though it be with fire and sword?"

The assembly gradually dispersed at these words, until Bertric and the old monk were left alone.

"Father," said the young man, passionately, "tell me what I shall do, and what I shall believe; for you seem still to retain your trust in God, although you see the world falling into ruins around you."

"My son," was the reply, "the ruin brought by the Danes is not the first ruin I have seen, nor the worst. I have seen abbeys founded by holy men for the service of God turned into palaces where men vowed to poverty lived in luxury and idleness. I have heard sounds of traffic and revelry in halls which were built to be houses of prayer. And the blackened walls of many of the abbeys which entomb their slaughtered inmates seem to me less terrible than the fair edifices where men's souls are entombed, as in whited sepulchres, in hypocrisy and sin."

"But all were surely not thus fallen," said Bertric; "and the Danish armies make no distinction in their vengeance."

"God makes the distinction, my son," said the old man. "Hast thou forgotten that death is not an exit only, but an entrance-gate, and a gate from which issues more than one path?"

Bertric was silent, and the old monk continued tenderly:

"When the flames consumed thy father's house, were there no holy angels present to bear the innocent babes and the souls of those who cried to God in prayer, safely into the paradise of God?"

For the first time the bitter calm passed from the young man's voice, and in trembling tones he said:

"The poor will wait at the gates of our home no more, to receive the alms from my mother's hand!" Then, hiding his face, he gave way to an uncontrollable agony of weeping.

The old man sat still beside him, and prayed silently. He knew that such tears are Heaven's best balm for such griefs.

At length Bertric composed himself, and said:

"Father, what shall I do? I have no vocation for such a life as yours. Since I stood by the ruins of my home I have had but one desire—a fierce longing to avenge my kindred on the Danes."

"As they avenged the massacres of Charlemagne on thy kindred!" said the old man, quietly.

"Do not speak to me of forgiving my enemies," exclaimed Bertric, vehemently. "I know it is in our Lord's sermon on the mount; but he could never have meant, 'See the powerful and wicked cruelly slay and torture the just and helpless, and stand by and pray that they may be forgiven.'"

"If I were young again," said the old monk, "I would deem the sword and bow more befitting accoutrements than the cowl and the pen for these days. I would seek the best and wisest prince in the land, and join myself to him, to serve him in defending the helpless people on our coasts from these marauders. I deem such a life would be nobler than to say any number of prayers, or accomplish any mortifications for my own spiritual glory in an abbey. But I may counsel thee wrong. We know best the dangers of the paths we have trodden."

The next morning, when Bertric came out in the early dawn, he found the old monk awaiting him on the burial-ground.

"My son," he said, "I watched late last night, thinking of thee, until I fell asleep and had a strange dream. I thought the holy Bishop Aidan himself appeared to me, with Saint Cuthbert, robed like the blessed, in garments white as the light. And he looked reproachfully at me, and said: 'Who art thou, to bear the sword of vengeance against those heathens of the north? What wouldst thou have been if God had sent me to thy forefathers with the sword instead of with the message of peace?' I would have justified myself, but with the effort I awoke and came out hither to St. Cuthbert's tomb, to keep my vigils better, and to wait for thee."

"What is the interpretation of the dream, father?" said the young man.

"I know not even if it was a voice from heaven," said

the old man, "and still less if it was a message for thee. Yet I have been thinking thou art but a youth as yet. Might it not benefit thee, if our abbot willed it so, to accompany some of our brotherhood who are bound on pilgrimage to Rome, there to learn what thou canst at the Saxon school, and so befit thyself for higher service at the king's court than thy youth might now obtain? Thou art not of the kind, I trow, who have only hands to offer in service; and those who are to lead others should be before them as well as above them. Learning might serve thee in the place of thy lost lands and thy lacking years, and give thee earlier the post in which thou mightest serve the people best."

"Thou dost not think, then," said Bertric, "that the saints meant me to abandon my purpose."

"I think only," said the old monk, "that they would have thee set it before thee to serve and defend thy Saxon people, and leave it to God to inflict vengeance on the Danes. Remember, also, that if a heathen man becomes a Christian, he is an enemy won over to thy side; and a foe reconciled is better than a foe slain."

The young man acquiesced, although with some reserve, and the next day he set sail with the pilgrims for Rome; and when he left, the old monk solemnly blessed him, and said:

"My son, darker days yet may be in store; but remember the darkest hour heralds the dawn. Forget not the Jewish proverb, 'When the tale of bricks is doubled, then Moses is sent.' To prayer and patience no cause is lost."

On their way they saw in the distance a fleet, which they took to belong to the Danes, bound for the Norwegian coast, and considered themselves fortunate in escaping.

But in that fleet was a young captive maiden, borne away by the Jarl Sidroc to be the slave of his wife in her home on one of the Norwegian fiords. Something in her had touched the spring of pity which lies in almost every human heart. Thus Hilda and Bertric, the brother and sister, passed each other unconsciously on the ocean; one to arm himself for the conflict in Rome, and the other to carry on the conflict with other weapons in the very home of the spoilers; as she told the children of the fierce pirate her simple stories of Mary of Nazareth and her Holy Babe, who of old took the little ones so tenderly in his arms and blessed them.

II.

THE pilgrimage to Rome did its work for Bertric. It gave him a new confidence in the final victory of truth and right, to see how the tombs of martyrs had become the glory of the city where they had been slain, and to watch pilgrims flocking in from those Gothic and Teutonic tribes which had overwhelmed old imperial Rome, to do homage at the graves of the men imperial Rome had doomed to ignominious deaths. Moreover, it made him, an orphaned wanderer from a land where heathenism seemed once more triumphant, step more firmly, and breathe more freely, thus to feel himself a member of the great community of Christendom which pagan Rome and pagan Goth had proved so indestructible.

As he knelt in the churches by the tombs of King Cadwalla, King Ina, and his Queen Ethelberga, and returned at night to the Saxon school, where, in the strange land, and among the strange people, he was greeted by the familiar accents of his mother tongue, the idea of the great central Holy City, where the devout of all Christendom might worship at one shrine, and the homeless of all nations might meet as in a common home—a city which should be as a family hearth for all Christendom, and a source whence light should radiate throughout the world—took possession of his heart. It had not then been proved—as centuries afterward proved it—that any human institution claiming to be the fountain-head of truth and holiness, cut off by the very loftiness of that claim from the inexhaustible fountain of grace which only flows for the lowly, must stagnate and become a source of corruption and death.

At that time Rome had surely, in God's providence, a great work to do for the nations of Europe. Those massive ruins of the proudest material empire the world had seen, now ruled over by a priest whose whole power rested on a belief, bore powerful witness to the rude warrior tribes of the North of a spiritual might before which all physical strength must bow. The Holy City, where all the contending and scattered Latin and Celtic and Teutonic races worshipped as members of one Church, ennobled them, by the force of its central attraction, from a conglomeration of tribes into a community of nations. At Rome, also, thoughtful men first learned to look into the great illuminated track of the historical past, so as to understand the unity of the human race, and the progression of God's dealings with man. Turning from the wild and disconnected legends of their fathers which glittered above the dark ocean of bygone time, but scarcely revealed it, at Rome they gazed back on the long vista of the four great empires, crossed and lit up at intervals by the white light of sacred history, and at one point made clearer than the scenes actually around them by the glory around the person of the Son of Man.

This, in her day, it was given to Rome to accomplish for Christendom. How many of the miseries, and sins, and superstitions of men and of humanity, proceed from anachronisms; from putting in the sickle before God's harvest is ripe; from seeking to stunt the youth into the measure of the child; from seeking to galvanize into immortality what has done its work, and is dead! When will men learn that a harvest gathered before God's hour is come is no harvest, but a devastation; that the man stunted in growth is no longer a child but a dwarf; that by refusing to bury the dead, we render them not immortal, but a source of death to the living? Not until all men shall have learned to say, as the second Man, the Lord from heaven, said in his agony, "Not my will, but thine be done." And then old things will pass away— old sins, old sorrows, the old history, the old world, the old man—and all things will become new.

But that future history of Rome, which is to us such a record of usurpation and corruption, was unknown to Bertric and the Saxon pilgrims around him. And looking back from the honoured graves of martyred apostles, he learned to look forward with a new hope for the future of his country. But whence the deliverance could come, as yet he could not conjecture. Saxon pilgrims continued to bring dreadful tidings of the ravages of the Danes. He longed to be at home again, in the humblest post, where he might help to stem the torrent of heathen invasion. At times he had misgivings as to whether he had any right to remain away. The connection between studying the Latin grammar and fighting the Northern pirates seemed very remote. However, he resolved to follow the old monk's counsel at least for one year.

Six months of that year had not passed when, in 753, Bertric met, at one of the gates of Rome, a company of horsemen appareled as if they were the attendants of some great house. As he paused in the narrow street to let them pass, to his surprise he caught the homely accents of his own Saxon tongue. His attention was aroused. One of the horsemen, evidently the chief of the company, carried before him on the saddle a fair-haired boy, four or five years old.

"Who is the young prince whom you are escorting with such honours?" Bertric asked of one of the attendants.

"It is Alfred the Atheling, youngest son of Ethelwulf, king of Wessex."

A few days afterward Bertric, with all the Saxons in Rome, was present at a ceremony in which that child bore the chief part.

Solemnly, in an assembly of the chief nobles and ecclesiastics, Pope Leo IV anointed the fair head of the Saxon child with the holy oil which of old consecrated kings and priests to their offices, and all Christians to their royal and princely calling in the ancient rites of baptism and confirmation, adopting him as his own spiritual son.

A strange unconscious prophecy lay hidden in that ceremony. Three elder brothers stood between that child and the throne, and half a lifetime of trial and humiliation between him and his kingdom. Yet a consecrating hand was indeed upon that childish head. Unknown to Israel, the infant Moses was indeed there, the hero and the lawgiver who was to break the iron yoke of the oppressor, and to form the divided multitudes of his people into a nation.

And as that evening, after listening to fresh tales of Danish outrage and oppression from the young prince's court, Bertric said bitterly in his heart, "O Lord, how long?" he little knew that in that unconscious child he had seen the answer.

More than twelve months passed, and once more the boy Alfred appeared in Rome; but this time it was in the company of his father.

The Saxon king came to lay his offerings at the shrines of the apostles; and to this day the records remain of his costly gifts of golden crown and chalice and paten, of silken and embroidered stoles and priestly vestments.

From King Ethelwulf's company Bertric heard again how, amidst the helplessness of East Anglia, Northumbria, and even (in a great degree) of Mercia, Wessex remained as yet secure from Danish oppression; how St. Swithin and St. Neot, the king's kinsmen, gave the people examples of austere sanctity; while Ealstan, the brave bishop of Sherborne, was ever ready to risk his life in defending his countrymen against the heathen invader.

To King Ethelwulf's service, therefore, Bertric devoted himself, and in his company returned to England.

III.

IN those days, when John the Baptist's life seems to have been the ideal of holiness far more than that of the Son of Man; when to renounce the common food and the common joys of humanity was deemed far nobler than to turn earth's daily bread to divine uses; when the Church demanded of her saints that they should come neither eating bread nor drinking wine, it is remarkable that the greatest and best man whose history has reached us should have been trained in quite another way.

Alfred the Atheling grew up, not in the wilderness, but in the home. His early lore was not the ascetic legends, but the inspiriting ballads of his people, learned by heart and repeated at his mother's knee, to win the jeweled volume in which they were written. His school was not the narrow convent under monkish discipline, but the royal home, with its recreations and its occupations. He was familiar with men and events before he became familiar with books; and therefore, to him books became, not the dry dust, but the living pictures, of the men and events of other days. The heroic conflicts of the Saxon ballads might be fought again in the England of his day; the field was there, and the foe, why not also the heroes? The chase was his great delight; not the mere pursuit of harmless creatures "preserved" for the purpose; but perilous pursuit of wolves and wild boars (such as in his day wounded Carloman, king of the Franks, to death), tracing them to their hiding-places, through unbroken forests, and following them till spear or arrow striking them arrested their flight, or they turned to bay as fiercely as any Dane on the pursuer, when the chase was changed into a struggle for life or death. Thus, eye and hand were trained, and muscle and nerve were braced; and with these physical qualities were strengthened insensibly the great intellectual and moral qualities so closely linked to them—quick observation, ready resource, and vigilant caution; patient endurance, steadfast purpose, and calm courage.

Alfred was successful in the chase; "and skill and good fortune in this art, as in all others," says Asser his friend, "are among the gifts of God." And after such days of toil, and peril, and triumph, in which every faculty of body, mind, and heart were called out to the utmost, the young prince might well turn with keen zest to the ballads of heroic dragon-slayers, whether couched in Saxon ballad or saintly legend.

"In look, in speech, in manners more graceful than all his brothers," the darling of his parents, and of all the people, he yet seems to have escaped the usual compensating misery of such popular favourites. There must have been a noble absence of self-assertion and self-seeking in a character which could be at once the example and the delight of young and old, of elders and companions. We find no trace of jealousies such as marred the early life of the father's darling of old Hebrew days; and, from what we learn of the character of King Ethelwulf, the merit can scarcely be ascribed to his judgment or forbearance.

The sunshine of those early days does not, indeed, seem to have been without its temptations. To Alfred, from his own confession, whatever may have appeared to others, the great sorrows of his after life did not come as an unaccountable crop of troubles, springing he knew not whence, but as a needed chastening, whose bitter root of sin he traced with penitent tears, while others, with rejoicing eyes, **bore witness** to their peaceable fruits of righteousness.

Yet from the first glimpses given us of him, a fervent and practical piety seems to have been interwoven with

Alfred's inmost being. Dear as his national ballads were to him, and all records he could glean of the wise and great of old, the book which "he kept day and night in his bosom" from his youth, as Asser himself saw, was one containing the Scriptures and hymns for the sacred hours, with certain psalms and prayers in Anglo-Saxon, psalms of praise and penitence of David the king, and Christian prayers pleading for grace in every time of need, and purification by the fire of the Holy Spirit "from that Lord God of truth who redeemed mankind, sold to sin, not by silver and gold, but by the blood of his precious Son."

Such words kept in his bosom, such words laid up in his heart day and night, were the hidden source of that self-sacrificing life to which England owes so much.

What tales that little well-worn volume might reveal, if it could but relate the scenes which must have been photographed on it—of midnight vigils and solitary hours passed in the churches before the first priest came to celebrate the first mass, in fervent prayer to God; prayer which, doubtless, no written nor even any spoken words could fathom, which often deepened into "groanings not to be uttered." For Alfred's was no apathetic nature, and his position was one shielded from no temptation. One who knew and loved him well has written, that so strong were his passions, yet so much stronger his dread of sin, that he entreated God to strengthen him against himself by any malady, however painful, only that it might not make him imbecile or contemptible in his royal duties.

Interpret it as we will, such prayers the young prince offered, rising often in the morning before the cock-crowing, and prostrating himself on the ground in the empty church before God. And from such a malady he suffered, tortured with sharp and often recurring spasms of pain, yet such as never hindered him in any service of God and of his people.

The suffering, however, became so intense and increasing, that while still a youth under twenty, Alfred was seized with a haunting dread of leprosy, or some other complaint which makes men useless or despicable. This fear pursued him at his studies, at his brother's court, and at the chase, until one day, when on a hunting expedition in Cornwall, he turned aside from his company, as was his wont, to offer his private devotions in a lonely chapel dedicated to St. Guerir (now St. Neot's), in a rocky valley among the Cornish moors. There "he spent some time entreating of God's mercy, that of his boundless clemency he would exchange the torments of the malady which then afflicted him, for some other lighter disease;" asking but for one condition, not a diminution or abbreviation of suffering, "but only that it might not show itself outwardly in his body, lest," in those rude and stormy times, "he should be an object of contempt, and less able to benefit mankind. When he had finished his prayers," writes Asser, "he proceeded on his journey, and not long after he felt within him that, by the hand of the Almighty, he was healed, according to his request, of his disorder, and that it was entirely eradicated."

By such discipline the Father of spirits saw fit to train a spirit, which, instead of seeking to manufacture penances for itself, committed itself unreservedly to Him. And to such ends did that divine discipline lead. By paths so rough to goals so glorious does God conduct his sons who trust him, and wish, above all things, to obey him.

Well may we tremble to ask God to teach and sanctify

us if we do *not* mean it. But we need *not* tremble at any possible discipline if we do.

IV.

AT this West Saxon court Bertric passed many years of his life, growing from youth to manhood, whilst Alfred grew from childhood to youth. Consciously or unconsciously, the hopes of the country, and its best and bravest men gathered around the prince. For meanwhile, in 860, "a large fleet came to land and stormed Winchester."* In 865 "the heathen army sate down in Thanet, and made peace with the men of Kent, and the men of Kent promised them money for the peace; and during the peace and the promise of money, the army stole away by night and ravaged all Kent to the eastward." In 866 "a great heathen army took up their winter quarters among the East Angles," who made peace with them, and supplied them with horses to ravage the rest of the land. In 867 the heathen army went into Northumbria, where, "by the instigation of the devil," Asser thinks, "there was much dissension on account of two rival kings;" and at York "there was an excessive slaughter of the Northumbrians—some within the city, some without—and the two kings were slain." In 868, "the heathen army took up their winter quarters at Nottingham." In 869 they were again at York, and there was a great famine and mortality of men, and a pestilence among the cattle; and in 870 this same terrible army, horsed by the East Angles, "rode across Mercia into East Anglia, and took up their winter quarters at Thet-

*Saxon Chronicle.

ford; and the same winter King Edmund (the martyr) fought against them, and the Danes got the victory and slew the king, and subdued all the land, and destroyed all the minsters (monasteries) which they came to. At that same time they came to Medehamstede (Peterborough) and burned and beat it down, slew abbot and monks, and all that they found there; and that place, which before was full rich, they reduced to nothing." For such involuntary discipline and unfeigned destitution were the poor monks compelled to exchange their comfortable voluntary penances and their vows of voluntary poverty mitigated by the charitable donations of the faithful. They had renounced the world, but it was rather a different thing for the world thus to renounce them. Yet, by such unexpected and uncompromising discipline, inflicted by no friendly hands, we may trust, were many true sons of God scourged into his kingdom.

Had not the chosen deliverer himself to earn his knighthood by discipline as little self-imposed, and scarcely less severe?

In 868, which was the twentieth year of King Alfred's life, there was a great famine. But at Nottingham there was great feasting; for Alfred the Atheling was married to the noble lady Elswitha, daughter of Athelred, surnamed Mucil (the Great), earl of the Gaini, and of Edburga, a princess of the royal line of Mercia, "a venerable and pious lady.".

Day and night the festivities, with banquet, song, and dance, were prolonged — the guests, royal and noble, prince and peasant, forgetting for awhile, in wild merriment, the cloud of misery and oppression which shadowed all the land—when suddenly, in the presence of all the guests, the princely bridegroom was seized by some mysterious and agonizing malady.

The noisy mirth of the revellers died away in alarm or in sympathy, as the report of his sudden attack penetrated among them. An anxious silence succeeded to the sounds of music and laughter, broken only by the running hither and thither of the attendants, as they vainly sought help, and the murmurs of hope and disappointment in the little circle immediately around the sufferer, as remedy after remedy was tried in vain. The skill of the physicians was baffled; none knew the cause of the disease, nor any means of alleviating it. Here and there among the courtiers, and still more among the serving-men and maidens, it began to be whispered that the prince was bewitched by secret magic arts, or that the devil himself was tormenting him in person.

Such was the close of Alfred's wedding-feast. From that day till his forty-fourth year—twenty-four years afterward—the terrible and mysterious malady, whatever it was, continually recurred; one agonizing attack succeeding another with dreadful certainty, yet at irregular intervals, so that he was never a day or a night free either from suffering or from the dread of it.

The darling of parents, of court, and people, had found the cross which was to make his earthly crown safe for him, and to fuse for him the heavenly crown.

"Often," says Asser, "he thought it rendered him useless for every duty, whether human or divine." But when Christ lays his cross on any who follow him, he takes care that, however it may hurt, it shall never hinder. For Alfred also, as for us, the rod and the cross are blended. The furnace which tries our faith scorches our sinful flesh. Alfred could not always see this as he suffered; but England has acknowledged it now for a thousand years, and Alfred, we may believe, not for less, casting his crown before Him who did not only bear the cross before us, but was nailed to it for us.

In such ratio are the multiplications of heaven when God turns our sorrows into songs.

V.

THERE was silence in the Danish camp in East Anglia. The sounds of revelry and the wild tales of plunder and slaughter had died away, and the warriors lay asleep around the camp fires. The captive women and children, weary with being driven all day like cattle across the devastated country, had forgotten their sorrows for a time in sleep, wrapped in such ragged garments as had been spared them; and the Danish women were at rest in the tents. Enemy there was none left within reach to offer resistance. The pirates were as safe in the land they had laid desolate as on their own northern shores, and the tread of no sentinel broke the stillness.

One Saxon woman only was awake—Hilda, the sister of Bertric—and she sat on the ground at the door of the tent of her young mistress, Gudruna, the daughter of the Jarl Sidroc the younger. All around the horizon the sky was lit up from point to point by the fires of burning villages and monasteries. She had been taken about with the heathen army through Mercia, Northumbria, and East Anglia, through scenes of plunder, bloodshed, and unutterable horror, until she seemed to have no tears left to weep; and as she sat and watched the flames of violated and burning homes, a dull hopelessness lay on her heart—she could neither pray nor weep.

A few weeks before, her heart had glowed with a hope she scarcely cared to conceal from her captors, and many bitter and taunting words had been launched at her for it. The brave Earl Algar had gathered a Saxon force in the south of Lincoln, and had well-nigh been victorious. Eagerly Hilda had watched the anxious consultations of the Danish lords; but that glimpse of hope had faded, like so many others. The gallant earl had fallen into the old Danish stratagem, and had been tempted by a pretended flight into a rash pursuit. The enemy had been reinforced, and some of the Saxons had deserted in the night; so that on the battle-field Algar and his faithful five hundred had accomplished nothing save the staying for that one day of the cruel work of plunder and ruin, at the cost of the best lives left in eastern England.

Then had followed days of fiercer slaughter than ever. The abbeys of Bardeney, Croyland, and Peterborough, with all their treasures and libraries, were burned, and such of the monks as could not escape into the woods and marshes had been massacred, with torture, on their altars.

Hilda could neither weep nor pray; for the fountain of tears, as of prayer, must be opened by some touch, however faint, of the hand of hope—and she had lost all power to hope.

The Christian faith, as she had learned it, had been bereft of much of its divine comfort. She had learned much of the wrath of God and of his judgments. The saints she had been taught to reverence were, for the most part, men of severe mould, who had spent life in making themselves holy by self-mortification and renunciation of all earthly joy. She had a certain dread of all natural human joys, as of things belonging to the sinful flesh and the doomed world; and with the meaning of joy she had necessarily become confused about the meaning of sorrow. Pain, voluntarily self-inflicted, or endured in martyrdom, had in it, she believed, something expiatory; but this agony and misery around her—was there anything expiatory and purifying in that? Was it not rather the scourging of a people that, having sinned beyond forgiveness, found its hell beginning on earth?

One thought alone preserved her from despair—that image of divine and undying love, that vision of Christ on the cross, which no corruption can quite blot out of Christianity, rose before her through the darkness and above the flames of vengeance. When she could feel nothing else, again and again the thought of that suffering Redeemer seemed to take the icy weight from her heart. She could not trace the connection between him and all this suffering; but blindly, helplessly, with little hope and less understanding, she clung to him. She felt she could trust him. It was of him she spoke to the young Lady Gudruna, the one Dane whom she loved. And it was seldom that this dim yet sincere trust left her so utterly prostrate as she felt to-night.

As she sat thus motionless, gazing unconsciously at the terribly glowing sky, a slight movement aroused her, and, looking around, she saw a young boy, not more than ten years old, creeping gently to her side.

"Christian woman!" he murmured, clinging to her dress, "let me speak to you. Sidroc the Jarl warned me to keep out of sight of the Danes, or he could not save me any longer."

"Who art thou, poor Saxon child?" she said; "and how dost thou know me?"

"I heard thee utter the name of Jesus just now," he said, "as I lay hidden here beside Sidroc's tent. I am Turgar, the child they spared at Croyland—the only one."*

Hilda shuddered.

"Thou wast there at the massacre?"

The child began to weep.

"Softly!" she whispered, hiding his sobbing face in her bosom as she folded him to her.

"I saw them all murdered," he murmured between his sobs,—"all: the children my school-fellows, the old monks who were too old to flee, the old abbot with his gray hair. They tormented many of them with dreadful tortures—children and old men—to make them say where the treasures were hidden; but they could not tell, for the young monks had carried them away. The old monks cried out in their great pain, but they asked for no mercy. But the children sobbed and begged for mercy; yet not one was spared—not one but me. I kept close to the good sub-prior, and when he fled into the refectory and they killed him there, I prayed them to let me die with him."

Hilda let the child talk, and her tears fell slowly on his fair head.

"But Sidroc the Jarl spared me," continued the child. "He spoke kindly to me, and pulled off my little cowl, and threw a Danish tunic around me, and bade me keep close to him. But he told me yesterday he can do little more for me, the kings and jarls are so angry because the brother of Hubba was wounded at Peterborough. Hubba killed the gray-haired abbot there and seventy of the monks, with his own hand; but Sidroc says that is hardly vengeance enough. What can I do?" And

---

* *Vide* Sharon Turner's "Anglo-Saxons."

tears covered the innocent face, whose childish beauty had moved the heart of the Danish chief to pity.

"Pray to God, my child," said Hilda, "for the Lord Jesus Christ's sake, and flee from this wicked camp the first moment that thou canst. God will help thee."

"But the monks of Croyland and the children my school-fellows prayed," said the child, "and God let them die in agony."

"Death is but a gate, my child," said Hilda, her faith gathering strength as she uttered it. "God heard those who prayed, and took them safely to himself through that blood-stained gate. Did you never hear of the Massacre of the Holy Innocents?"

The boy grew calmer as he listened to the old story of death; and as she said to him the sweet old hymn about the flowers of the martyrs, whom on the threshold of light the enemy of Christ cut off, as a garden of budding roses, those first victims of Christ, those tender lambs of sacrifice, who at the altar innocently played with their crowns and their palms;—the memory of the massacred innocents of old, long in paradise, leaving only the fragrance of their morning sacrifice on earth, threw a sacred light on the massacres of yesterday.

"King Herod has been dead eight hundred years," said Hilda, "and Hubba and the Danes, and every one around us, will soon follow. Your beloved and mine have only gone a little before, and they have gone to Christ."

"*Your* beloved?" said the boy.

And then she told him the tale of her old home on the heights near London, where, she had been told, all her kindred had been slain. And as, in low whispered words, she related the long story of her griefs, for the first time for years her thoughts went back into the past, and the present vanished from her altogether, until, by the heavier pressure of his head upon her shoulder, she knew that the child had fallen asleep.

Then with the heart she had comforted beating close to hers, once more she could pray. "King Herod died," she thought, "and the Holy Innocents are in paradise, and the blessed Lord could not be slain until his time came; and then he died to redeem us, and rose again, and is ascended into heaven. Yes, we may not see it pass, but this night of terror will not shadow the earth for ever."

So she repeated the Creed, and the Lord's Prayer, and some portion of the Saxon Te Deum, which she had learned more than twenty years before in the convent at Canterbury, and then fell peacefully asleep beside the child.

The chill of the dawn awoke her. Tenderly she wrapt a warm mantle round the sleeping boy, and kneeling down beside him, repeated her morning hymn of praise. There was a sad silence in the dawn. A few song birds sang from a wood near them; but no lowing of cattle or bleating of sheep came up from the wasted fields—no hum of labour from the sacked and smouldering villages.

Before long she awoke the child, and making him say his morning prayer beside her, she sent him to another part of the camp to avoid suspicion.

That day, as the army were crossing the river Nen, two of the wagons laden with plunder were overturned in the river, and during the confusion the child of Croyland escaped into a wood on the river banks. All day and night he wandered on, until he came to his own monastery. There, amidst the burning ruins, he found the fugitive monks, who were endeavouring to extinguish the flames. But as they listened to the child's tale of horror, and learned the meaning of the stains of blood on altar, and wall, and chapel floor, for a time they lost heart for their work, and could do nothing, strong men as they were, but give way to an agony of grief.

Then, collecting the mutilated remains of their murdered brethren, they buried them among the smoking ruins of the abbey, which a few days before had stood so strong and fair, looking out over its fertile island amidst the fens.

But Hilda was carried on with the Danish army until they came near Bury, in Suffolk.

There she was sitting one morning with the young maiden Gudruna, in a house from which the Saxon owners had been lately driven.

As they sat spinning in the hall, Gudruna said,—

"Was your home like this?"

Hilda answerd sadly,—

"Like this *was!*"

"I would give anything to make you feel at home in our home," said the maiden; "but I suppose you never can."

"There is no place on earth so much like home to me as where you are," said Hilda, quietly. "Have I not served you from infancy?"

"Faithfully," said the maiden; "yet there is a gulf between us. I feel it. How can you forget what your people have suffered from mine?"

Their conversation was interrupted by a party of Danish horsemen, who came to ask a drink of ale or mead in passing.

They were courteously invited in; their horses were held when they alighted; ewers of water and basins were brought by the slaves to wash their feet; and a repast of bread and honey, with ale, was spread in the hall.

As they ate, they talked to each other. The first sentence enchained Hilda's attention as by a terrible spell.

"He died bravely, the young king," said one of them. "If the Christians had a walhalla, he endured enough to earn it."

"Yes, they were of our blood," growled another, "before their Christianity spoiled them. Better to have shown his courage on the battle-field than tied to a tree and beaten like a hound. Scarcely a death that, for a hero."

"How did this young King Edmund die?" asked a third; "I came too late to see. When I arrived, the corpse was lying covered with blood at the root of the tree. I missed the rest."

"First, they counseled him to submit," said the first speaker; "but he said, his most faithful followers were dead, and the loss of them made him weary of the light of heaven; and that he felt it nobler to die for his country than to forsake it. 'Tell your commander,' he said, 'I am neither terrified by his threats, nor deluded by his promises. Death is preferable to slavery. You may destroy this frail and perishing body, like a despised vessel; but my spirit shall fly to heaven from this prison of flesh, unstained by a degrading submission.' The old blood spoke out there, I trow. How he died you may ask another. I am sick of such sights, and have no taste for torturing helpless victims."

"They bound him to a tree and scourged him, and then pierced him with many arrows. But life was tenacious in him; he would utter no complaint, so that at last King

Hingwar, the son of Regnar Lodbrok, wearied with his patience, struck off his head."*

Gudruna turned as pale as Hilda, and was leading her from the room, when one of the warriors claimed to pledge his countrywoman, the fair hostess, in a cup of mead.

"I am a Dane," said the maiden, passionately, "but I am a woman; and no monsters or beasts of prey are kindred of mine. Drink, if you can, with the moans of the patient, tortured king in your ears; but I will take no pledge from you."

There was an angry murmur, and some of the guests rose; but the man who had spoken with respect of the murdered Edmund, spoke out boldly.

"The maiden has spoken to my mind. Touch her who dare!"

In a few minutes the hall was cleared, and Hilda and Gudruna stood there alone.

"Hilda," said the Danish maiden, "my heart bleeds for you. Until we came to England I knew nothing of these horrors. The tales of victory brought from across

---

* The legend which grew up around the death of King Edmund is a curious specimen of the instruction our Anglo-Saxon ancestors received by way of sermons. It is from a homily for St. Edmund's Day, November 2, in the Salisbury Breviary, quoted in Soames' "Anglo-Saxon Church." After the young king's death, his followers went to search for his body, in order to give it a reverent burial. "They went out seeking together," says the homily, "and constantly, as is the wont of those who oft go into the woods, cried, '*Where art thou, comrade?*' And to them answered the king's head, '*Here, here, here.*' Thus all were answered as often as any of them called, until they all came through calling to it. There lay the grey wolf that guarded the head, and with his two feet had embraced the head; and, greedy and hungry as he was, he durst not taste the head, and held it against wild beasts. Then were they astonished at the wolf's guardianship, and carried the holy head home, thanking the Almighty for all his wonders. But the wolf followed forth with the head, until they came to town, as if he were tame; and after that turned into the woods again."

the sea made me feel nothing but pride and gladness. I received the spoils, and looked on them only as the proofs of my father's prowess, and the gifts of his affection. If I thought of the poor plundered people at all, it was only as my father's foes—cowards, probably; and at all events, being of another race. But now all is changed. I have heard the cries and moans of the dying. I have stood on thresholds stained with the life-blood of murdered parents and little ones. And Hilda," she said, passionately, "I would rather be one of your people than one of mine: for, except my father, who spared the child of Croyland, these men around us seem to me more cruel than beasts of prey. If I knew any of our gods who are tender-hearted, and would listen, I would pray them to grant us no more victories, but to take us home to Norway, and leave this Saxon land to the Saxons. But there is no god who would listen. Balder, the beautiful, the kind, for whom all creatures wept, might have heard me, but he is shut up for ever in the halls of Hela, the death-goddess. Loki, the black-hearted, slew him; and among all the gods I know not one who would have pity."

Hilda was silent.

"There is One who has pity," she said at length.

"Yes, I know whom you mean," said Gudruna. "But how can I trust in one who lets those who serve him die such deaths, and suffer worse than death before they die? One thing only I know," she added; "you have told me there are houses among the Christians where maidens can live apart from the world, and never marry. Rather than wed one of these savages I would fly to such a refuge to-morrow, if I knew of one."

"But you are not a Christian," Hilda said, sadly.

"Nay," said Gudruna. "I cannot understand your Christian faith. You suffer patiently, I see, and have a hope beyond death; but if all the good men are only to suffer, and let all the wicked men do as they please, I cannot see what the world will come to. Why did not this poor King Edmund gather together his people and fight with them before it was hopeless?"

"I know not," said Hilda, mournfully. "Christianity used not to make men cowards. Some are called to suffer, and some to fight; and perhaps as God sees it, the martyrs do help forward the victory. It is something if the sufferer's patience teaches his enemy to hate cruelty."

"But if your Saxon people and your Christianity are to be saved," said Gudruna, "I think your God must send you heroes of another kind."

"For this I pray day and night," said Hilda, in a low voice. "Of old, God always rescued his people by some one deliverer; and if England is to be Christian England still, He will raise us such a hero yet. Be he king, or priest, or peasant, I have sometimes faith to believe the deliverer will come; but when and how, we know not. Joseph (the nuns of Canterbury taught me from the Holy Scriptures) was sold into slavery before he reigned for his people's good: Moses was trained in the very house of the tyrant he was to overthrow. I think the deliverer will come, for God is good, and the misery is so great. I only pray the people may know him when he comes. The Jews did not even know their Christ when he came; but God grant we be not like them."

VI.

NOT more than a year passed after the murder of King Edmund, near Bury, when Hilda heard tidings which gave her the first glimpse of hope that her prayers were answered.

The Saxons had won their first victory at Ashdune, among the chalky downs of Berkshire.

King Ethelred and his brother, Prince Alfred, led the English forces; Ethelred against the king's, Alfred against the earl's. The Saxons were posted in the valley. The Danes held the hill. The front of their position was marked by an old stunted thorn, which in after days men who spoke of that battle remembered well as the point around which swayed the battle.

Both armies raised their shields and demanded battle; but King Ethelred was hearing mass in his tent, remembering, perhaps, the early lessons of good Bishop Swithin, his father's friend. Alfred deemed the moment for attack was being lost, and urged him not to wait for the conclusion of the service. The troops were ready and eager to advance. On such moments the fate of battle hangs. A pause might enable the Saxons too well to measure the peril, and might bring a panic. The Danes might think they feared to advance, and might rush down on the hesitating Saxons from their vantage-ground. But Ethelred would not be hurried. He must reverently hear the sacred office to the close, he said, and then he would come. God gives victory.

Alfred delayed no longer, but advanced boldly up the hill. His attack at first seemed succeeding, but the Danes rallied, and were overpowering him by the weight of numbers, when King Ethelred, having finished his mass, came to the rescue. The "heathen men" were routed with great slaughter. Some said, by the prayers of King Ethelred; others by the prowess of Prince Alfred. The corpses of the invaders lay piled around the stunted thorn on the hill of the Ash, where the battle was turned, and all along the Berkshire hills, where all night and next day the Saxons pursued them till they found shelter within the walls of Reading. Long afterward, the shepherd, leading his flocks across the green slopes, came on scattered corpses lying stiff as they had fallen, wounded in that desperate rout.

All through the land went a shout of triumph, as if a terrible spell had been broken. From the harrow and the plough, where Saxon thanes and yeomen toiled hopelessly as slaves of the conqueror, went up at evening deep thanksgivings when the tidings came, and the next morning there were no slaves to till the soil for Danish oppressors. Husbandmen and herdsmen had gone off to join King Ethelred of Wessex, and the young prince, who could vanquish the invincible.

Widow and orphan heard it in their bondage, and gave God thanks in prayers, where curses were strangely mingled with blessings. All England heard it and took heart again; and in the Danish court the captive Hilda heard it, and said in her heart,—

"God has answered our prayers. Surely the deliverer is come."

The deliverer had indeed come, but not yet the deliverance.

A few months afterwards, defeat followed victory. Three years afterwards, the monks of the burned and wasted monastery of Lindisfarne still gathered around the bier of St. Cuthbert in the forests of Northumbria, homeless exiles. And the pilgrim band which assembled to sing and pray around that wandering bier were almost the only company in England who ventured publicly to celebrate the Christian worship of God.

To the victory of Ashdune succeeded the defeat of Merton. The Danes held the field of carnage. Ethelred the king was slain, and the land was so steeped in misery that the king's death scarcely deepened the mourning.

Alfred became king in his brother's place, and the accession of England's darling could scarcely win a note of rejoicing; so long, and heavy, and hopeless was the weight of ruin and fear which rested on all the people.

The deliverer had come; but the deliverance had yet to be wrought. Nay more, the deliverer himself had to be trained. The iron for the sword of warfare was there, but it had yet to be tempered in the fire. The Moses had been sent, but he had yet to be trained in the wilderness.

HAMPSTEAD, *July*, 1863.

VII.

Alfred the Truth-Teller.

SCENES FROM THE LIFETIME OF
ENGLAND'S DARLING.

VII.

ALFRED THE TRUTH-TELLER.

I.

THE uncontrollable joy and thankfulness which Hilda the Saxon captive had felt at the tidings of the first victory of her people, under Ethelred and Alfred, had within a few hours been followed by other tidings, which filled her with sorrow.

In that first victory of the Christian over the pagan forces on the hills of Berkshire, had fallen Sidroc the younger, the only Dane of whom it is recorded that his heart was touched with pity for the miseries of the plundered people, the generous rescuer of the Saxon child from the massacre at Croyland.

There were bitter wailings that night in the fortress at Reading, whither the vanquished Danes had retreated—those wild heathen wailings of sorrow which has no hope, whose only consolation is the fierce promise of revenge.

Gudruna had not even this bitter consolation. She went out alone at midnight to the mound where the slain were buried, and made her hopeless moan to the cold night winds.

"He was gentle and generous to all," she sobbed, in

her anguish, as she wept over the grave in which they had laid her father's body hastily among the other fallen heroes and kings. "There were thousands of pitiless and cruel men who might have perished, and I would have said, 'It is just.' But, oh! why must *he* die? Surely it is neither the God of the Saxons nor our gods who decide the destinies of men, but the passionless Norns, some of whom are daughters of the gods, and some of the elves of darkness—the cold and pitiless Norns, who weave and break the destinies of men, and water the tree of life from the fountain where float the heavenly swans. They water the tree of the world's life; but what to them are the lives of one man or another? Only as the leaves of the tree which unfold in spring and fall in autumn. The leaves fall, but the tree lives; and the Norns are content. The world is their care; but what are *we* to them—what are the best of men or the worst? They neither love, nor hate, nor pity, nor heed."

Thus Gudruna made her death-wail over her dead, in the night, by the funeral heap which covered the slain of her people, on the banks of the Thames at Reading. Then, her heart growing bitterer as she spoke, she went on—

"Nay, it is not ye even, cold and stately Norns! who have robbed me of my joy, the only shelter of my orphan youth—of him who was to me both father and mother. It is an enemy who has done me this wrong. It is Hela, the death goddess, the daughter of Loki, the father of lies and misery. It is Hela and Loki, who could not endure that one so merciful and pitiful should enjoy the light of the sun—one so like Balder the beautiful, the brave, and gentle, whom the gods love, and they the black-hearted hate. It is Hela who has taken thee, my beloved, my father, and imprisoned thee in her dark halls within her barred gates—Hela, 'whose table is hunger, whose servant is delay, whose knife is starvation, whose threshold is the precipice of sudden woe, whose bed is care, and whose chambers are hung with burning anguish.' But I rave!" she exclaimed, suddenly bursting into another strain; "didst thou not die in battle? The halls of Hela are not for thee. Skuld the Future, youngest and fairest of the Norns, has chosen thee from the battle-field. Thou feastest in Walhalla among the heroes, in the dwellings of Odin; thou feastest on the boar Sæhrimnir, ever slain and ever renewed, and drinkest the milk of the goat Heidrun, better than mead. Thy days are glad with the joys of the fight, and thy nights with the joys of feasting."

Then she paused, and burst into uncontrollable tears.

"But we who loved thee, thinkest thou of us?" she moaned. "Walhalla would scarcely be home to thee without thy child. And Balder, gentlest and best beloved of the gods, is no longer there. Loki has banished him to the dark kingdom of Hela. When will Balder the good return? Then Walhalla might be like home, and there would be some one to listen when we pray; not only when heroes pray, but *we*, even poor desolate maidens and orphans such as I am."

Her last words did not fall only on the ears of the dead. Hilda had followed her, and kneeling beside her, drew the poor child to her, murmuring softly and half unconsciously the words that had been in her heart since she heard of Sidroc's death—"In that ye did it to the least of these my brethren, ye did it unto Me!"

Gudruna suffered herself to be led from the grave, and through the night the two women sat watching together in the tent.

11*

After a long silence, Gudruna said:

"Hilda, what words were those you breathed over my father's grave?"

"They are the words of Christ," was the reply, "the gracious, compassionate Lord, who was once slain through the arts of the father of lies, and imprisoned in the dark dwelling of death; but who has burst the iron gates, and ascended into heaven, where he reigns for evermore, and looks on us and pities us, and heals and saves us if we call on him."

"But what made you think of those words?" said Gudruna.

"They are in my mind constantly, since the good Earl Sidroc was slain," replied Hilda. "I think of his kindness to the child at Croyland—the one who had courage to be pitiful among the pitiless; and I think it will not be forgotten."

Gudruna said no more; but she kissed Hilda tenderly, and lay down, for the first time since her bereavement, to sleep.

In the morning, when Hilda awoke, Gudruna was standing in the morning sunlight at the door of the tent, looking, Hilda thought, like one of the virgin goddesses of whom she used to speak—Fulla, the darling of Frigga, queen of heaven, who glides through the golden halls, with her fair hair flowing round her, bound with a golden fillet. So fair and bright did Gudruna seem, leaning against the door of the tent, with her fair hair clustering in wavy tresses from the golden ribbon which bound it, her large violet eyes looking out to the dawn.

Hilda softly uttered her name; and then the maiden turned to her, and kneeling beside her, said—

"I have had a golden dream. I thought I stood before the black gates of Hela, the death goddess, weeping bitterly, because none could burst those heavy bars; when softly, without a sound, or the touch of any hand, I could see the gates flung asunder and opened wide; and through them came a flood of light, as if it had been Walhalla, and not hell, that was opened. As I gazed, however, I saw that all the light beamed, not from those dark halls, but from the glorious being who came forth from them. His face and his raiment were brighter than the sun. Yet it was not the light that filled my heart with joy when I saw him; it was the look in his eyes. He looked at me. I knelt at his feet, and said, 'Balder! Balder! the beautiful and the good!' But he pointed to the sky, and rose into the heights, and vanished from my sight. Then I seemed to hear, floating down on me in tones of the most joyous music, the name, not of Balder, but of Christ. And so I awoke."

Hilda made the sign of the cross, and said—

"It is very strange. Can it be possible that that lost god of your fathers, so beautiful, and good, and beloved, was like a fair dream in their night, to point them to Christ the Lord?"

"How do I know?" said Gudruna; "but my dream has filled my heart with comfort. If those impenetrable bars have been broken once, they are no more impenetrable."

From that time she listened with ever-increasing interest to all Hilda could teach her of Christianity.

Not long afterwards, at the Easter time, a young Danish maiden stood with Hilda the Saxon captive among the little Christian band gathered round the bier of St. Cuthbert in Northumbria.

It was in a retired glade in the depths of a forest, far from any Danish encampment. Gudruna and Hilda had secretly found their way thither, at some peril, through the dusk before the dawn.

It was the first public Christian service at which Hilda had been present since her captivity, and the first Gudruna had ever attended.

Both women were deeply moved as they listened to the prayers and the hymns of praise chanted to the grave Gregorian music.

All the past came back on Hilda in a flood of memories—the chants of the slaughtered nuns at Canterbury, the hymns in her father's ruined home, steeping her whole heart in that mingled tide of unutterable feelings which sacred music can unseal.

But to Gudruna all was new. Rapt at first into a mysterious awe and tenderness by these solemn and pathetic chants, every faculty of her being awoke as she listened to the words of the Gospel for the day—afterwards read in Anglo-Saxon by the priest. It was one of the narratives of the resurrection.

She heard of the empty sepulchre and the risen Lord; but when for the first time she listened to the story of her who sat still by the sepulchre weeping, entreating but to be suffered to bury the lost dead, her lost Lord, until at last the dulness of her hopeless sorrow was pierced by that voice uttering her name, and all her heart burst forth in that "Rabboni," Gudruna turned to Hilda and whispered—

"It is my dream! it is my dream! He is risen indeed, and has spoken also to me—even to me."

Silently the two women returned through the forest to the Danish encampment—silently, but heart bound to heart by ties stronger than those of nation or kindred; even by the might of that redeeming name.

II.

SEVEN years had passed away since the death of Sidroc the Earl—years of pitiless pillage and feeble truces. Year after year in the chronicles of the time we read, "the West Saxons made peace with the army;" "the Mercians made peace with the army;" and then, immediately afterwards, of that same indestructible army "taking up winter-quarters at London, in Lindsey, at Ripton, by the river Tyne," subduing the whole midland country, driving helpless King Burhred from Mercia to die at Rome. What was meant by the Danish army taking up winter-quarters, or "sitting down for a year" in any place, the famines and pestilences which follow may explain. Having drained all the joy and life out of a district, that terrible army abandoned it for a time, till the desert they had made should once more, in the course of years, gather prosperity enough to make it worth while to plunder it again.

With pity, which in its helplessness was almost bitterer than the woes it wept, Hilda and Gudruna watched that army in its desolating course. They could only now and then creep out to the field of carnage, which the victorious Danes so often held, on the night after the fight, and dress the wounds and relieve the dying thirst of some Christian sufferer there, surprising the dying into thanksgivings with unlooked-for words of Christian faith and hope. Their own faith made them objects of suspicion in the camp. Their movements were jealously watched, and nothing but the honour in which the memory of the Earl Sidroc was held sheltered their own lives. Often they spoke of flight; but whither could they flee? The monasteries were levelled to the dust, the walls of the cities were broken down, and for a Christian Danish maiden there was no refuge either among Saxons or Danes.

One name, however, gradually rose into distinctness to the ear of Hilda, among the multitudes of captains. "In the summer of 875, *King Alfred* went out to sea with a fleet, and fought against the forces of seven ships, and one of them he took, and put the rest to flight." The name which had been most loudly cursed by the Danish fugitives from Ashdune began to be honoured constantly by their angry murmurs. The first victory at sea, as well as the first victory on land, was attributed to Alfred. Great was the excitement in the Danish camp at the tidings of this defeat on their own element. Their whole attention began to be directed to the kingdom of this daring young chief. The patriot had succeeded in turning their fury on himself.

The next year " the army stole away to Wareham, in Dorsetshire, a fortress of the West Saxons. And afterwards the king made peace with the army, and they delivered to the king hostages from among the most distinguished men in the army ; and then they swore oaths to him on the holy ring, which they never would do before to any nation, that they would speedily depart the kingdom. And, notwithstanding this, that part of the army which was horsed, stole away by night from the fortress to Exeter." Yet the king trusted them again, the "Truth-teller" himself, and generously incapable of believing that other men would not be true. In 877, again, one hundred and twenty of their ships were wrecked at Swanwith. King Alfred and his horsemen chased the army to Exeter. Then again, more hostages, "as many as he would," and many oaths. And in a few months again, oaths forsworn, and rapine and slaughter. "In 878, during mid-winter, after Twelfth Night, the army stole away to Chippenham, and overran the land of the West Saxons, and sat down there; and many of the people they drove beyond sea; and of the remainder, the greater part they subdued and forced to obey them, except King Alfred; and he, with a small band, with difficulty retreated to the woods and the fastnesses of the moors."

Into these few lines does the Anglo-Saxon Chronicle compress the story of unutterable misery, and of indomitable courage; of a whole people broken and subdued, a land wasted and ruined, the bravest exiles beyond the seas, the rest hopelessly "harrowing and toiling" for an army whose glory it was to consider all work menial except the work of the locust and the vulture; until at last all were subdued except only King Alfred, and he abandoned by court and people.

Once more the captive Hilda kept her sleepless watch in the Danish camp near Glastonbury, in the heart of plundered Wessex, looking out on the midnight lit up into a lurid glow by the fires of the burning villages and homesteads, where the corpses of her murdered countrymen had found a funeral pile among the blackened ruins of their homes. Gudruna stood by her.

"The deliverer has come," said Hilda, with bitter tears. "God sent him, and my people have not known him. They have rejected the deliverer, and accepted the bondage. Henceforth there is nothing left but to bow to the yoke, and to look for the better country,— the heavenly."

The long pressure of trial, those seven years of hope deferred, and at last thus crushed, began to tell on Hilda's spirit as well as on her hollow cheek and emaciated frame. But those same seven years had matured Gudruna from the bright impulsive girl into the thoughtful steadfast-hearted Christian woman. She had proved the strengthening power of the services of love to those who serve; and without attempting to use words of comfort, she gently led Hilda before dawn, attended by one faithful old servant of her father's, to a field near the camp, where, on the day before, there had been a skirmish.

Through all the field of carnage they went, but heard no moan, so well had the work of slaughter been accomplished, until as they were turning from the sight of horror which nothing but prayer and the hope of giving relief to the sufferers could have nerved them to endure, in passing the ruined wall of a farm-house around which the fight had raged, they caught a feeble sound, which, as they stood still and listened, they perceived was not a moan nor even a plaint, but a prayer,—words spoken to One who listened.

It was the 102d Psalm, "the prayer of the afflicted when he is overwhelmed and poureth out his complaint before the Lord."

Hilda drew in her breath and listened, each of the words dropping like balm into her heart, in her own Anglo-Saxon tongue:

> "Hide not thy face from me when I am in trouble
> My days are like a shadow,
> But thou, O Lord, shalt endure for ever;
> Thou shalt arise, and have mercy upon Zion:
> For the time to favour her, yea, the set time, is come.
> So shall the heathen fear the name of the Lord,
> And all the kings of the earth thy glory.

> He will regard the prayer of the destitute;
> For he hath looked down from the height of his sanctuary;
> From heaven did the Lord behold the earth;
> To hear the groaning of the prisoner;
> To loose those that are appointed unto death."

A power she could not resist drew her to the voice, and motioning to Gudruna to remain where she was, she crept round the wall—

> "To loose those that are appointed unto death,"

she murmured, taking up the last words the wounded man had spoken.

Then kneeling down beside him, she found that the danger of his wounds lay chiefly in the loss of blood they occasioned. These were many, but none of them mortal, and with bandages of linen, and the simple medicaments of the good Samaritan, "pouring in oil and wine," in an hour or two the sufferer was much relieved.

"I have not felt a touch so gentle since my mother's," he said; and then flowed out those recollections of home which so crowd on the heart when the body is brought down by weakness.

Hilda listened at first with the compassionate interest of one who had long ceased to have any hopes and fears of her own. Her life history had closed, it seemed, twenty years ago, when she had been carried away a captive exile, a friendless orphan to be a mere "thing" in the household of a stranger, a mere accessory to the life of others. Bitter as the lot had been at first, she had long acquiesced in it, and had grown not merely passively to exist, but actively and vividly to live to the life of those around her, really to mourn in their sorrows, and really to rejoice in their joys.

But deep in her heart, unknown to herself, lay the old fountain of natural affection, and one touch of that wounded man's suddenly rolled away the stone from the brink.

"Never have I known such care as this," he said, "since my mother dressed a wound I had received in hunting on the last evening I ever saw her, before I went to rescue my sister in the nunnery at Canterbury."

"Bertric!" she exclaimed.

And the wounded man's arm was folded round her, as she leant sobbing joyful, thankful tears on his breast.

Then remembering Gudruna and the peril in which a longer stay might involve them, Hilda went to the other side of the wall, where she was waiting, and telling her in a word the discovery she had made, led her to Bertric's side.

"This is the comforter God has given me all through my long captivity, Bertric," she said, in a broken voice, "Gudruna, the daughter of Sidroc."

"Of Sidroc, the merciful, who saved the child at Croyland?" he said, "the merciful Lord bless thee, lady, and show thee kindness, as thou and thine have shown kindness to me and mine."

And raising himself, he reverently took her hand and kissed it.

"She is a Christian," murmured Hilda.

"Then God has given thee a better vengeance on the oppressor than I, my sister," Bertic said. "Better, as the old monk of Lindisfarne said, to win one foe to Christ than to slay thousands."

A brief consultation decided what step they should take next.

The morning was fast passing into day. Hilda could

not leave her brother, and Gudruna could not safely linger, if she was to return to the camp at all. Hilda's first thought was that neither of them should ever return, but remaining together, seek some place of refuge in common. But to this Gudruna would not consent.

"They would search diligently for me," she said, "but might perhaps be content to let you escape. My flight would double your danger. Besides," she added, "I am a Dane, and I cannot separate myself from the fortunes of my father's people."

Hilda pleaded the solitude of Gudruna's life as the only Christian in the Danish camp, the pain it would be to her to part from one who had been to her as a child and a sister, and yet the impossibility of abandoning her wounded brother. But Gudruna said—

"I shall not be more alone than thou wert for years. Christians, we know, are never alone; and besides," she continued, with a kindling eye, "how do I know that I am the only Christian among my people, or that if I am, I may always be so?"

"The lady Gudruna is right," said Bertric, firmly, "the noblest course is the right one, and she has chosen it."

Once the women embraced each other, and then Gudruna inclining her head courteously to Bertric, drew her linen veil closely round her, and moved rapidly away. His eyes followed the retreating figure until she disappeared behind the broken wall, then he said to Hilda—

"If ever the tide should turn, and a Saxon court be a refuge for a Danish maiden!—But now she is safer where she is. She is noble in every word, and look, and movement. Her heart has moulded her face and form."

A shadow passed over his face, and for a moment a happy dream flitted through Hilda's mind, but the next instant, glancing on her pale and suffering brother, and looking on the wasted fields around them, all dreams, and well-nigh all hopes, vanished before the hard reality of their position.

"How can the tide ever turn, brother?" she said. "Is not Alfred lost? Has not God sent our people the deliverer, and have they not disowned him?"

"God has not disowned him," was the reply. "Is it not written that in the wilderness Moses was trained for his work, and from the wilderness he came forth to do it."

"You think, then, there may yet be hope," she said.

"I have heard King Alfred *pray!*" he said, "and I have seen how God answered him. Never shall I forget the morning when we missed him from the chase in Cornwall, and at last I found his horse fastened to a stone outside the little chapel in the rocky valley of St. Guerir, among the moors. Within I heard a voice pleading fervently with God. 'Any suffering thou wilt!' was the burden of the prayer, 'only strengthen me against sin. Any suffering but such as might disable me from serving the people!' The morning sunbeams slanted through the small eastern window on the prince's form as he knelt prostrate before the altar. I deemed it treachery to listen any longer, and mounting my horse, I rode silently up the hill-side, and bid the rest of the company wait for the prince. It was nothing new to us that he should thus seize an interval for solitary prayer; but there was something new in the light that beamed in his noble and earnest face when he rejoined us, at least I thought so. And all day, as we pursued the chase, the prince foremost among us, I felt as those must feel who, according to old legends, have seen heavenly saints mingling in the fight, and leading them on. Since then he has become king, and some have complained bitterly of his bearing to his people. They say he is impatient and severe, not willing to hearken to complaints, and bent on carrying out his own plans at any cost to any one. It may be so in some measure. One who risks everything of his own may claim too rigidly that others should do the same. One who sees with such a quick glance to the heart of a matter may be impatient of the slowness of others. One who sees his country in ruins, and is spending life to restore it, may be severe with the selfish murmurings of those who, while rescued from a burning city, complain that the deliverer has pinched their fingers in the rescue."

"You think, then, the king is blameless, and must triumph in the end?"

"I do not think the king is blameless," was the reply, "nor can I be sure whether God will glorify him with the crown of the victor or with that of the martyr. But I am sure he is the noblest man England has seen for centuries; and I am sure God is training him to be nobler yet. And I know King Alfred lives still, and while he lives, lives for England, and therefore I cannot despair."

He spoke so eagerly that Hilda began to wonder whether her medicaments, or the king's name were working these wonders, and whether he might venture to walk. He tried, and, with her help, crept across the fields to the entrance of a forest which stretched for many miles around them; but there his strength failed, and he could scarcely move a step further. She dreaded the effects of another night in the winter air on her brother's wounds, and pressed on a few yards deeper into the wood, across the top of a little hill, when Bertric said,—

"I see there a wood-cutter's hut. I know the man. If we can reach it, we are safe."

And before night-fall they were sheltered under the friendly roof.

III.

AS Bertric's wounds healed, his one intense desire became to rejoin the king, who, he believed, was concealed in some of the neighbouring forests. His eagerness hindered his recovery. In spite of Hilda's remonstrances, he insisted on leaving the wood-cutter's hut while his wounds were scarcely healed. As they wandered through the marshy forests, wet, and cold, and insufficiently fed, a low fever seized his weakened frame, and they were once more obliged to seek refuge under the roof of a peasant.

The owner of the hut was absent when they reached it, leading his herd of swine to their pasture among the acorns, and the wife did not welcome them very cordially. "The times were very bad," she said; "and they had enough to do to feed themselves, to say nothing of the stranger that was under their roof already. If they liked, they might warm themselves by the fire; but as to the rest, she could promise nothing until Denewulf her husband came home."

Bertric was too ill for Hilda to be repelled by mere discourtesy of manner, and she thankfully availed herself of the permission. But, as she sat beside her brother, she smiled inwardly to see how the good woman (while carrying on a continuous grumble about the times, and the unreasonable claims made on poor people, and the inconvenience of strangers wandering idly about the country, expecting others to give them food), nevertheless piled up the fire, and brought a sheep-skin to throw over Bertric, and, finally, prepared him some savoury broth, which she peremptorily insisted on his swallowing.

Denewulf the swine-herd soon returned, and then their welcome was secure. The good woman asked when their other guest would return, but Denewulf could not tell her.

"Hast thou found out who he is?"

"He is no common man," was the evasive reply. "A day of his talk is worth a year's schooling from the monks, when monks there were."

"Common man or no," said the housewife, "matters little to us. He eats and drinks for all I can see, like any of us common folk; and food and drink are not so plentiful in these days."

"Dost thou grudge the food, wife?" he said. "Remember the old monks' lessons. 'He that giveth to the poor lendeth to the Lord.'"

"Nay," she said, "he is welcome to the meat for that; but I like not to see thee toil thy life away that strangers may eat in idleness. Between the Danes and these wandering thanes, there is little left for such as we. Thou canst not say I ever grudged a sup to the monks; but the days are evil, and it is long since I heard any good words, since the old minster was burnt and the good priests scattered. Dost thou think the stranger may be a monk, belike?"

"His talk is wise and holy as any monk's," was the reply. "But I never saw a monk who knew so much of wild animals, of the chase, and war. In good sooth, he seemed to know my own calling as well as I do."

The next morning, Bertric lay in a delirious fever in

the inner chamber, and Hilda was sitting beside him, when a stranger entered the outer room. The housewife welcomed him in her way, with rough words and kind deeds.

"Heaven knows how long we may have enough for ourselves or for thee," she said, placing bread and ale before him. "Here are new guests arrived, and one a sick man—wounded, the woman says, in a skirmish with the Danes."

A voice replied in low, quiet tones; but the moment Bertric caught them, he started up and listened.

The next moment the stranger entered the inner chamber, courteously greeting Hilda, and approached the straw couch on which Bertric lay. Bertric seized his hand and kissed it, and would have risen from the couch, but he was unable, and sank fainting back. The stranger gently felt his hand, and recommended some concoction of herbs, which the housewife brought.

There was something in the stranger's manner which at once made Hilda yield to his directions, and gave her a kind of instinctive confidence that, while he remained in the house, all would go well. All that night Bertric continued delirious, but at the dawn he fell asleep.

For a few hours all was quiet, when, as Hilda sat watching him, dreading any sound which might break that healing sleep, she was greatly disturbed by hearing the sharp voice of the housewife (to whose absence she had been not a little indebted for the silence) say angrily, as she re-entered the hut,—

"Why, man, do you sit thinking there, and are too proud to turn the bread? Whatever be your family, with such manners and sloth, what trust can be put in you? You will not turn the bread you see burning, though you will be very glad to eat it when done."

Hilda could see through the doorway the bread on the hearth, while the stranger sat beside it, mending a broken bow. She listened in terror, dreading a louder and more angry reply; but the gentle tones of the other voice were as calm as before. The stranger she was reproaching seemed to be gently acknowledging the justice of the rebuke; and, the soft answer turning away wrath, no altercation followed.

Bertric did not awake for some time; he only moved in his sleep; but when he woke, and looked at Hilda once more, with grateful eyes, in which the light of consciousness was fully restored, the first words he said were,

"Where is the king?"

For an instant Hilda thought his mind was still wandering; then suddenly the truth flashed on her, and she brought the stranger to her brother's couch.

From that day Bertric steadily gained strength, and was able to enter into King Alfred's plans for the future. From day to day, one and another of the king's faithful followers found their way to the hut, until at length it was decided to retire to the island of Athelney, close at hand among the marshes, and there to form a camp of refuge.

LENT AT ATHELNEY.

LENT was wearing fast away at Athelney. King Alfred had made such shelter there as he could for his wife and little children, with one or two brave and patient women of the royal family who chose to share the perils of their sovereign. Poor indeed that shelter was. Not three months since they had kept their festive Twelfth Night in the royal palace of Chippenham; and now, without kingdom, without army, almost without subjects, the queen and the royal children were thankful to find a refuge in a hut scarcely raised above the marshy lowlands on the banks of the river Parret. Yet, in the hearts of all around the king there was a power of renewed life, as strong as that which, invisibly but irresistibly, was flowing upwards through every brown branch and twig of the willows and alders around them. Not one visible augury of the better days coming for England was to be seen in the land around them, any more than in the grey, colourless copses of low, stunted trees which rose here and there on little grey hillocks, above the reedy green of the marshes, or in the alder groves which fringed the sluggish streams as they crept round Athelney. No time had been spent on constructing dwelling-houses. All the labour of the few hands they could muster, and all the scanty building materials they could gather, had been spent on a rude fortress, which guarded the only bridge by which access was to be obtained to their little isle of refuge.

One evening in Passion Week, Hilda sat at the threshold of the wooden hut where she and her brother lived, anxious to catch the last light for her spinning; for candles were scarcely to be had, and clothing was as scarce as food.

As she span, she chanted softly to herself an old hymn on the Passion:—

HYMNUM DECAMUS DOMINO.

Come, let us sing unto the Lord,
   A song of highest praise to God,

Who, on the accursed and shameful tree
    Redeemed us by his blood.

    The day was sinking into eve,
        (The blessed Lord's betrayal day,)
    When, impious, to the supper came
        He who would Christ betray.

    Jesus, at that last supper, then
        Tells the disciples what shall be:
    "For one of you betrayeth me,
        Of you who eat with me."

    Judas, by basest greed seduced,
        Seeks to betray Him with a kiss;
    He, as a meek and spotless lamb,
        Denies not Judas this.

    Thus, for some thirty counted pence,
        The impious bargain Judas made,
    And Christ, the harmless, blameless Lord,
        Is to the Jews betrayed.

    Pilate, the governor, proclaimed,—
        "Lo, I in him no fault can find."
    Washing in water then, his hands,
        Christ to his foes resigned.

    The blinded Jews rejected him,
        And chose a murderer instead,
    Of Christ, "Let him be crucified!"
        With bitter spite they said.

    Barabbas then is freed, as, bound,
        Guilty and doomed to death he lies;
    And the world's Life is crucified,
        Through whom the dead arise.

As the whole story of wrong and ingratitude, patient, voluntary suffering, and redeeming sacrifice came before her in those simple words, her distaff fell from her hands, and her hands were clasped on her knees, and she sat gazing across that wild landscape, not consciously looking at any part of it, yet its desolate loneliness, and the slow, steady wailing of the March wind across the marshes, insensibly blending with her meditations.

"Thou hast borne the cross for us," she thought, "and we are thy redeemed. Thou hast borne the cross before us, and we are Thy disciples. Oh that for us, and above all for that royal heart which has already suffered so much, submission to our heavenly Father's will may transfigure suffering into sacrifice! It is the submission of the will, which can only be proved by suffering, and not the suffering itself in which Thou delightest. Is not the king submissive? And will not his sorrow soon be turned into joy?"

As she mused, a man came towards her hut in the dusk, with a pilgrim's dress and wallet. He seemed weary and emaciated, and she wished her brother was returned, with the rest of the warriors, from the foray they had gone forth that morning to make against a force of Danes reported to be near, that she might have bread to give the poor wanderer.

"Would that I had a crust in the house to offer thee," she said.

But the pilgrim smiled and replied—

"I have just received half a loaf from him who bides in the hut yonder."

And crossing himself, he passed on, with a benediction on her.

"It was the king," she said to herself, "and it must have been his last loaf. I wish Bertric were come." Just then she caught the tramp of horses' feet in the distance, and in a few minutes the foraging party returned across the bridge into the island. Their foray that day had met with little success. But the king met them with a cheerful mien and encouraging words. "It was Lent, and they should not wish to break their fast thoroughly before Easter." And with eager interest he listened to all the tidings they brought. The Danes were encamped in scattered bands here and there throughout the country, plundering in detail whatever the passage of their larger armies might have spared. The peasants had scarcely heart to trust the few grains left them to the ground, whose harvests the oppressor would devour. Yet there was a kind of unquiet expectation through the country (they said) not quite like the lifeless submission of a few weeks since.

The Danes kept more together, as if uneasily conscious that they were no longer sole possessors of a ruined and conquered land. One peasant, of whom they sought tidings, had asked if they were the band who rescued his father's homestead, a few weeks ago, from the heathen plunderers. Another had inquired in a mysterious whisper of Bertric whether it could possibly be true that the king was yet alive.

"The spring is not come," said Bertric to Hilda, as they sat alone in the hut by the fire of dried twigs and branches she had piled up for him, "but it is at work in secret."

The hope in the king's heart had spread itself to every heart of the little band around him.

The Easter morn dawned on Athelney. Few birds greeted it, for Easter fell very early that year, on the 23d of March. No church-bells pealed forth their welcome to the resurrection morning from minster or village church, far or near. Neither minster nor village church, scarcely indeed any village, was left in the land.

As Hilda and Bertric rose early that morning, a wintry silence reigned in the clear cold air around them. The course of the river was traced by a blue mist slowly creeping through the woods and marshes. Here and there a little column of smoke began to rise from a lonely herdsman's hut, and the lowing of cattle sounded from time to time through those marshy lands among which the Danish plunderers had not been able, or had not been tempted, to penetrate.

Yet dreary as the scene and the landscape were, Hilda was full of gladness.

"I scarcely know how it is my heart is so light to-day," she said to Bertric, "Easter hymns seem ringing through it, for the first time since our nunnery was burnt, without being responded to by the bitter wail for those over whom no Christian dirge was chanted. Silent as the land is, to me there seems a stir of distant music in the air. Every bird that twitters seems to say, 'I am only the first of a countless choir.' Every cold wind that sweeps through the branches seems to say, 'Do not misjudge me. I am only clearing the air for the perfumes of a thousand flowers.' And the river as it trickles softly through the shallows seems to say, 'Soon you will not hear me for the pealing of the minster bells.'"

As she spoke the king passed through a willow-copse near them. He held a book in his hand, from which he seemed reading. Hilda thought she heard a faint murmur, and saw his lips moving as he walked on.

"It is the little book with Anglo-Saxon Psalms, and hymns for the hours, and prayers, which he always carries in his bosom," said Bertric softly. "In that heart

God has kindled the light which shall beam summer once more on all the land."

"Because in that heart is treasured the Word of the King of kings," said Hilda, thoughtfully, and she continued in the words of the ancient Ambrosian Easter hymn,—

> "For He, the strong and rightful King,
> Death's heavy fetters severing,
> Treads 'neath his feet the ancient foe,
> Redeems a wretched race from woe.
>
> Vainly with rocks his tomb they barred,
> While Roman guards kept watch and ward;
> Majestic from the spoiled tomb,
> In pomp of triumph, He is come.
>
> Let the long wail at length give place,
> The groanings of a sentenced race;
> The shining angels as they speed,
> Proclaim, 'The Lord is risen indeed.'"

"Yes," answered Bertric, "the darkness of the cross endured but three hours; the darkness of the sealed tomb but three days. And Easter morning began an eternity of light and life. I have seen Rome in ruins," he continued, "around the tombs of the martyred apostles. And I have seen the nations who ruined Rome worship the God of the martyrs Rome slew. King Alfred fights not for England only, but for Christianity. And be the struggle for a day or a year, or a century, the triumph will be infinitely longer. And I think it is near."

A few days afterwards the little guerrilla-band returned to Athelney from a successful sally, bringing with them store of provisions for men and cattle, and tidings better than any spoils. The copses resounded with shouts of victory and with the broken thanksgivings of women weeping for joy, as the warriors told how the Danes had been repulsed from the feeble walls of Kynewith, a fortress they were besieging on the Taw in Devonshire, by a sally of Odun the Saxon earl; the fierce leader Hubba, son of Regnar Lodbrok, being slain, and the raven-standard taken.

The names of Regnar Lodbrok and his three invincible sons were known on all the coasts of England and France, as names of more than mortal terror. The death of Hubba was far more than the mere destruction of a ferocious enemy; it was the dissolution of a paralysing spell of terror. And the loss of the raven-standard was even more to the Danes than its capture to the Saxons. Woven in one day, with charms and songs of incantation by the three maiden daughters of Regnar Lodbrok, the terrible raven-standard spread its ominous wings over many a field of carnage.

Full of courage and hope that night were the little heroic band at Athelney. They were no more alone in the land! England was awaking from the stupor of despair. The bird of Odin had turned against the Danes.

The Danish army was encamped at Ethendune in Somersetshire, spreading from the summit of a hill which they had entrenched over the plain below. Near it they had placed their women and wounded in a fortress for security. The days were passed when the heathen men could roam fearlessly whither they would throughout the land. Guthrum, their chief, who had seized the throne of the martyred Edmund in East Anglia, had heard rumours of a coming army of the Saxons, which made him vigilant, although no Saxon force had been seen such as to warrant serious apprehension.

One evening as Gudruna joined a group of Danish maidens in the fortress near Ethendune, she noticed a "hush" pass from one to another; and silence succeeded the clatter of busy tongues. This was not the first time her coming had been the signal for such a pause. She knew she was regarded with suspicion by her people on account of her Christian faith, and she bitterly felt the injustice.

But this time the glances directed against her were unusually black. At length one said sarcastically, "Why conceal the tidings from the Lady Gudruna? It must give her joy to know that the raven-standard is in Christian hands."

"It is no joy to me," said Gudruna, gently, "to hear that my people are overcome by the Saxons; but it would be joy unspeakable to hear that they laid down their arms at the feet of Christ. Am not I the daughter of the earl Sidroc?"

"It were time for us to seek some other gods, truly," said another woman, "when Odin abandons us. Of old, when the sacred raven but drooped in the fight, the hearts of the bravest were smitten; what will they do now it has gone over to the foe? I would we were back by my father's house beside the sea in Norway."

"There are rumours in the air," said another. "Some have heard the sounds of the Saxon horn afar off in the forests, where not a Saxon troop has been seen for years."

"And others say King Alfred, who won the fight at Ashdune, is alive."

"Impossible! Was he not slain months since?"

"All thought so," was the reply, "but last night a

12*

harper came into our camp at Ethendune, and was admitted to the table of king Guthrum, so great was his skill, and so many old songs could he sing. But my husband said this harper's glance seemed to him all the while he sang to have more of the quick fire of war in it than the quiet light of song, and after dusk he saw the stranger creep quietly away, looking carefully around him on all sides. And my husband, who was at Ashdune, says there was something in the harper's eye and port which reminded him of Prince Alfred, who met the Earls in the shock of battle and drove them back."

Among the Saxons, also, strange rumours were floating, rising, as among the tumults of the people is so often the case, no one knows whence, like gusts of wind in tempests, the vague hopes and fears of men shaping themselves into wild tales of marvel, which again arouse their hopes and fears. King Alfred, it began to be rumoured, was living still. St. Neot (some said) the holy monk, the king's kinsman, not many years dead, had appeared in a dream to the king, and told him that his trial had now endured the necessary time to purify him for the triumph which was close at hand. Others told how the saint in person had visited the king in his hiding-place at Athelney, in the guise of a beggar, and being greeted with humble words and merciful deeds, had told him that the arrogant self-will for which in old times he had warned him he must suffer, having evidently been purged from his heart in the fires of affliction, God would speedily send him better days. Others indeed shook their heads, and said the people had abandoned their chief, and he would never be restored to them.

Meantime the faithful little band at Athelney continued to make sudden sallies from their hiding-place among the marshy woods, appalling the Danes and succouring the Saxons by appearing here and there, at all kinds of unexpected times and places, and then disappearing, none knew whither—the mystery and suddenness of their movements giving them much of the charm and terror of the supernatural.

At length the time came when the king's name and the assurance of his life would be worth a victory to his people; and then some of the best-proved men among the band at Athelney were sent forth one by one through the land, east, and west, and south, to the king's faithful thanes in Wiltshire, Hampshire, and Somersetshire, to desire them to meet their sovereign in a forest at the stone of Egbert, the first founder of the glories of the West Saxon royal house.

Thus, about six weeks after the lowly Easter at Athelney, not five months after the flight from Chippenham, when kingdom, king, church, and people all seemed lost, hope burst forth afresh, and all England went a-Maying in the forest around Egbert's stone to meet her king. The life which had been lying hidden in the silent woods and in the hearts of the people, broke forth at once into joyous sound and sight. Arms clashed, horns rang, and trumpets pealed their royal salutes to the new-found king, through the forest-glades green with the young leaves, and bright with the countless flowers, and musical with the countless songs of May.

From all quarters the people flocked to King Alfred's standard, and in a few days he who, not three months before, had been hiding in a swine-herd's hut, rode at the head of an army to confront the Danes at Ethendune, under King Guthrum.

To the heathen men it was like being called to meet

an army risen from the dead. A mysterious terror no doubt prepared them for panic ; no magic raven-standard waved them on to victory. On the other hand, the Saxons, confident in heaven, in a cause as sacred as any for which men ever fought—in a leader as noble as men ever followed—seemed to see before them their golden-dragon standard borne in immortal hands. It was no mortal standard-bearer (they thought) that led them on, the aim for every Danish arrow, yet scathed by none, but St. Neot, their countryman, the saintly kinsman of the king!

What could be too great for the Christian host to hope from the heaven which had given them back their king! Had not Alfred, who led them on, risen, as it were, from the dead, to save them from the heathen foe? It was the conflict of a loyal Christian nation with a barbaric horde. Individually the Danes fought bravely, according to the intrepid nature common to Saxon and Dane ; but they could not long withstand the steady and continuous rush of the Saxon phalanx. The fatal flight of Saxon arrows was followed by the determined charge of Saxon lances ; and from lances the fierce combat deepened to the hand-to-hand conflict with swords, till the Danish ranks were broken. Then the desperate desire of safety replaced the eager strife for victory. The terrible heathen army which had so long ravaged England, melted into a crowd of despairing men, each possessed only by the passionate longing to save his own life. Thousands of Danish corpses strewed the plain, and those who escaped took refuge in the fortress they had secured not far from the camp.

Gudruna stood alone one night a few days after the battle of Ethendune, looking out at one of the narrow windows of the fortress where the remnants of the Danish army had taken refuge. All day she had been tending her wounded countrymen, proving the efficacy of such simple remedies as she had learned from Hilda, and Hilda from the nuns. Now and then, also, she had been able to tell the sufferers, as they cursed the gods, who they said had failed them in their need, of Him who never fails those who trust in him—whose death had made death the gate of endless life to his disciples. To most of those wild marauders the name of Christ had grown familiar in their twelve years' ravaging of the land. From tortured and dying sufferers, monks and nuns, and even little children, in burning minsters and ruined homes, again and again they must have seen the power of that name to sustain and to console. They must have felt the beauty of the orderly Christian social life they had been laying waste, in comparison with their own career of destruction. The best among them must have felt the mercy with which King Alfred pursued his victories, his generous trust in their false oaths, his truth to his own word. Imperfect as the Christianity of the Anglo-Saxons may have been, it had nevertheless life in it to bring forth fruits their fierce creed had never known.

Gudruna mused on these things as she stood by the window of the fortress, and wondered whether King Guthrum would sue for peace, or whether the hunger they had now been enduring for some days would have to be endured unto death, rather than yield to the Saxon. Then her mind turned to Hilda and her brother, and she thought how all was changed between them; how she had now become the lonely orphan exile who might have to sue for the mercy of a victorious enemy. And as she mused, her thoughts reached those depths of conscious helplessness where springs the fountain of prayer. "Have mercy on me," she said, "O Jesus, Son of Mary, Son of God! Have mercy on us!"

The next day King Guthrum sent in his submission to King Alfred, offering the noblest among his forces as hostages. He was permitted to leave the fortress which had become a prison to him and his starving followers.

Among the throng of Saxons who watched that emaciated and humbled band issue from the fortress, stood Hilda, pressing close to the gate to catch the first glimpse of Gudruna. Before long a slight and drooping form appeared among the Danish women. Her eyes were not fixed on the ground like those of the countrywomen, but often glanced upward as from a heart whose tendency was toward heaven. Her cheek was more wan, and her form more wasted even than any; for she had often shared her scanty portion with the sick and feeble; but there was a patient calm on her brow such as only one hope can give.

Hilda saw, with a glance, not only enough to enable her to recognize Gudruna, but to trace the history of the time that had passed since they met. In a moment she had folded her in her arms.

A few weeks afterwards King Guthrum and thirty of his nobles repaired to Alfred's camp to receive Christian baptism. It was surely no mere political expediency which led to this. Guthrum had seized the throne of the murdered Edmund of East Anglia. Who knows how deep the impression of the young king's patient and heroic death may have sunk in his heart, or how the patience he may have despised in the victim may have at length won his homage, when he saw it transformed from the endurance of the sufferer into the forbearance of the conqueror? The mercy and truth, and ill-requited trust of King Alfred, which seem to have lost him the fruit of some victories, must have contributed at last to an end better than any mere military victory.

The religion which made suffering noble, strength forbearing, and oaths sacred, was a religion his foes must have felt worth listening to; and on that baptism day they paid the deepest homage to its power, when they, the chiefs of the heathen army which had rendered England desolate for years, trusted themselves, unarmed and unattended, in the heart of the Saxon camp, among men whose kindred they had robbed and murdered, guarded from the vengeance they so well deserved, only by the sanctity of the Christian promise, by the word of "Alfred the truth-teller."

The summer of that eventful year, whose spring had seen Alfred a forsaken fugitive, had not mellowed into autumn when, at Aulre, near Athelney and within his own camp, he stood sponsor for Guthrum at the font.

How much the Danish king and his thirty pirate chiefs understood of the faith they were professing, cannot now be known. They had been instructed for some weeks, and Alfred was not one to offer a mockery to God. Something, no doubt, they had learned of the majesty and grace of the glorious name into which they were baptized. It was something to pass from the service of gods whose rites were bloodshed and plunder, to the furthest outskirts of the courts of Him whose service is love and truth.

There was a deep hush in the camp that summer noon, as the Saxon army listened to the low question of the priest, and the response of the heathen warriors, and saw the sign of redemption traced on the brows of the destroyers meekly bowed to receive it, and heard the Christian benediction breathed over those who had so long been the curse of the land.

Emotions deeper than any warrior's triumph must have stirred the heart of the Christian king, as he saw in that solemn rite the promise of peace to the Saxon, and salvation for the Dane.

The Saxons were rescued, and Christianity had triumphed, and from the union of Saxon and Dane that day cemented at the font, our country rose from a collection of petty kingdoms into England!

Once more the Saxon patriots who saved their country from her most imminent peril, could indulge that love of home which is at the root of the love of country.

One morning, soon after the chrismal fillet had been loosened from the baptized Danes, the baptismal robes laid aside, and the last guest had departed with royal presents from Alfred's palace at Wedmore, Hilda and Gudruna sat under the shade of a beech tree, on a farm of Bertric's, arranging some medicinal herbs they had been culling from the fields, when Hilda suddenly desisted from her work, and said,—

"I may wait for months before anything will lead to what I want to say to thee, unless I make a way. Thou must surely have seen that my brother's happiness is bound up in thee. And yet I know not when he will say so to thee, so sacred is his respect for the asylum he offered thee in his house. He fears, if thy heart could not freely be given to him, and so his home become thine, this house would cease to be thy refuge. But he need never know that I have spoken thus to thee. He is older than thou art, Gudruna," she continued in a deprecating tone, " and sorrow early scattered gray amongst his hair, and furrowed his brow."

"I like gray hair in a man," said Gudruna, colouring deeply; "and where there are no furrows of thought, how can there be any harvest of noble deeds?"

They fell for a few moments into silence, and then Gudruna said suddenly, looking up, and fixing her clear eyes earnestly on Hilda,—

"Hilda, you have always been true to me; are you sure your brother does not wish me to be his wife only that I may not be left to wander homeless through the world? If it were thus, I would rather be a bondmaid in any home than the lady of his."

Hilda smiled, and thought her task was done; and laying down her work without answering, she fetched her brother from the field. And the next day Bertric and Gudruna were betrothed.

The field of England had been won from the foe. It had yet to be reclaimed from the desolation to which the Danes had reduced it. The waste and ruin of years could but slowly be repaired. Scarcely a city remained unruined throughout King Alfred's dominions, scarcely a monastery unburnt, scarcely a judge who could read the laws, a priest who could read the services of the Church.

Laws, lawyers, churches, priests, books, readers, the king had to make them all. And he did it—not in the uninterrupted leisure of a tranquil and vigorous life, but with a body worn by continual weakness (worn out in fifty-three years), in the pauses of incessant contests with the Danes by sea and land. His biography is a record of work so varied, so hindered yet so successful, that it might seem a mere legendary tale of the heroes, if we did not know how much of the most effective work in the world has been done in the intervals of brief and busy hours.

Once more, the home of Bertric began to rise on the fertile range of hills to the north of London, where lay his father's estates. Some fresh horde of predatory Danes, owning the force of no treaty made with other bands of their countrymen, had retained London, and were not dispossessed by Alfred until after a regular siege in 886. Then Bertric ventured to reclaim his home, and the wooden homstead of the Saxon thane rose on the summit within the ancient moat. In spite of all its perils, the free life of the country attracted our Saxon forefathers more than the restraints of the city. Bertric and his men gladly followed the king as he rode among the charred remains of the dwellings of London, and once more cleared the site of the great church of St. Paul's; and lent their aid to the work. But his home was on the heights looking northward, over the range of forest and heath, broken by green glade and forest pool, which wild birds haunted, and where deer and wild boar came to drink; and southward over terraced vineyards and golden corn-fields to the Thames. The age of great cities had not yet come. But it must interest the dwellers in London of to-day to remember that while the origin of the city dates back to far-off unrecorded British times, the form of the first Founder that rises distinctly out of the dimness of the past is that of Alfred the Great. It is something for town or city to trace back its beginning to hands so pure.

It was not the lot of Bertric, however, or of any brave man in those days of mingled conflict and restoration, when, as in Jerusalem of old, men had to build with their weapons beside them, to lead a tranquil, stationary life. As one of the king's thanes, he and his family followed the king from one town or royal residence to another.

The court of King Alfred was no mere state palace, nor even only a royal home. It was at once a travelling university, a British association, the great court of justice, the Board of Trade, the Admiralty, and the Horse Guards of the kingdom. The learned men, themselves pupils, or pupils of pupils of great Englishmen, such as Alcuin, who were induced by the king's liberality and love of learning to come from the continent to instruct the youth of England, had to share this wandering life. The children of Bertric and the courtiers were brought up with the king's children. The future bishops, and judges, and warriors of England, were trained under the eye of the king. Often, indeed, they received instruction from his own lips. It was his wish (and with him to wish was to endeavour) that all the free-born youth of his people who possessed the means, should persevere in learning so long as they had no other affairs to prosecute, until they could perfectly read the English Scriptures; and that such as desired to devote themselves to the service of the Church should be taught Latin.

His law-book began with the laws of God as given by Moses to the Israelites (the Ten Commandments,* with the 21st, 22d, and 23d chapters of Exodus), followed by these words: "These are the laws spoken to Moses by Almighty God himself, who commanded him to keep them; and afterwards the only Son of God, who is Christ our Saviour, came upon earth and said that he did not come to destroy those laws, and to abolish them, but in every way to fulfil; and he taught mercy and humility." This epitome of the Divine laws concludes with, "Whatsoever ye would that men should do to you, do ye even so to them. By this one commandment man shall know

* Exodus xx. 23, was inserted in place of the second, which was omitted.

whether he does right; then he will require no other law-book."

The year of our Lord 987 was one of great rejoicing in England. For three years the king had lived at the head of his army to repel the invasion of Hastings, the daring and able Danish chief, who had laid Europe waste from Holland to Italy.* In Devonshire, Shropshire, Kent, and Hertfordshire, King Alfred had met and defeated the invaders, until at length, "without lucre and without honour," the baffled Vikingr had taken his final flight for the less defended shores of France, with the wife and children who had been twice captured by Alfred, and twice restored to the invader with courteous words and royal gifts. Once more the farmers of the country around London could gather in their crops without being under the protection of a royal army. Old cities and old minsters rose from their ashes; and the king being thus wonderfully free from troubles of his own, found leisure to think of the troubles of his fellow Christians of the ancient churches of St. Thomas in India. The Bishop of Sherborne was sent to them with gifts and a message of Christian sympathy; and thus, the first time England came in contact with India, it was with the clasp of Christian fellowship through the hand of Alfred the Great.

Four peaceful years followed, marked by one of the happy silences of history; and then came a day of mourning for all England, when the body of their best king, worn out by suffering and ceaseless toil—suffering which he never permitted to hinder his toil, and toil almost entirely for others—was laid in the church of the monastery which he had founded at Winchester.

---

* He captured the ancient city of Luna, in the Gulf of Spezia, *mistaking it for Rome.*

In May, twenty-three years before, the nation had at length awakened and recognized her deliverer, and had rallied round him in the forest, dating the new spring-tide of her life from that spring-time of the new earth.

Nature had her forest garlands and her songs for King Alfred's triumph; and now on this 28th of October she had her funereal pomp of autumn, and her boding silence for his tomb.

History has recorded no death-bed scene of Alfred the Great; and no legendary vision has attempted to open the heavens above his grave. It is remarkable that all the legends which the grateful affection of after and less happy times gathered around his memory in the hearts of the Saxon people are connected, not with death, but with his life. The traditions that float around his memory are popular, not ecclesiastical. The greatest king and the noblest man of his days has not attained the lowest step of monastic canonization. Monks who attained the perfection of saying their prayers in ice-cold water, and priests who had physical encounters with the devil, and who exercised their courage in maiming a poor young Saxon queen, have their due record in ecclesiastical legend. The king who set an example, not of celibacy, but of a Christian married life, who won England back to Christianity, and brought the Danish pirates to Christian baptism—who chose any suffering rather than sin should vanquish him, who spent his life and early wore out his strength in ceaseless labours for the spiritual and temporal good of his people, is left to secular history. We may well be thankful that monastic ingenuity has been exhausted on St. Neot rather than on his royal kinsman, and that such stories as that of restoring broiled fish to life, and bending a wild stag's neck to the yoke of the plough, have been withheld from the memory of England's first and perhaps her purest hero. Happily for him, Alfred himself, as well as the ecclesiastical historians, looked on St. Neot as the saint, "not as other men," and on himself as "the sinner" needing "mercy," and thankful for the chastisement that assailed his sins. Grand as an old Greek statue amidst a theatrical group of waxwork; simple as a Bible story amidst a mass of monkish legends, the history of King Alfred comes down to us. Neither the splendour nor the gloom of the middle ages is upon it.

It is not the want of detail in his biography which gives this simplicity and grandeur to our impression of him. We are not left to fill up the breaks of a broken outline with ideal lines.

His character and life stand out with a singular clearness from the legendary days which preceded it, and from the romantic tales of crusade and conquest, of castle and convent, which follow. We know the delight of his childhood in ballads, his ardent love of the chase in youth, his sympathy with the studies and recreations of his own children, and the children of his thanes. We know even the way in which he divided his time, and how he constructed the horn time-lantern which measured it. We are told how he apportioned his revenue. We can sit with him as he listened to the daily lessons and psalms from the Scriptures. We know how, often at midnight, he went alone into the church, which in his busy and crowded palace was his best closet, and having shut the door, prayed to his Father who seeth in secret. The echo of one of these solitary prayers has even reached us, and the rewards of how many! We know how he learned to read, and the books he loved best.

We know even much of the contents of the little manual of Scriptures, hymns, and prayers, which he always carried in his bosom.

We have, in the original passage which he inserted in his translation of Boetheus, a touching tribute of his affection for his wife: "She lives now for thee, thee alone. Hence she loves none else but thee. She has enough of every good in this present life, but she has despised it all for thee alone. She has shunned it all, because only she has not thee also." Does not the memory of the exile in Athelney, which his wife Elswitha shared, quiver through every word of this passage? We see it also in the peculiar pathos which breathes in his version of the story of Orpheus and Eurydice, and in the provision of his will, which among other estates, left to Elswitha Wantage and Ethendune; his birth-place, and the great battle-field on which he conquered the Danes.

From his will also we learn how carefully he provided for his servants, and how earnestly he insisted on the liberation of his slaves, that when he died they might be free to choose any master they would.

We know also what a burden the crown was to him,— the crown which to him had always hung over his head "suspended by a small thread;" how hard he found it to make his people work with a tithe of the energy for their own good with which he worked for them; what sorrows he felt to be the accompaniments of power; and what emptiness he found in mere "clothes" and state.

We know how his mind grappled with the great questions of human free-will and divine foreknowledge. We know his tastes, his pleasures, his sicknesses, and his fears.

We know something of what his conflicts were, and we know where he found his rest.

"The true blessedness is God," he writes. "He is the beginning and end of every good, and He is the highest happiness."

"There is no man that needs not some increase but God alone. He hath enough in his own self. He needs nothing but that which he has in himself." "By these things we may manifestly understand that every man desires this, that he may obtain the supreme good, when he can know it, or is enabled to seek it rightly. But they seek it not in the most right way. It is not in this world." "There is no creature that does not desire it may proceed thither whence it came before. This is rest and felicity. Its rest is with God; God is its rest."

"In God, the beginning, and the fountain, and the root of all good," was the rest and the spring of life of that aspiring mind and that tried heart.

"No necessity has taught Thee to make what thou hast made; but of thine own will and thine own power thou hast created all things; yet Thou hast no need of any."

"Most wonderful is the nature of Thy goodness; for it is all one, Thou and thy goodness. God comes not to thee, but is thine own. Thou hast created all things very good and very fair; and thou thyself art the highest and the fairest good."

Yet, rising above Manicheanism as above materialism, he says, that "because the creatures are not complete and self-suffering, they are not for that reason not good; for everything would go to nought," he concludes, "if it had not some good in it."

"God is wisdom, the supreme good, the highest eternity. All eternity is present to him."

"His riches increase not, nor do they ever diminish. He is always giving, and never wants. He is always almighty, because he always wills good and not evil. He is always seeing; he never sleeps. He is always mild and kind. He will always be eternal. He is always free."

Most expressive is the silence with which the biographers of mediæval saints have done homage to this holy memory. He built monasteries; he endowed churches; he honoured the great ecclesiastical metropolis of Rome. He translated Pope Gregory's Pastorals, full of legends after the monk's own heart, for the benefit of his clergy. But his own life was set by a higher standard, and nourished by deeper springs than these narratives could reach.

His bones, desecrated by no embalmer's arts into a poor monastic mummy, have been suffered to mingle with the dust of the country he saved. If any perfume hangs about his tomb, it is that of the fresh grass and lowly wild-flowers, with which the earth honours the remains committed trustfully to her sole keeping. His memory, profaned by no decorating hands of theatrical historian or legendary chronicler, comes home to our hearts, not as that of the canonized saint or the crowned hero, but of the faithful husband and father, the generous foe, the true friend, the devoted patriot, the Christian king, in himself all that he desired as the elements of a kingdom—"the prayer-man, the army-man, and the workman."

Silently he passes into the eternal world to which so many of his thoughts had arisen, his death but one simple unrecorded act of his patient and obedient life.

Of ordinary vanity he seems to have been absolutely

destitute. His chief literary works (except his laws) were translations, for the good of his people; and the noble original thoughts and eloquent original words, by which we see into his own mind, are hidden among the thoughts he translated without any distinctive claim, only to be disentangled from these by a careful comparison of the translation with the book translated.*

In thinking of all he was and all he accomplished, it is scarcely possible to avoid running into a panegyric, which would be an insult to that grand and simple character.

We must turn to his own confessions, recorded by his friend Asser, to learn what were his faults. From his own words we may best understand the purpose of his life. "I have desired," he says, "to live worthily while I lived, and after my life to leave the men that should be after me a remembrance in good works!" His ambition, to live worthily; his monument, good works. How lofty the simple words are! Duty, not romantic achievement, is the aim of his life; not to do "some great thing," but the right thing; the right thing being simply what God gave him to do. The subtle spiritual vanity, which makes some lives a disappointment and a failure, seems to have been absent from his. He seems to have felt in his inmost being, that each man was sent into the world, not to be like some one else, but to do his own work, and bear his own burden, precisely the one work which God has given him, and which can never be given to or done by any other.

The great Christian ideal, not to do this or that work, but to do God's will, seems to have been his. He aimed not to live remarkably, but worthily; and so, uncon-

* Sharon Turner's Anglo-Saxons.

sciously, he became Alfred the "Great," wept in every Saxon home, throughout the bad and bitter days of the early Norman conquest, as the Shepherd and Darling of England; honoured by Saxon, Dane and Norman, as the man who could be trusted—Alfred the Truth-teller.

HAMPSTEAD, *August*, 1863.

VIII.

VIII.

Saxon and Norman:

A Story of the Conquest.

VIII.

SAXON AND NORMAN.

A STORY OF THE CONQUEST.

I.

THE doors and windows had just been closed and barred in one of the few Saxon homesteads remaining in the great wilderness made by William the Conqueror out of fertile Northumbria. The aged master of the house, Aldred the Thane, gathered his household around him, in those stormy times, for prayer, (according to a simile of an old chronicler,) "as a ship's crew is gathered in the seas in the stormy tempest." Bows and arrows, pikes and swords were laid together where they could easily be found in case of sudden attack, and each was retiring to rest for the night, when a low knock was heard at the door. Aldred, the blind old thane, was the first to hear the sound, and grasping his daughter Editha's hand, they stood still to listen. The knock was repeated more forcibly, and then voices were heard. This time it was Editha who was the first to catch the sound, and, with a flush of pleasure, quickly followed by a look of anxious fear, she said,—

"It is Siward. What can bring him here so late, and who can be with him?"

In another moment the heavy bolts were let down, and through the cautiously opened door entered a young man in a common peasant's dress, and a priest.

"Welcome, Father Osyth," said the old thane, grasping the priest's hand, while Editha bent for his blessing.

After a brief conference, the fire was piled up in the hall, the table was spread, the house was once more fast closed, the household was dismissed, and Aldred and Editha were left alone with their guests.

The subjects talked of were not of a cheering kind and yet Siward's face seemed to Editha to have more of hope and determination in it than she had seen there for many months. A bitter sense of wrongs, terribly common to all, and yet, while familiar to each, too deep to be often floating on the surface of intercourse, pervaded that little company.

Aldred, the old thane, although, by a rare exception, suffered to remain in the homestead of his fathers, had had the sight deliberately scorched from his eyes, while Editha was yet a child, for killing some of the king's deer which wasted his fields. Siward was the last of a noble Saxon family which had been slain in one of the many brave but disconnected insurrections with which after the death of Harold, the Saxons vainly resisted the united host of Norman plunderers. His father and elder brothers had perished fighting with Hereward in the camp of refuge at Croyland, among the fens; and he, a child of four years old, had fallen to the lot of the knight Bertrand de Garenne, whose serf he was. So early inthralled, his mind might have grown down to his circumstances, had it not happened that the lands assigned to De Garenne were in Northumbria, and included the home of Aldred the Thane, whose family had of old been allied to that of Siward; so that thus, much of his boyhood he had been suffered to pass under the roof of his father's friend. He had shared with Editha such teaching as Father Osyth, one of the wandering priests from a ruined Saxon monastery, could give them in his occasional visits; and thus the memories of the noble and the saintly men and women of their race had been kept alive in the hearts of these Saxon children. St. Cuthbert of Lindisfarne, the good Abbess Hilda, the venerable Bede of Jarrow, the great and holy King Alfred, with Hereward, the last Saxon national hero, were names dear and reverend to them—loved with a tender and pathetic reverence which at once ennobled and softened the hearts in which it dwelt. Saxon ballads and proverbs, and, what was better, Saxon gospel, psalm and hymn, were their heroic and sacred literature. And gradually, by the fireside in winter, and among the free forests in summer, as Editha spun or gathered medicinal herbs, and Siward made or tried his Saxon bow and arrows, an ideal of character rose before them which moulded their own as they looked up to it—an ideal truer and nobler far than that of the Norman chivalry around them—an ideal which made nobleness possible for the peasant as well as for the knight, and saintliness attainable for the layman as well as the monk. Gradually also grew up between them that deep affection, unquestioning because undoubting, gently intertwined with every fibre of being, which made life simply not life at all to one without the other.

So tranquilly their youth passed on until the old knight

Bertrand one day awoke to the fact that Siward was of an age to be of service. Then began the bitterness of bondage for them. All in their hearts and lives seemed to spring at once from unconscious, tranquil happiness, to agonizing consciousness. They had to descend into the common destiny of their oppressed and down-trodden people—they, with their free Saxon blood and their Saxon reverence for freedom. Thus Editha's affection for Siward grew into that union of passionate reverence and indignant pity which becomes so unconquerable in a woman's heart when all she most reverences and loves is subjected to unjust humiliation.

She who had been wont to give herself little imperial maidenly airs with him in happy days, watched him now when they met, to render him little services, and spoke of him in the presence of all as her betrothed.

But with him it was otherwise. It scarcely seemed a pleasure to him to meet her. Generally his manner was abrupt to roughness, except when the fear of having pained her made him forget all but herself, and for a moment all the old gentle tenderness came back.

But to-night all this was changed. Editha felt it at once, although he said nothing until Father Osyth and Aldred the Thane had seated themselves by the hearth, and he drew Editha to the little narrow window, through which one streak of moonlight fell on the stone floor, beaming quietly across the flickering glow of the firelight, as the purpose of God crosses the fitful purposes of man.

"Editha," he said, "my love, my betrothed,"—he had not called her by an endearing name for months,—"to-morrow I shall be a thrall no longer ; I shall be free !"

Her hand trembled in the strong grasp of his, and she was too much moved to answer him by word or look.

"The knight Bertrand has resolved to join the Crusade to the Holy Sepulchre, to do penance for his sins. He has given all his serfs the choice to follow him to the Crusade; and whoever takes on him the Crusader's cross, is from that instant and forever free."

Editha did not say anything. To her the boon seemed very mixed, and yet she knew too well how unattainable it was by other means, and how precious, not to share his enthusiasm. Still she could not speak a word to send him from her. He felt her silence like a passive resistance, and resumed with a vehement earnestness,—

"Editha, for your sake I have given up every other way by which brave men, wronged as I am, seize their freedom. Better and more patient men than I have taken to the forest for wrongs less than your father's or mine. The forest is the Saxon freeman's castle. The Conqueror founded it for us when he laid the whole land waste from the Swale to the Tyne. When his army marched, divided into many columns through the north, slowly destroying everything in their track, they little thought that in levelling cities and burning villages, in turning meadows into marshes and fruitful fields into forests, they were making the whole wilderness a fortress for our people. The Norman robber builds his castle on the height, with its winding passages and its dark torture-dungeons. But beside him God slowly rears the forest-fortress of our race. Time, which slowly wears away the hardest stones of the invaders' walls, ceaselessly strengthens our rampart, raising the sapling into the mighty tree, and intertwining the gnarled branches. The Norman horsemen sink in the marshes they have made, or, if they venture into our woods, they have to fell their way at every step along the narrow forest-paths until sword and battle-axe are blunted ; and then when they reach the open glade, unseen arrows bring down their bravest, until, weary and dispirited, they return ; or perhaps never return, lost in the mazes of the woods, which only we Saxons know. Meantime, our countrymen dwell safely in some deep glade the foe has never reached, and make their sallies on their oppressor, rescuing many a Saxon home from wrong, and winning many a ransom from the Norman. I think this life is noble, Editha. We fight for the oppressed against the oppressor. No feeble or helpless one ever complains of the Saxon foresters ; the widow and fatherless welcome them like angels ; and on Sunday, Saxon priests read them Gospel and hymn in the old free mother-tongue. Shall we join these, my love? If you will come, my cousin Frithric will welcome us to-morrow. His wife and sisters are there, of race noble even as thine. Shall we go to the forest? Thy father will be honoured as a prince among them, and Father Osyth will visit and bless us there as here. This would please me best. No infidel to me so hateful as these worse than heathen Normans! no crusade to me holier than to redress the wrongs of my people. Editha," he continued, " shall we go together to the forest, or shall I join the Crusade ?"

Editha hesitated.

" I cannot tell why, Siward," she said, at length, in a very sad and quiet voice, " but it seems to me the Crusade is best. Our people of old always conquered through keeping the laws, not through breaking them. Now the laws seem all on the wrong side ; but in some way or other I feel it would be worse that there should be none. I see how noble Frithric and many of these outlaws may be ; but their life seems to me too much like that of the old Danes to be Christian, or to do good in the end."

"Did not Alfred, England's darling, once live thus in the Isle of Athelney, and so begin the deliverance of England?"

"But Alfred was king, and fought for his people," said Editha; "and he had a great right, and a great purpose; and these foresters seem to me to have no great purpose, no great national hope. They harass the Norman knights and sheriffs in their neighbourhood, and rescue some innocent, oppressed people, and avenge others, but there it ends. The Normans avenge their vengeance on some other helpless Saxons, and the laws continue unchanged, and the evil really unredressed."

"But," said the young man, impatiently, "there is not one of our race who does not wish well to the free foresters. Would Father Osyth visit them if they were so much in the wrong?"

"He may be afraid of their becoming worse," she said. "It would be an evil thing if the priests only ministered to saints."

For an instant a fear which had often crossed Siward's heart took possession of it, and he said, abruptly, "Editha, can your heart be grown cold to your people? A better home, in good sooth, than any I can ever offer, may easily be yours!"

"Siward!" she exclaimed, in a voice trembling with feeling, as she withdrew her hand from his.

"Nay," he continued, in low rapid tones, "if I do not say this now, I never shall; and, Heaven knows, nothing but a love stronger than I am could make me speak. The young knight Bernard de Garenne is not like his father. He is, I believe firmly, a true knight according to their Norman chivalry, brave and true, and reverent to women; at least, to fair and noble women such as thou. He has seen thee, and, I know, thinks thee fairer than any other maiden. He says the Norman ladies may be fair as mortals may be, but thou art fair as Mary, our Lady. In thine eyes, and thy fair hair, and on thy white, calm brow, he sees the beauty as of heaven. Hast thou seen him?"

"I have seen and spoken to him," she said. "He seems good and true as any Norman can be. But I had rather live in any forest glade among the outlawed Saxons than in the fairest castle of any Norman robber in the land. There are no torture-chambers in the forest; and besides, Siward, what is any home but thine to me?"

For a little while Father Osyth and Aldred the Thane had the conversation to themselves. And then it was without any remnant of bitterness or anxiety in his voice that Siward resumed, although in tones not calculated at all to disturb the two old men by the fire,—

"Yet thou wouldst rather have me join the Crusade than the free foresters?"

"Yes," she said; "I think it is nobler for thee; and I had rather we should suffer anything so that we choose what is right."

The next day Siward knelt before the missionary monk who was preaching the Crusade through England, received the liberating cross, and was a freeman. Even in its faintest and coldest reflections such power for blessing lingered around that symbol of redeeming grace.

II.

A FEW days afterwards the young night Bernard de Garenne was riding alone on the outskirts of the forest in the early morning, when he caught the murmur of a low chant from the ruined church of one of the many Saxon villages which the Normans had burnt in Northumbria. The peasants had been massacred, and their poor wooden houses had easily been reduced to ashes. There was nothing to mark the site of the village but a little undulation of the ground, where the ashes of village and villagers had been lying for nearly twenty years, as if the bosom of the Earth had heaved a gentle sigh as she took them to her keeping,—and a little deeper richness in the tint of the wild herbage which had replaced the gardens and cultivated fields. The chancel of the church being of stone still stood. It was from under its roof that the sound of the low chant came.

"Some of the shrines of those old Saxon saints of whom no one else ever heard," thought the young knight, "yet to which these old Saxons so obstinately cling. Dangerous haunts, my father says, for the spirit of discontent and insurrection."

He dismounted, and, leading his horse, moved softly round to see what was going on.

An aged priest stood at the altar; and before him knelt three motionless figures,—an old white-haired man, a man-at-arms with the red cross on his shoulder, and a young maiden in white linen dress and veil. The priest held their hands united, and then laid a hand on each of their heads as they bowed before him, blessing them and their love for life and death. In a few minutes they rose, the white veil fell from the maiden's brow, and the young knight recognised the calm fair face of Editha, the daughter of Aldred, as she held the hand of Siward and looked up to him. He turned quickly away, remounted his horse, and rode silently homeward. The whole scene left a deep and sacred impression on him;—the calm of the dewy morning in the forest; the clinging of the Saxon people to their ruined sanctuaries and desolated homes; this marriage, so different from the glitter and pomp and wild revelling of the weddings he had seen; the pure sweet face of the Saxon maiden, so full of love and trust,—all seemed to open to the young knight a deeper world and a higher life than any he had yet dreamt of.

That very day he left his father's castle, riding with the old knight Bertrand at the head of a goodly troop of mounted retainers. Behind him rode Siward, the Saxon man-at-arms. Both had the same vision in their minds, and both went silently on among the gay and jesting company. But it was long before either spoke to the other of what lay deepest in the heart of both.

Two weeping women watched that departing company, unknown to each other,—Marguerite, the sister of Bernard de Garenne, and Editha; one from the windows of the new and stately Norman castle on the hill, the other from the door of the lowly Saxon homestead among the meadows.

Marguerite's Norse ancestors had married into Frankish and Breton families; and there was little in her clear, dark complexion, her flashing hazel eyes, and her small supple figure, to mark the original kinship of her Norman fathers with those of the Saxon Editha, with her tall majestic form, her fair broad brow, and pensive blue eyes

Marguerite had thrown her embroidery silks impatiently on the floor of her room, and sat leaning her face on her small delicate hand, as she watched her betrothed, her father, and her brother, with their men, wind round the hill from the castle gate. Her colours were in her knight's helmet, scarcely less sacred, he had said, than the cross on his breast. He lingered behind the rest to wave one last farewell, and then, as a winding on the road hid him from her, she turned from the window and threw herself on the couch in a passionate burst of unrestrained weeping. Grief was new to her, and she had no sorrow as yet which she dared not fathom. She would listen to no consolation; she would drink this her first cup of bitterness to the dregs,—in its bitterest drops there was so much of the sweetness of hope and memory. Therefore Marguerite was inconsolable; perplexed her maidens by refusing to taste any food; cried until her nurse feared her beautiful eyes would be blinded; and declared all occupation, from the lute to the embroidery frame, a mockery for one so utterly desolate as she was.

Meanwhile Editha stood with quietly clasped hands at her father's doorway till the troop passed. One face turned for one minute to her, and she saw no other. When that last silent parting look was over, and Siward was hidden from her in the throng, she clasped her hands with one suppressed sob on her breast, and then turning to her father laid her hand in his, and looking up in his blind face said,—

"These Normans have brought us very low; but Father Osyth says it is by bringing us into the low place God brings us near him."

"It is in the song of the Blessed Virgin herself, my

child," said the old man. "You will chant it to me this evening, and we shall be comforted."

Editha went to the farm-yard, where the calves were waiting to be fed, and the cows were lowing for the milking. And the homely household work and the fresh evening air relieved her heart of the strain on it, so that afterward she could take her spinning-wheel and talk quietly to her father as he told old stories by the hearth. For the first time, as the tears fell fast over her work, she was glad he could not see. But she could not prevent his hearing the trembling in her voice as she tried to chant him one of her Saxon evening hymns.

"Say it, my child! Your voice is always sweet as a song to me."

And she said in a low voice,—

"He hath scattered the proud in the imagination of their hearts.
He hath put down the mighty from their seats, and exalted the humble and meek.
He hath filled the hungry with good things, and the rich he hath sent empty away."

"Not yet, father!" she said, after a brief pause when she had finished. "God has not done that yet; the proud are not scattered, nor the mighty humbled, nor the meek exalted yet."

"Mary the most blessed is exalted," he said, thoughtfully, "but that is in heaven; and the Lord who was born of her, the Lord of all, who was lowly in heart, was lifted up—but it was on a cross. Perhaps, my child, it is the same now. And perhaps," he added, "we are not lowly. It is not quite the same to be low and to be lowly. Many thoughts come to me in my blindness, Editha, as Father Osyth says the angels used to come in the night."

"Thou art lowly enough, father, at least!" said Editha, kissing his thin and withered hands. And she added in her heart, "God grant the time be not near for thee to be exalted in heaven. I could never bear to be left alone like that."

But that sorrow also came, and Editha was strengthened to bear it. Comfort came with it she had never dreampt of. She had anticipated the bitterness of the cup, but not the compassionate touch of the Divine hand that gave it her to drink.

When she saw that noble and patient face lying still in death, and the lids closed over the sightless eyes whose blindness she never more should mourn, a strange feeling of repose came over her heart. All her grief seemed silenced in the thought, "He is at rest, and he is seeing God."

And when at night a large number of her oppressed countrymen gathered, from many miles around, to do honour to the memory of the old thane, and Father Osyth chanted funeral psalms over his grave under the ruined Saxon church, where, a few months before, she had been married, Editha felt as if one goal in the pilgrimage of life had been reached, and she were nearer home, now that one so dear was safely there already.

Only, on returning to the old homestead the emptiness and loneliness struck coldly on her heart as she moved among the farm-servants, quietly directing every one, with no one's will to consult but her own.

III.

AFTER the old knight Bertrand left, the country around became unsettled, and scarcely a safe dwelling-place for lonely maidens, whether in castle or cottage.

The Saxon foresters grew bolder in their sallies, and the Norman barons more reckless in their revenge. Thus it happened that both the Saxon bride and the Norman demoiselle took refuge in the same convent, far from the troubled region of wronged Northumbria, within the walls of the ecclesiastical city of Canterbury. A kinswoman of Editha's was sub-prioress, and an aunt of Marguerite's was abbess, so that both found a welcome and a home under the same roof.

Marguerite came with a stately train of retainers, and brought rich gifts to the abbey. The great gates were thrown wide to admit her, and the abbess stood at the door to receive her noble guest with courtly hospitality. A cheerful room was assigned her and her waiting-woman, which in a few hours acquired quite a luxurious aspect under the tasteful French fingers of Marguerite and her maiden. Silken shawls from the East were thrown over the couches, and tapestried hangings draped the walls. Chased silver jewel-boxes and perfume-cases propped up the steel mirror in its carved oaken frame; and as Marguerite's small fingers ran over her lute, while she hummed a French chansonnette, she felt quite at home.

She did not hear the low knock at the postern-gate by which, that same evening, Father Osyth obtained admittance for Editha. None of the usual convent arrangements were disturbed by the arrival of the Saxon maiden. Father Osyth bade her a kind farewell, and blessed her; and the sub-prioress bid her welcome, and kissed her for her likeliness to her mother, and led her to a little cell which looked on the convent garden.

Editha's cell was very bare and plain, yet she also had her treasures. An old worn copy of the Saxon Gospel

of St. John, translated by the venerable Bede, with
hymns at the end, which she had often read to her
father; King Alfred's Boethius; and a book of Saxon
ballads, out of which she and Siward had learned to
read; the harp to which her father had been used to
sing in the old days when Saxon homes were homes of
feasting, and every guest had a song. Simple, time-
worn things, yet with more of the true elements of
genuine civilization in them than all the rich *bijouterie*
of Marguerite's chamber. A Bible and a literature, and
the sacred ancestral memory of holy men and heroes—
these were treasures such as no Norman possessed in the
days when the Conqueror subdued Saxon England.

Editha felt it, and not a shade of envy passed across
her mind when, a few days afterward, she was summoned to Marguerite's fairy bower to accomplish a pretty
fancy which the young lady had adopted, of learning to
spin. She honestly felt on a higher level than her pretty,
wayward pupil, and contemplated her various dainty
little affectations with the kind of tranquil dignity with
which a lion might observe the gambols of a kitten.

Marguerite was at first sure that her hands were too
small to grasp the distaff, and then that it was too difficult for any one that was not born to it; and finally the
secret of her purpose was revealed, as she confidently
told Edith that her betrothed, the young Lord Walter
de Richemont, had said a woman's hands never looked
so dainty and small as when flashing to and fro at the
spinning-wheel.

"Your hands are very white and well shaped," she
said, speaking Anglo-Saxon with a French accent; "though
they are rather large. They look really pretty as you
spin like that. Did any one ever tell you so?"

Editha coloured, and said people had sometimes praised her work, but that no one had ever taken the liberty to admire her hands.

"Ah," sighed Marguerite, "your Saxon people have no *galanterie*, no romance! I will sing you a chansonnette that was once composed in honour of my hands."

And she took her lute, and sang in a warbling, flexible voice.

"Is not that *gentille?*" she said.

Editha smiled.

"But you have no poetry; perhaps you do not understand," said Marguerite.

"I do not understand French," said Editha, proudly. "Our poetry is about something else than pretty fingers."

"About what?" asked Marguerite.

"About brave men, and fair and loving women," said Editha; "about battles, and heroic deeds, and life and death."

"Very grave," said Marguerite, slightly raising her eyebrows; "in French, we put all that in sermons."

"Life has become very grave in England lately," said Editha.

"I am sure I think so," sighed Marguerite. "From what my aunt says, it must have been much pleasanter in France. For my part, I wish William of Normandy, and my grandfather and father had stayed at home and left England to the Saxons. What with the Crusades and these wild foresters, life is anything but a *fête* to me."

"You have kindred at the Crusade?" asked Editha, for the first time aroused to interest.

"My father, my brother and my betrothed are there,"

was the reply. "I am expecting a messenger with tidings and gifts every day."

"They will send you messengers to say how they speed!" said Editha, for the first time tempted to envy her pupil.

"Doubtless," said Marguerite. "How could I live without that?"

"Other women have to live without that," said Editha.

"You mean the relations of the people who have no messengers to send," said Marguerite. "I never thought of that. I suppose the men-at-arms and bow-men have also brides and sisters to leave behind. But then," she added, languidly, "they do not feel as I do. I am sure they cannot. For the very evening the knights left, when I was crying so that I could not taste anything, my nurse went as quietly about her work as ever, although her husband and son had gone with my father."

"Perhaps, lady, your nurse kept her tears back," said Editha, quietly; "then they show less, but hurt more."

"Perhaps," said Marguerite, as if a new light was breaking upon her. "I remember afterwards she had a severe illness." Then glancing quickly at Editha, she said seriously, watching her as she plied the distaff, "It must be terribly sad to be separated from those we love and never to hear of them. It must be like death."

"It is," said Editha, quietly. "If it were not for the hope, death would be easier to bear."

"Easier!" exclaimed Marguerite, with a shudder, as if she had felt an icy touch on her heart.

"Yes," said Editha, looking up, and fixing her large, thoughtful eyes on Marguerite, "I have found it almost easier. We know more about the dead; at least, more about those they are with."

"More about those they are with!" said Marguerite.

"Certainly," said Editha, looking gravely at her, yet as if she was looking beyond. "You know, they are with the holy angels and the blessed saints, and Mary, the mother of the Lord, and with the mild and gracious Saviour himself."

"If they are saints," said Marguerite; "but otherwise! Were all your friends, then, saints, who died?"

"I have only lost one," said Editha, "and he was noble as King Alfred, and humble as Bede or St. Cuthbert. If the holy angels carried Lazarus to his rest, I am sure they were waiting for my father. Besides, since Lazarus died, the Son of God has lived on this middle earth, and has died for our sins. And we must surely be sure to find a welcome in paradise now that the Lord and the penitent thief are there."

"You know a great many things," observed Marguerite.

"I have a Saxon Gospel of St. John," replied Editha.

"Were all those good men you speak of in the Saxon Gospel of St. John?" asked Marguerite. "I did not know there was so much good written in Saxon."

"King Alfred, and Bede, and St. Cuthbert are not in the Gospels," replied Editha. "They are our Saxon king and saints."

"Are there, then, Saxon saints in the calendar and in heaven?" asked Marguerite.

"There certainly are in the calendar," replied Editha; "but I am not sure whether they are called Saxon and Norman in heaven. My Gospel speaks of one fold and one flock there."

"You know a great many things," repeated Marguerite, humbly. "You can spin, and read, and repeat the Holy

Scriptures like a mass-priest. Who taught you all this?"

"My mother first," replied Editha, "and then Father Osyth."

"I never knew my mother," said Marguerite; "and no priest ever taught me anything but the Creed and the Paternoster in Latin. Can you write?" she exclaimed, interrupting herself; "and will you teach me? I should like it better than spinning. And I might send a letter to Walter or to Bernard. Yet, what would be the use of that?" she added, laughingly; "neither Walter nor Bernard can read or write, and they might not like me better for knowing more than they do."

Editha was summoned by the sub-prioress, and so closed for the time the intercourse of the Norman and Saxon maidens.

There was both mutual attraction and repulsion in it. Editha felt a motherly pity for the frank and trusting child who had never known a mother. At the same time her pride was roused by seeing the substantial advantages of wealth and power in the hands of what seemed to her the lower and shallower race. Yet the pride thus wounded was appeased by Marguerite's acknowledgment of inferiority; and she could not help admiring the tact which led the maiden, apparently so childish, instinctively to glance away from any subject that might give pain.

That outward refinement and grace which she was inclined to despise seemed, she felt, to react inward, and give a considerateness to the feelings. And that night, kneeling down by her hay-stuffed bed on the floor of her cell, her father's words came back to her, "It is not the same to be low and to be lowly;" and reproaching herself for her pride, and contrasting it with Marguerite's graceful self-depreciation, she concluded that the Norman maiden was holier than herself, and penitently seeking forgiveness, resolved at their next interview to be less bent on the glorification of her people.

With Marguerite the process was different. Her contented self-complacency, clouded for an instant by comparison with the accomplishments of the Saxon, rallied quickly on a brief survey of herself in the mirror, as she recalled the various compliments which had done homage to her beauty; and how, when Bernard, her brother, had said that Saxon women were like alabaster images of saints, Walter had replied that one diamond was worth many pearls, and the flash of a Norman eye was better than the whiteness of any Saxon eyelid.

Moreover, Marguerite had further recourse for consolation to her waiting-woman, who assured her that the Saxons were for the most part little better than beasts of burden or clowns. Saints they might have had, she could not say; it was said that some even of the holy apostles had not been born gentlemen. Books they might have, such as monks read in monasteries; but knights they certainly had not, nor *trouvères*, nor castles, nor anything that made life gay and fit for young seigneurs and dames.

Thus, in their various ways, the maidens were consoled. The fountain of Marguerite's humility was not so deep as Editha in her simplicity supposed. Editha had as little idea of the consolations of vanity as Marguerite of the bitterness of pride. Yet, in spite of dissimilarity and mutual misunderstanding, the two were drawn to each other. Editha took much pains to instruct her quick, but by no means patient, pupil; and Marguerite, on the other hand, never had an opportunity of seeing any brilliant show or pageant that she did not offer to share it with Editha. Royal processions and pompous Norman festivities, however, had no attractions for Editha; and she so steadily declined to attend them, that Marguerite said one day,—

"You have learned to read Latin, you will not have anything to do with worldly pomp—it is plain you must be preparing to be a nun, if you are not one already."

"I am not a nun, and I trust I never shall be one," replied Editha, with a solemnity which seemed to Marguerite very disproportionate to the occasion. All her little treasures of memory and hope had long since bubbled up to the surface in conversation, and she had no conception of the hidden springs of love and recollection that lay deep in Editha's heart. But the jest with which she was prepared to dissipate Editha's gravity died from her lips as, looking up, she saw in Editha's eyes, not a lofty determination, which she could have ridiculed mercilessly, but tears.

For some time after that she did not venture to invite Editha to any festivity, until at last she induced her to attend the consecration of a new church by Archbishop Anselm.

There was all the pomp of silken banners, crimson and purple, of gold and silver crosses, priests in gorgeous robes, knights in glittering armour on richly-caparisoned steeds, ladies in silks and cloth of gold on ambling palfreys; and within the church, music, massive carved porch and window; solemn shade broken by mellow light through stained windows, by the gleam of altar-plate and the flash of arms, and the shining of many tapers; all harmonized to the senses by the echoes of the lofty aisles, and the dreamy aromatic perfume of the incense swung from silver censers. All this, and Archbishop Anselm's sermon.

For once, as the maidens sat together in Marguerite's chamber on the evening of the festival, the same feeling seemed to possess them both.

In the twilight they sat together, hand in hand in silence.

"How glorious the music was, and the light, and the incense! I felt as if I were in paradise," said Marguerite at length.

Editha was silent still, but Marguerite felt tears falling on her hand.

"Did anything give you pain to-day?" she asked, gently.

"Oh no," was the reply; "it was the words, Archbishop Anselm's words."

"The sermon?" said Marguerite, hesitating. "Yes, his manner is majestic, but he looked more like a monk meditating in his cell, than a princely archbishop, although they say he has maintained a bold contest with the king for the rights of the Church. His voice was very solemn, but what were the words which touched you so deeply?"

"He said," replied Editha, (speaking slowly and softly, as if she were still listening, and merely repeating the words after the preacher,) "'The mercy of God, for which there appeared no place when we were considering the justice of God and the sin of man, we find to be so great and so harmonious with justice that nothing can be conceived more righteous than that mercy. For what can be imagined more merciful than when to the sinner doomed to eternal punishment, and unable to redeem himself, God the Father says, Take my only-begotten Son—I give him for thee; and the Son says, Take me, and redeem thyself.' And afterwards," she continued, "he looked up and said, 'Holy Father, look down from the height of thy sanctuary, and behold this mighty sacrifice which our great High Priest, thy holy child Jesus, offers for the sins of his brethren, and have mercy on the multitude of our transgressions. Behold the voice of our brother Jesus crieth to thee from the cross. See, O Father, this is the coat of thy Son, the true Joseph; an evil beast hath devoured him. The monster hath in his fury mangled the beautiful garment and steeped it in blood; and see, he hath left in it five lamentable wounds. But now, O Father, we know that thy Son liveth, and he ruleth throughout all the land of Egypt, nay, through all places of thy dominion. Raised from the prison of death, and having exchanged the prison-garment of the flesh for the robe of immortality, thou hast received him on high; and now, crowned with glory and honour, at the right hand of thy majesty, he appears in thy presence for us. For he is our own flesh and our brother. Look, O Lord, on the countenance of thy Christ, who became obedient to thee even unto death; nor let the prints of his wounds ever recede from thy sight, that thou mayest remember what a satisfaction for our sins thou hast from him received. Nay, even let those sins of ours by which we have merited thy wrath be weighed in a balance, and over against them weigh the sorrows suffered on our behalf by thy innocent Son. Assuredly those sorrows will prevail, so that for their sake thou wilt rather let forth thy compassion upon us, than for our sins in wrath shut up thy tender mercies. Thanks, O Father, for thy abounding love, which did not spare the only Son of thy bosom, but did deliver him up to the death for us, that we might have him with thee an Advocate so mighty and so faithful. And to thee, Lord Jesus, what thanks shall

I repay, a worthless thing of dust and ashes? What couldst thou have done for my salvation that thou hast not done? To snatch me from the gulf of perdition thou didst plunge into the sea of thy passion, and the waters entered in even to thy soul. For to **restore my lost** soul to me, thou didst deliver thine own soul to death. And by a double debt thou hast bound me to thee. For what thou didst give, and for what thou didst lose on my behalf, I am thy debtor; and for my life twice given, in creation first, in redemption next, what can I render? For were mine the heaven and the earth, and all their glory, to render these were not to repay thee what I owe. **And even that** which **I ought** to render it is of thy gift if I do give it. To love thee with all my heart and soul, and to follow in the steps of Him who died for me, how **can I** do this except through thee? Let my soul cleave fast to thee, for on thee all its strength depends.'"[*]

Editha's face kindled as she repeated these words with a deep and joyful enthusiasm which broke through her reserve.

"It seemed to me," she said, "as if music, incense, priests, people, solid walls, all vanished like a dream, **and I saw** only the unseen—God the Almighty giving his Son **for** me, Jesus the Lord giving his life for me. I knew before that God had loved us, but I never knew how much. I knew there was a Redeemer, but I never understood we were really redeemed. It seems as **if I** could give or suffer anything in return for love like that."

Marguerite awoke the next morning with a feeling of awe in her heart, as Editha's words came back to her. It seemed as if an invisible presence had touched her for

---

[*] From Anselm's Meditations, quoted by Dr. Hamilton in his "Christian Classics."

the first time, and as if her former life had been a dream, and this were waking.

Editha woke with a heart full of lowliness and joy. It seemed as if all her former life had been spent in the night, and this were day. And she felt a strange new delight in the thought of the humble labours to which she was called in the convent. "For God, for Christ," seemed written on every duty; and the lowlier the sweeter to her who had been redeemed by the shame and agony of the cross.

Not long afterward she saw Father Osyth, and told him how the words of Archbishop Anselm had entered into her inmost heart.

"Yes, yes," he said. "Dearer to Archbishop Anselm, they say, to hold communion with God in his cell than to sit on the archbishop's throne; and yet he hath courage to resist the fierce king for what he deems right. Moreover," continued the old man, "he doth honour to our Saxon saints; for once when Archbishop Lanfranc spoke slightingly of our archbishop, the martyr St. Alphege, (who suffered the Danes to kill him, his gray head falling under the cruel missiles, rather than exact an enormous ransom from his poor plundered fellow-citizens,) and said it was unreasonable to call a man a martyr who died not for the Christian faith, but because he would not ransom his life from the enemy, Anselm replied: 'Nay, it is certain that he who died rather than offend God by a small offense, would much rather have died than provoke him by a greater sin. Alphege would not ransom his life, because he would not allow his dependents to be distressed by losing their property for him; much less, therefore, would he have denied his Saviour if the fury of the people had attempted by fear of death to force him to such a crime. He who dies for the cause of truth and righteousness is a martyr, as St. John the Baptist was, who suffered, not because he would not deny Christ, but because he resolved, in maintaining the law of God, not to shrink from speaking the truth.'"

"I see," said Editha, "it is then obedience in which God delights, whether in little things or in great. That makes so many things plain and easy to me, Father Osyth."

"It is well, my child," was the old man's reply. "Archbishop Anselm also saith that the heart is like a mill, ever grinding, which should only grind the Master's grain, but oftentimes an enemy throws in sand and gravel, or pitch, or dirt and chaff. The mill ever grinding is the heart ever thinking; the gravel and dirt are evil thoughts, and the good grain meditations concerning God and holy things. Keep thou thy heart then full of the fine wheat, my daughter, and there will be no room for the enemy to throw in his chaff."

IV.

WHILST Marguerite de Garenne and Editha the daughter of Aldred the Thane were thus passing tranquil days in the convent, the young lords Bernard and Walter, and Siward the man-at-arms, were faring very differently. Deeds rather than thoughts were their fare, or, if thought came, it was of that rude and intense vitality which springs up amidst the tempest in the crevices of active life.

The Crusade was set in array among the forests and vineyards on the hilly banks of the Moselle, under the leadership of the brave and devout Godfrey of Bouillon; the only successful crusade—the only crusade which could boast of "Jerusalem delivered."

Both Bernard and Siward found the names of their races everywhere as they wandered through Europe, the great expedition necessarily dividing itself into various bands, so as to find shelter and food by the way, and not by their mere numbers prove a curse to the lands they traversed.

On many a rocky promontory along the southern shores of Europe, Bernard found some of his daring and restless kinsmen established in castles overlooking some captured town or guarding some fair harbour. Siward, on the other hand, found the names of his countrymen not among the living terrors of mankind, but among their sainted dead. Along the Rhine, in remote corners of Germany or Switzerland, in abbey and church, in city and village, he came on the name of his countrymen among the benefactors of the country. The shrines of the Saxon Willibrord, the Saxon Winfried (Boniface and Clement), the evangelist of Friesland, and the apostle of Germany, were only second in the reverence of the people to those of apostles or martyrs of apostolic times.

One evening when the troop were riding silently along the banks of the Rhine, relying on their privileges as crusaders to bear them safely past the robber strongholds which were then beginning to bristle on the heights, the bell of a village church called them to vespers.

As soldiers of the cross, they dismounted, in turn, to pay their devotion at the altar and to receive the priestly benediction. When the service was finished, the priest, hearing that they came from England, gave them a cordial welcome, and a blessing in the name of the patrons

14*

of his church, the Black and the White Hewald, who, four hundred years ago, had come, he said, from Saxon England to preach the faith to the heathen on the Rhine, and on that spot had laid down their lives in martyrdom.

"This honour is due to you," said Bernard turning to Siward; "our Norman pedigrees have contributed little, I fear, to the list of the saints."

It was decided that the little troop should accept the good priest's hospitality, and remain that night under his roof, Siward and the other Saxon men-at-arms, by the alliance of their mother-tongue with that of the villagers, being moreover able to make their wants understood.

The rest of the troop were soon asleep for the night on the rushes strewn in the priest's kitchen; but the incident of that evening had awakened many thoughts in Siward's mind. The priest and he prolonged their conversation late into the night, discoursing of names well known to both, of Boniface and Willibrord, and of the last mission of the Saxon Church; how at his own request English priests and teachers were sent to king Olave of Norway, and how he embraced the faith and was baptized; how afterward he showed his gratitude by helping with his ships to drive the Danes from London, destroying London Bridge, which linked the Danish armies at Southwark and London together; and how at length he proved the sincerity of his faith by dying for it—king Olave, saint and martyr. Long after the conversation ceased, Siward lay awake thinking how times had changed, and wondering over again David's old wonder at the prosperity of the wicked.

"We were not the Pharisees," he thought. "We did not seek to shut others out of the kingdom of heaven.

Our fathers opened its gates to nations. Norway, Friesland, Rhineland, and Old Saxony, trace the first dawning of their Christianity to Saxon England. And now these Normans, who never did good to man or nation—a people without books, without saints, without a purpose in the world except selfish wealth and selfish power—drive us out of home and country, plunder our towns, ruin our homes, desecrate the shrines of our saints, and none come to our help in heaven or earth."

It was the old bitter cry of human impatience, "Our life endures but a day, and shall the steps of God's justice be measured by centuries?"

"Why sayest thou, O Jacob, and speakest, O Israel, My way is hid from the Lord, and my judgment is passed over from my God?"

Siward rose softly from among his sleeping comrades, and went into the little church. There, by the graves of his martyred countrymen, larger and less bitter thoughts came to him.

"It is on the graves of martyrs I kneel," he thought, "and the graves have become shrines of the very faith for which they died."

Eternity seemed to expand around time, like the starry, boundless heavens above the earth. Going back over the past, he thought how long it was since the last mission had gone forth from Saxon England. Then this cheering thought came:

"Perhaps God thought our nation *worth chastening*. He does not waste his ploughing on the barren sand. Perhaps we are but living in one of the seed-times of the ages, and the harvest will be better than we can think."

Then recurring to his own life, he thought how far

sweeter and better his Editha was than any woman he had ever seen, and how sorrow had made her so. And humble thoughts followed—such as spring naturally from true and deep love—of his own unworthiness. He who knelt on the graves of martyrs and claimed them for his kindred, and their deeds as his people's heritage, what end had led him hither? Was it truly for the wrongs of his people he felt, or for his own? What right had he to claim the sacred name of a soldier of the cross, he whose purpose in this war had been simply to regain his own freedom? Were his aims, although purer and more legitimate, really more disinterested than those of the Normans he so denounced?

A large cross rose before him in the moonlight. It seemed for the first time revealed to him what it meant—the sins and selfishness that had brought the sinless One to his cross—the love and fullness of sacrifice.

The vows and the pomp of chivalry were unknown to Siward. No princely hand gave him the accolade of knighthood; but there rose that night from the lonely shrine of the martyred Hewalds as true a knight as ever strove to defend the innocent and the helpless.

"I go a pilgrim to the Holy Sepulchre," he thought; "yet if my heart fixes its highest earthly hopes on a Saxon home, I think it is no desecration—the desecration has been in my proud and murmuring heart. The expiation is not in the cross I bear, but in the cross borne for me. I have heard Father Osyth say that the true pilgrimage is that to the Holy Jerusalem above; and that can be carried on everywhere. Day by day, wherever I am, may I have grace to be a true soldier of the cross, to do what good I can, and redress what wrong I can. And then I trust each day, whether I reach the Holy Sepulchre or not, will bring me nearer God, and nearer Editha, who serves God better than any one I know. What place thou wilt on earth!" he prayed, "O Lord Christ, who didst bear for us the cross, only let me be thy servant like these thy martyrs of old!"

A new dignity came into Siward's life from that night—the dignity of eternity. For the bristling armour of pride, strong only to wound, and powerless to guard from wounds, he became clothed with humility. Many a rude jest which would have pierced him to the quick, glanced lightly from him, as from one who treats lightly the slights of a strange country through which he is only passing to a home where he will be known.

And Siward's humility was not that of an angel who, having stooped from heaven, has no measurements small enough wherewith to measure the little degrees of earth. It was the humility of a man awakened to feel not his sinfulness only, but his sins; who has discovered in his own heart the sins he has been despising in others, and from the depths of humiliation to which repentance has brought him, finds any step God leads him in life a step upward.

Thus unconsciously the hearts of Editha and Siwald were drawn closer to each other, even whilst their steps were being sundered farther and farther.

V.

IT was the evening before the final assault of the Crusaders on Jerusalem. Three years of common peril and mutual aid had taught Bernard de Garenne and Siward the Saxon to understand each other. Siward had learned the true courage and feeling that lay under the gaiety and lightheartedness of the Norman. Bernard had discovered the fervour of affection and power of thought that were hidden under the reserve and silence of the Saxon. On many a weary march, and in many a perilous encounter, the steady persevering courage of the one had blended well with the quickness and daring of the other. Siward had grown to honour the gaiety which made light of privation and peril, and the ready wit which found a way out of many an ill he would have met simply by endurance. Bernard had learned to reverence the unobtrusive unflinching valour, which needed no pomp of splendour or fame to feed its steady fire. The qualities which, in the fusion of centuries, were to mould Norman and Saxon into Englishmen, already proved the strength of their alliance in the deeds of that little crusading troop.

It was Holy Thursday, the 14th of April, 1099. All had been made ready for the assault. Confessions had been made, vows had been renewed. The holy sacrament had been received. Arms had been sharpened and repaired to their highest point of efficiency, and now, except a few on guard, the besieging host lay slumbering outside the walls of the city. Bernard and Siward were on guard. The strange brilliancy of a Syrian night lighted up the hills around which should have been green and glowing then with the burst of the Syrian spring, but were brown and bare with the devastations of the besieging army. Before them rose the lofty walls, surmounted by the domes and roofs of the sacred city, to them still mysterious and untrodden ground.

But their thoughts wandered far away to the land which was the home of both. Words sealed up at all other times came naturally to the lips which might be silent for ever in death on the morrow.

"Siward," said the Norman, "on that morning of our departure, in the chapel in the forest, there was a witness you knew not of. If you should be among to-morrow's slain, I swear upon this relic of the holy cross, your widowed bride shall be a charge as sacred as my own sister; and if I should fall, I have my father's promise that the lands of old Aldred, her father, shall be yours. And in after years, you can tell your bride that the thought of her, and of some words she once spoke to me, have been like sacred relics in my heart, guarding me in many an hour of temptation. I ventured once," he added after a pause, "to speak lightly of her betrothal to you, and to urge her to transfer her affection to one who could offer her a home worthier of her. But she said, 'If ever you love truly you will know that woe binds hearts as weal never can, that the heart is not nourished with *things*, and that, from God himself and Christ the Redeeming Lord, to every heart in which his image is, love has a joy in sacrificing greater infinitely than any of the poor joys of receiving.' Tell her that her words and her acts, and her pure, heavenly face as I saw it that morning at the altar, have again and again stripped off the disguise from empty pomp and hollow pleasure, and raised my life to another level altogether; and that if I die here, at the Sepulchre of the Lord, it will not be without having learned something of the love of Him who sacrificed himself for us, and something of the joy of sacrificing self for him."

"She never told me of this!" said Siward.

That night they said no more to each other. Before long the guard was changed, and Siward and Bernard did not meet again until the assault began on the morrow.

The night of Good Friday closed over Jerusalem. The crusading assault had succeeded. The banner of the cross floated over the battlements. Where once the rude cross of wood had risen outside the silent city and above the sepulchre not yet empty, but enshrining the body of the Redeemer, the red-cross banners waved over a city not silent, indeed, but echoing with the moans and cries of men and women in their death-agony. Of all the horrors witnessed on those hills, of all the despairing anguish echoed by those rocky valleys, probably none were surpassed by the events of that day. Jerusalem that night was one huge sepulchre. Of seventy thousand Mohammedans who had possessed the city before the assault, it is said not enough were left after it to bury the dead.

Siward and Bernard were separated in the assault. It was not until dusk, when the fight was over, and while the slaughter was proceeding, that Siward succeeded in finding his chief. Where the slain were piled thick at an angle of the wall, Siward first recognized the corpse of the young knight Walter, Marguerite's betrothed, the hands clenched, and the white face turned up to the sky. Then a low moan guided him to Bernard, and leaning down towards him, he caught the words,—

"O God, let me die somewhere out of hearing of those shrieks of agony."

Gently, Siward, and a Saxon bowman who accompanied him, raised their wounded lord, and carried him to a house which had been built of old for pilgrims, where they found a quiet, empty room in which to place him.

There Siward watched him night and day until the fever of his wounds began to give place to the conscious weakness of recovery. And very close was the attachment which thus grew between them.

"The capture of the Holy City has been no festival to thee!" said Bernard one day, as the Saxon brought him some savoury soldier's mess he had prepared with his own hands.

"A more Christian festival to me than to most," was the grim reply. "I know not with what heart men can plead for mercy at the very Calvary of the patient suffering Lord, whose ears were deaf to the cries for mercy of tortured women and children."

"But they were infidels; they would have crucified the Lord himself!" said Bernard.

"I know not," was the answer. "Mohammedan little children are so like others. Their little wailing, piteous voices ring in my ears still."

"But they were unbaptized," said Bernard.

"So, for aught I know, were the babes who sang the hosannas," replied Siward; "and yet the Lord would not have their little lisping songs silenced."

"Is Godfrey of Bouillon crowned King of Jerusalem yet?"

"Nay," replied Siward; "they say he will not be crowned with gold where Christ the Lord was crowned with thorns."

"He is a brave and Christian knight," said Bernard.

A few days afterward, Siward supported Bernard's still tottering steps to the Church of the Holy Sepulchre. The wreck and bloodshed of the terrible Good Friday had still left traces within the walls; but once more silver lamps were burning before the Tomb and the Hill which have been the shrine of so many centuries; and the perfume of the incense filled every recess of that irregular building, with its many sanctuaries.

Bernard, keenly sensitive to external impressions and associations, was absorbed in devotion. Reverently he knelt at every shrine, kissing the stones which covered the sacred earth.

When they reached their home again, he said fervently,—

"It is worth while to have encountered perils and privations tenfold what we have endured, to have seen and felt what I have felt to-day!"

Siward was silent.

"It is not the first time you have experienced the overpowering emotion of that sacred place?" Bernard added, looking to his friend for a response.

"I am appalled at my own coldness," said Siward at length, abruptly. "I have felt nearer God, and more full of adoring gratitude to our Lord, at almost every church I have worshipped in, than at the Holy Sepulchre, the sanctuary of sanctuaries. Between me and the face once crowned with thorns there, and bowed in death for us, intrude perpetually the crowd of agonized, imploring human faces I saw there after the assault. The unheeded cries of those helpless sufferers drown to my ears the echo of that voice of supremest agony and tenderest pity. I long," he concluded, bitterly, "to be out of Jerusalem again, that there may be silence enough in my memory for me to hear once more the voice of the Redeemer."

Bernard sighed.

"My wounds must have saved me much," he said. "But I also long to return. I would not that Marguerite should hear of her bereavement from any one but me.

Poor little tender sister, full to this day, doubtless, of her happy dreams!"

The next Sunday, Siward took Bernard to one of the lonely heights of the Mount of Olives.

There, under the shade of an old olive which had survived the siege, they looked across the Kidron valley to the city—the towers of Sion rising behind the sloping platform of Moriah. The sunset, which beamed back from the west on the eastern hills of Moab, touched dome, and minaret, and all the dreary ruins of the shattered walls with beauty, and lighted up here and there the white and crimson banners of the cross, waving from tower and battlement.

"This is my sacred place," said Siward, softly. "Just below, among the olives, is the Garden of Gethsemane. We are standing on the foot-path to Bethany. From the height above us, where the church stands (then bare and lonely), the Lord ascended. Such a cloud as that we see floating on the golden sea where the sun has set, hid Him from the apostles' sight. Hidden from our sight still, but no more lost than the sun which has sunk below these western hills, He is there in heaven now, looking down on us, on his own empty sepulchre, on these sepulchral valleys heavy with countless dead; and looking down on England, on suffering Saxon England! In that crime-laden city, the echoes of despairing human voices seem to me to drown all heavenly music. But here upon these lonely hills, where His feet have trod, I seem to see the stain of that atoning blood blotting out in its deeper dye all other stains. I seem to hear His cry, 'Why hast thou forsaken me?'—His prayer, 'Father, forgive them, they know not what they do'—His triumphant dying words, 'It is finished,' deep beneath all the din and tumult. I can bow and think, 'Thou hast suffered, thou hast triumphed, thou livest!' and wait to have all the rest answered when I see His face."

VI.

MANY years afterward, Bernard brought a Norman bride to his castle on the hill; Siward and Editha lived tranquilly in the homestead of Aldred the Thane; and in the valley between the castle and the farm was slowly rising, on the green meadows by the river side, a Cistercian nunnery, of which Marguerite was abbess.

There was much still to separate the Saxon home from the Norman fortress; yet there were sacred recollections and honoured names common to both. The links of the chains which were to bind Saxon and Norman into one English nation were being slowly fused—although, meantime, there was more to be seen of the forge fires, and more to be heard of the forge hammers, than of the result.

A middle class was growing up, with ancestry nobler and worthier far, in their belief, than that of the stranger race who had so suddenly seized the position of the upper class. Saxon franklins, whose grandfathers had been thanes or ealdormen, or even of right royal race, could not look with complacency on Norman barons whose fathers had been penniless adventurers, or mere men-at-arms in the Conqueror's army. To the Normans, on the other hand, the noblest Saxon names were such a jest as Pilate would have made of the royal title of Israel. As yet, the fall and the defeat, the wrong and the plunder, were too recent for any one to perceive the advantage to the nation of a middle class, whose origin was as high as that of the aristocracy, and whose history was far nobler.

Thus, as yet, everything was seen under two aspects throughout the land. To the Norman, the massive and elaborate churches, rising everywhere on the sites of the old abbeys, were a boon to England, enough to compensate for countless ruins; to the Saxon, they were the vain attempts of old age to atone for the devastations and crimes of youth. The old unadorned shrines of dishonoured Saxon saints were more sacred in their eyes than the most magnificent Norman piles.

The church was the great place of meeting for the two races; and yet the church itself was not precisely the same to the conquered and the conqueror. While the Norman abbot entertained noble guests with princely hospitality in the refectory, and won their admiration for the lofty arches and rich carving of the new church, which he had summoned foreign architects to design, the Saxon monks jealously guarded the relics of the Saxon saint, whose memory had originally consecrated the place, and kept alive in the hearts of farmer and peasant the good deeds of better times.

Religion was the great bond of union between the possessor and the dispossessed; and yet religion itself took a varied colouring from their various circumstances and national tendencies.

The words of Wolfstan, Saxon Bishop of Worcester, who died in 1050, were no doubt echoed in many a Saxon heart. On the very day that he began to rebuild his cathedral at Worcester, he was observed by one of his monks standing mournful and silent in the church-yard. The monk endeavoured to console him by comparing the beauty of the buildings of those days with the simple erections of old Saxon times. "I judge otherwise," said the bishop. "We pull down the labours of holy men to glorify ourselves. The good old time was when men knew not how to build magnificent piles, but thought any roof good enough if they could offer themselves a willing sacrifice to God. It is a miserable change if we neglect the souls of men to pile stones together." These words have doubtless been recorded as the utterance of many a silent conviction; and in them lay the germ of the Puritanism which in after days took such deep root among the Saxon people of England.

Once more the heavy bolts were drawn within the doors of the old homestead of Aldred the Thane. A motley group was gathered around the fire. The younger children were asleep; the eldest boy, Wilfrid, sat mending his Saxon bow beside his mother Editha, and his sister, who were carding wool. The warm corner by the hearth, where the blind old thane had been used to sit, was occupied by Father Osyth, now a feeble and white-haired old man. The rest of the party were Siward, his cousin Frithric the forester, and a pale young man, scarcely more than a lad, with a frank and gentle expression.

The boy Wilfrid was listening breathlessly as Frithric told the history of their latest adventures; how he had come forth at dawn from the forest with his men, and scattered a party of the sheriff's men, who were leading off the pale stranger to cut off his right hand in the market-place, as a punishment for stealing the king's deer.

"That same right hand shall despatch many a royal stag yet!" he concluded, laying his hand on the lad's shoulder. "That is the way the Normans recruit for the bold foresters. Thou shalt lead a merry life yet among us, my son."

But the young man did not seem exhilerated with the prospect.

"They will do my mother some mischief yet for this!" he said. "She is a widow, and is alone in her farm, and has none but me to care for her. I would my right hand had been cut off before it shot the king's deer."

Editha looked up compassionately.

"Where was thy mother's farm?" she said.

"On the meadows on the other side of the river," he said.

Editha was silent; but the boy Wilfrid exclaimed,—

"Mother, that was where we saw the flames last night. They must have burned the house down already."

"Hush, Wilfrid," said Editha; "we cannot tell. There is more than one house on the meadows."

"But, mother," said the girl Alice, "a poor woman was brought this morning into the convent while I was at school, and they said her house had been burned because her son had killed the king's deer. And the poor woman was ill with fright; but the Lady Marguerite spoke very kindly to her, and said she would nurse her herself."

The lad's composure gave way.

"I shall never see my mother again," he said; "and the poor cattle that knew my voice, and my father's horse that would follow me like a dog—poor beasts, they must all be dead!—for no one but me could have got them out of the fire."

"Thou shalt have thy vengeance yet!" said the forester. "The Norman lips that had their jest, no doubt, at the agonies of the poor dying brutes and at the terrors of thy mother, shall be set to another tune before long. There are men in England yet who will see justice done, in spite of baron and sheriff, according to the good old Saxon laws. And there is another home for thy mother yet than the French lady's convent."

"Do not say anything against the Lady Marguerite, Cousin Frithric," said Alice, colouring. "She is my godmother, and she is good to all alike."

"I say no evil of her, child," said Frithric. "It is not her fault if she is a Frenchwoman; nor yours," he added, with some bitterness, "if you are her godchild."

Editha felt the sting of the words, but answered gently—

"Thou knowest, kinsman, what ties bind me to that poor lady, and how sorely she has been smitten. How could I refuse any comfort I could give to a heart which sorrow has made tender to all and bitter to none? I would sorrow did as much for all as for her?"

"Sorrows are different," said Frithric; "some soften and some harden."

"And characters are different," rejoined Editha; "the fire which melts ice hardens iron."

"And water and steel both are needed in the world," said Siward. "Our kinsman Frithric, I deem, my wife, has his work as well as thou hast thine. Go to the forest, boy," he added, "since the Norman laws have outlawed thee. But let the thought of thy widowed mother and thy poor dumb beasts make thee as merciful to Norman women as brave against their men. It was not the Norman cattle nor Norman widows who have done thee wrong. Thou shalt have tidings of thy mother often, I promise thee."

Far into the night the little party sat. Frithric had many a thrilling tale to tell of Norman tyranny baffled, and Saxon widows and fatherless children dowered with ransoms won from captured Norman knights. And Father Osyth kindled up, and told how the Saxon monks of Glastonbury had won the victory over their avaricious and tyrannical Norman abbot; how, after proving their monastic obedience by suffering themselves to be nearly starved, and robbed of their costly library, they had risen in open mutiny against some new fashionable church music the abbot attempted to introduce from Normandy, and had held the church in defense of their Gregorian tones; how the abbot had called in the soldiery, and the arrows from outside had pierced sacred screen and sculpture, yet the monks stood firm; how at length, when the abbot and the soldiers forced an entrance into the church, the monks had driven them out with such weapons as candlesticks and forms, and finally had compelled the Conqueror himself to withdraw the abbot and restore the Gregorian tones.

"It is for law," Frithric said, "and not for lawlessness, the Saxons fight in forest or abbey—for the good old music and the good old Saxon laws. The Normans made the fruitful field a forest, and we make the forest a city of refuge and a hall of justice."

And so the party separated for the night; and before the dawn the forester and the widow's son were away among the secret passages and in the hidden recesses of the Saxon castle, the free forest, which no Norman could safely penetrate.

The next day Editha went with her young daughter Alice to the convent.

The Lady Marguerite met her at the door of the infirmary, and embracing her as a sister, led her in to see the sick widow.

"Say some words to her—you will cheer her better than I can. The Norman accent makes my best words, I fear, bitter to her."

Editha had tidings wherewith to console the widowed mother; and a few whispered words brought a new light into the poor woman's face.

Afterward she and Marguerite went together alone to prepare some herb cordials, of which Editha had learned the secret in her childhood.

Marguerite's thin, white face was very sad as she bent over the herbs; and at length she said, "Will nothing ever bridge over the gulf between my people and yours, Editha? Or shall I never have suffered enough to find the key you have to sorrowful hearts? I have so little wisdom."

Editha told her the secret which had given her the power to cure the widow. Then she said, "I think every kind word and holy loving work is a stone in the bridge which is one day to bind my people to yours. But it takes longer to repair a cottage than to ruin a cathedral. Are there not links already between some of my people and thine? Did not I receive the message which has made my life glad from the Archbishop Anselm, appointed by your Norman king?"

"And did not I learn all the good I know from thee?" said Marguerite. "Truly, if true love between one Norman and one Saxon can form one link in the chain, thy heart and mine have begun it."

"I have heard," said Editha, "that, on the western shores of England, where the sea beats in the sand so as to cover and overwhelm wall after wall, there is a grass which grows in the sand itself, whose slender stalks and roots, silently entwining around each other, form a barrier which keeps back the sand and preserves the fields. How hopeless that little grass plant might feel its work as it looked up to the massive stone wall! and yet together they do what no walls can. Is not love like that?"

"It seems very little just to love and try to do little kind deeds," said the Lady Marguerite.

"And yet," said Editha, "I think your beautiful great abbey church, with its lofty arches and pillars, and your brother's castle, with its massive walls will perish long before the fruits of your quiet acts of mercy."

That night it was debated in the castle of Bernard de Garenne what measures should be taken against those daring Saxon foresters who had assaulted the sheriff. Some said no good would ever be done while one Saxon homestead was left to give shelter to the outlaws, and proposed a renewal of the old wars of extermination.

But Bernard said,—

"I owe too much to the faithful services of a Saxon man, the owner of such a homestead, ever to hunt down the Saxons like brutes."

And a few days afterward, when, in the secret councils of the outlaws in the forest, some of the fiercer spirits spoke of effectual vengeance on the Normans, and made dark allusions to the massacre of the Danes, the feeble voice of the aged widow interposed,—

"The Normans are Christians after all—not heathens, like the old Danes. Whatever you do, let warning be sent to the Lady Marguerite, who waited on me with her own hands as if I had been a queen."

History records the building and the ruin of the stone sea-walls, the irruption of the sands, and, finally, the mysterious checking of the enemy's progress; but it speaks not of the little lowly grass which wove the barrier. She records the struggles of kings and barons, the conquest, the misery of the conquered; and, finally, after many generations, she notes that the name of Englishman replaces those of Norman and Saxon. But of the little every-day human kindnesses, the sympathies, and services, and homely charities, slowly linking race with race, she can see little. The battle-cry, the stormy debate, reach her ear through the ages; but the soft words of peace and consolation, the voice of thanksgiving and of prayer, die away in the little circle for which they were spoken. She sees the church built and levelled, but knows little of the worship that went up within its walls to God. She sees the homes reared and ruined, but can tell little of the joys and sorrows, the sacrifice and service, of the home-life by which hearts were trained there for heaven.

These are for another history, to be read in a day to which probably much of our most pompous secular history will be as idle gossip, and much of our church history will seem secular—a thing not of eternity, but of the age—from a volume which shall be, not a record of death and destruction, but a Book of Life.

IX.

A STORY OF THE LOLLARDS.

IX.

A STORY OF THE LOLLARDS.

CUTHBERT'S TALE.

IT is scarcely ten years since I entered the order of St. Francis, the Friars Minorites, against all the prayers of my kindred, believing surely in my inmost heart that I was thereby devoting myself, in the most entire way possible, to God and to the good of my brother man. And now I sit here in the prison of the Grey Friars in London, on suspicion of holding what they call the heresy of the spiritual Franciscans, the "Everlasting Gospel" of the Abbot Joachim, and the prophecies of Oliva. Whether they accuse unjustly or not, I can scarcely myself say. It would be very pleasant to believe, as the "Everlasting Gospel" says, that this age is about soon altogether to pass away, and be succeeded by a time of progress and peace—the age of the Spirit; but who knows? From my heart all certainty of good and truth is utterly gone. Only the certainty of wickedness and falsehood remains. The gloom of this prison is nothing compared with the horror of great darkness in my soul. I would be content to bear any severities those false Franciscans—dark spies on men's thoughts, well named Black Friars—could inflict, to win back my early unquestioning faith, to obtain but one glimpse of something on earth worth living for, or in heaven worth dying for.

But if the earth be indeed the chaos of wickedness, and lies, and hypocrisy it seems to me, where can be the reality? Can it be possible that this world has been given finally over to the devil? Oh for the sign of the Son of man in heaven, even though it were a sign of unmingled terror, to sweep this evil earth away, and proclaim some better time! Oh for one more of those "Woe unto you, scribes and Pharisees, hypocrites!" spoken, not with pathetic human tones on the hills of Judæa, but with divine thunders from the heavens, shivering for evermore all lies and hollow seemings into nothingness!

Yet who am I, to denounce fire from heaven on hypocrites—I who, it may be, am a worse hypocrite than any I denounce? For have I not proclaimed heavenly pardons to poor trusting souls, by the right of an authority which I know to be a fountain, not of truth and equity, but of iniquity and falsehood?

Oh that anywhere I knew of such a decree of pardon as those poor men and women received with grateful hearts from me!

Yet, would I wish to kneel where they knelt? Would I believe what they believe, since it cannot be true? Would I, if I could, have the magic veil drawn over my eyes again, and go forth as these do, smiling, trusting, with lying pardons in my hand, to meet death and eternity, when I am sure that not a line of those purchased absolutions will be recognized by God?

Yes, *I am sure.* Here my doubts end, and my terrible

certainties begin. I am certain that the pardons which are issued in unlimited numbers, not to spiritual Franciscans to bestow on burdened consciences, not to humble parish priests to declare to those they know to be penitent, but to wandering friars to hawk about like ballads to those who have a few pence to spare, for money wherewith to furnish luxurious convents and gorgeous churches for these same poverty-vowed beggars—I am certain they will be of no avail in the day of wrath with the Judge of dreadful majesty.

Were there ever such evil times as these? Peasants ground down until their despair gives them a brutal courage for worse than brutal revenge; nobles living in alternate revelry and bloodshed; priests only abstaining from war to indulge themselves more at leisure in every sensual indulgence they have forsworn; friars, vowed to poverty, rivalling the priests in splendour and luxury. This I have seen everywhere in Germany, France, and Lombardy. How different this, to the hopes with which I entered the order!

I had read in my childhood a life of St. Francis, how he forsook father, and home, and fortune, to follow Christ—not seeking merely to obtain a solitary crown of sanctity for himself by self-mortification in the desert, but devoting himself to the poor, the outcast, the lepers; converting publicans and sinners into saints by his loving example, and startling false saints into true penitence by the vision in him of the reality they simulated. Most heavenly and beautiful the life seemed to me, and most Christ-like. At first scorned and buffeted alike by saint and sinner, at last he was reverenced alike by all. Eden seemed to spring up around his child-like heart; the very beasts and birds (it was said) owned his gentle sway, as when they came to innocent Adam in the garden and he gave them names. But none of these things were his reward. The wealth of the wealthiest would willingly have been thrown at his feet, who had renounced all for Christ; but this was not his reward. Fame, gold, homage, were absolutely worthless to him whose heart had become like that of a little child. They gave him no joy. Poverty was his bride; all created things—rivers and streams, clouds and storms, fire and cold, forest trees and the wild creatures that found shelter among them—were his brothers and sisters, creatures of his Father, sure to minister to him all that his Father knew him to need. Not from gold-filled coffers he drew his maintenance—exhaustible when fullest, and at best mere lifeless stores—but from that open, ever-full hand of God, whose touch in giving made the smallest gift bliss unspeakable. Then there were mysterious, wondrous stories, about the likeness to our Lord, so matured in his heart, being outwardly stamped on his emaciated frame— of the prints of the nails being indented in his thin hands.

Poverty had been his chosen bride. At length Death was his sister; all terror vanished from her face, she gently took him by the hand, and led him into the presence of the Father. On earth there was the weeping of the wretched he had succoured, and left orphaned again. In heaven there were the singing and the welcomes of the happy saints who through him had been lifted from the lazar-house to the golden streets.

Nor had St. Francis scaled these heights as a daring and inimitable adventurer, to plant a trophy on some inaccessible summit, for other men to gaze at from below and wonder. Close in his footsteps followed a few devoted men; and in a short time the few grew to an army, swarming eastward, westward, northward, and southward—not like the Crusaders, streaming to one point, but seeking everywhere strongholds of Satan to storm and enemies to conquer, in Barbary, in the East, in the forests by the Rhine, on the heights of the Apennines, on the French and Lombard plains, and here in this England.

On the Cornhill in the city of London was still pointed out to me the site where, little more than a century before, the first Franciscans had built their little huts, stuffing the crevices with hay and straw to keep out the unwonted damp of our climate. There in these huts they had been heard at all hours of the day and night chanting their joyful hymns or pathetic litanies, and had been seen issuing forth to the lazar-houses and the haunts of lowest poverty—embracing the lowest as their brethren, dressing the wounds of the diseased, sharing their crusts with the meanest, and winning them to the loving Saviour by the force of love. When the authorities threatened to hang them as vagabonds, they offered their own rope-girdles as halters, and the death which had no terrors for them was thus through wonder or contempt averted from them. When the jealous stationary monks, from their well-stocked tables, sent them broken scraps and sour beer, they were heard making merry over the churlish fare as children at a feast. And then their sermons! Men and women, who had crept in twos and threes to church, to listen sleepily to the four annual homilies of the priests, in the same style and on the same themes, crowded in thousands to the open-air sermons of the friars. They wept to hear of their sins and their peril, and they repented. They wept to hear of the love of

Christ. They brought their most precious things as willing offerings to those who had brought them blessings more precious far.

It is true I had not myself seen exactly such men nor heard such words; but the order existed, the rule continued, and somewhere, I thought, I was sure to find such men, and in some way to become such myself.

Bitter, bitter years! as slowly one by one the veils fell from my eyes, and I learned that the old framework indeed endured, but the life was gone!

I only learned this slowly; because I always hoped to find my paradise of simple and devoted hearts somewhere beyond, and yet beyond.

In the world I had expected to find hollowness and wickedness. It did not, therefore, surprise me to see in Germany, France and Lombardy, what I had seen in England—the powerful tyrannizing over the weak; the weak revenging themselves on the weaker still; prince, noble, burgher, peasant, all striving to climb to those above, to press down those below; and those who were lowest of all enduring like brutes, until the time came when they could take a brute's revenge. Petty wars of nobles with each other and with the cities; fierce insurrections of maddened peasants, springing from despair, and crushed by atrocious punishment into despair again —these things did not surprise me, though they made my heart ache. This was the world—the world which the earlier monks had sought to *flee*, and St. Francis to *save*.

Nor did the secularity of the secular clergy much amaze me. From my childhood I had heard enough of that.

The bitter disappointment was, to find that everywhere

among the followers of St. Francis himself the endeavour to follow him truly was looked on as a folly, if not as a heresy.

The nearer I approached the centre of light, the greater appeared the confusion and failure. To us in England the Pope's court may still seem a holy tribunal, where appeal can be made from the injustice of man to the justice of God; in Avignon, where the Pope lived, the Papal decisions are said to be determined by nothing save money or fear. Avignon itself was a place none could stay in with safety.

Italy, when I was there, was to the rest of Europe what the thick of the battle is to its outskirts. There the strife was more incessant, the crimes more inhuman, the vengeance more atrocious, than elsewhere. Under the sacred banner of the Pope (although it is said, not in his pay, because the Pope disliked paying), Sir John Hawkwood and other chiefs of the free companies ravaged the country and sacked the cities.

Rome, after the brief attempt to restore the old freedom by Rienzi, was abandoned, the palaces burned, and the churches lay open to the wind and rain.

In the midst of all these horrors, occasionally wild troops of penitents would march, wailing and shrieking litanies, through forest and city, scourging themselves as they went, and tracking their path in their own blood.

In the south of France men could still remember how for the last century one horror had succeeded another, and how in fair Languedoc a whole prosperous nation had been crushed into despair by the crusade against the Albigenses. I saw the ruined cities and the castles blackened with fire. Then had come an insurrection of the peasants, turning into a crusade against the Jews.

I saw the pestilential marshes near the Rhone where at last the peasants, entrapped thither by the idea of going into the Holy Land, perished of disease by thousands, until the remainder were weak enough to be massacred. All this the Pope might almost have heard and seen from his gilded palace at Avignon.

Within men's memory, also, was the destruction of the Templars and of the lepers. Everywhere accusations of frightful crimes, followed by atrocious vengeance! In those wicked times nothing seemed too monstrously wicked for men to believe. The torturing and burning of noble knights and crusaders was followed, in a few years, by the torturing and the burning throughout France of the poor outcast lepers, the wretched sufferers St. Francis sought to cheer and save.

And with these dreadful deeds sprang up all kinds of monstrous belief. In Milan, not long before I was there, Wilhelmine, a Bohemian lady, calling herself daughter of the Queen of Bohemia, had declared that in her the Holy Ghost was incarnate!

At length, one day, when I was walking in a mountain path between Lombardy and Switzerland, a man joined me in a slight and scanty dress, not like the flowing robe of any of the orders, nor yet like any peasant's rags. Its poverty seemed intentional. He had not even the friar's wallet. He would not even carry provision for the day. As we walked on together, he began to discourse on the wickedness of the world and the holiness of St. Francis, themes which naturally drew us together. More than once before, in lonely hermitages, or in the solitude of great cities, I had met men who professed to have found the truth all the rest of the world were vainly searching for. Some of these were peaceful and even joyful in their aspect; others were severe and bitter against the age; but I had so often been warned against the friends of God in Switzerland, the Albigenses, Paulicians, Waldenses, and other heretics, who were said still to linger in the south of France; I had, indeed, seen so many burnt with visible fire, and condemned to eternal fire, for so many heresies, that I had grown suspicious. It seemed so exceedingly difficult to pursue vigorously the way to heaven without running unintentionally against some doctrine of the Church, that of late I had grown hopeless and apathetic, striving to drive away the heresies which seemed so naturally to spring from thought, by not thinking, but mechanically reciting to myself litanies and psalms, at once to silence my own wandering thoughts and the wail of anguish, the tumults and blasphemies of the world.

But this stranger was so simple and orthodox in his discourse, and withal so devoted a Franciscan, that my suspicions were lulled; and in the evening, when he drew from his bosom a roll containing the Everlasting Gospel of the Abbot Joachim, I listened in a trance of delight. It seemed to me as if this might explain all. The true age of the Gospel, it is said, was not over—it was to come. There had been the age of the Father, the age of the law. The second age, the age of the Son, was rapidly, amidst convulsions and storms, drawing to its close. St. Francis, conformed in all things to Christ himself, came to usher in the true age of blessing, the third age—the age of the Spirit. The disorders, and miseries, and crimes around us were not to be wondered at; they were quite natural—they were the death agony of the old, the birth-agony of the new. We were living on the verge of the dawn of the days of peace, and holiness, and love, of freedom, brotherhood, and community of all things.

I listened, hoped, longed to believe—I thought I did believe—that I had found the lost truth, the hidden treasure. For joy of it I told it to all who would listen. I came home to my country to tell it to those I had known and loved of old ; and therefore am I here in this prison of the Minorites in London, on suspicion of heresy.

But, alas! here my Gospel seems to fail me. On what are its promises founded? Who can assure me the voice that spoke them is divine—that they are not merely the echo of our cries for light—not an answer, but an echo? The heart wailing, "All things here, how bitter and false!"—the seeming prophecy responding, "Bitter and false." The heart crying out, "Who will bring the day?"—the false Gospel replying, "I bring the day! the day!"

And if this be indeed a heresy, then am I not worse, more despicable, more criminal, more pitiable, than the most luxurious priest at the Papal court, the meanest purchaser of pardons, the most covetous seller of pardons, the worst leper, the vilest sinner who has kept pure in his poor distracted heart the holy faith I have lost?

The "nays" seem indeed to me plain enough! William of Ockham, defender of the spiritual Franciscans and glory of our order, seems to me to have proved plainly enough that the Popes are not infallible. My own eyes have seen that neither Rome nor Avignon is the heavenly Jerusalem. The Everlasting Gospel states that the outward corrupt Church is Babylon, the very antithesis to truth and holiness. Oh for three or four plain "yeas and amens," such as they say our Lord spoke on earth!—for but one!

So far I wrote yesterday, life seeming to lie like a chaos behind me, and the future like an unfathomable abyss before me. And this morning once more hope seems to dawn for me.

In the night I had a dream of my home in the days gone by, of my father and my mother walking out with us beyond the city in St. Giles' Fields on Easter Day; the river winding round the meadows to the great Abbey at Westminster; the meadows green with the first green of spring, and full of buttercups; the woods on the northern hills just softening into tender, delicate colours; my little sister Cicely yielding to my mother's care the precious posy of buttercups her little hands were too small to hold; my father telling me of his achievements with bow and arrow as we watched the apprentices shooting at the targets; my mother taking a silver penny from her purse to give to the Grey friar, and crossing herself reverently at his benedicite; I with the life of St. Francis in my heart, thinking how he would spend that alms in purchasing comforts for the sick and outcast.

I awoke with a great longing in my heart to see my home once more; and as I woke I heard a woman's voice in the still morning singing a low sweet chant. The sound awoke me. The singer must be a sister in the Franciscan convent of the Poor Clares, which was not far from my prison. I rose and listened. It was a new hymn I had heard in Italy, said to be composed quite lately by Jacopone de' Todi, who, on the sudden death of his good and beautiful wife, had suddenly renounced the world, and joined our order in its strictest rule. A wonderful hymn it was, moving men's hearts like thunder wherever it was heard—like thunder with a human voice

in it. Solemnly now again the words fell on my heart.
It was the Dies Iræ:

> "Tuba mirum spargens donum,
> Per sepulchra regionum,
> Coget omnes ante thronum.
>
> Judex ergo quum sedebit,
> Quidquid latet apparebit,
> Nil inultum remanebit.
>
> Quid sum miser tunc dicturus,
> Quem patronum rogaturus,
> Cum vix justus sit securus.
>
> Rex tremendæ majestatis,
> Qui salvandos salvas gratis,
> Salva me fons pietates.
>
> Recordare Jesu pie,
> Quod sum causa tuæ viæ,
> Ne me perdas illâ die!
>
> Quærens me, sedisti lassus,
> Redemisti crucem passus,
> Tantus labor not sit cassus.
>
> Qui Mariam absolvisti,
> Et latronem exaudisti,
> Mihi quoque spem dedisti."

Then the voice broke off, and the convent-bell sounded for matins. The words mingle strangely with the recollections of childhood brought by my dream. They are not, indeed, an amen from heaven, but they bring to my heart a hope, a tenderness in which its bitterness seems to dissolve away—a dim trust that underneath the tumult, and the heresies, and the confusion, there may be a tide of love and pity, and piety yet flowing in the world ; and if underneath, then may I not be sure also above? With such hopes and memories it seemeth worth while to live. And since in England there is no statute for the burning of heretics, nor any precedent for their punishment, I may yet escape.

Father, and mother, and little Cicely, shall I ever see them again?

Hymns of faith and hope, shall I ever indeed sing them again, as I used in my childhood?

CICELY'S TALE.

IT is now ten years since my only brother Cuthbert left us to become a Franciscan friar. One morning he came not to breakfast; and when they sent me, then a little maid of eight or nine years old, to fetch him, I found his chamber empty. His holiday clothes lay on the bed, and on his little table an open book, with his silver-mounted dagger and his silken purse beside it. I ran down, crying, to tell my father and mother, not knowing what to fear. My mother turned pale, and my father red. She spoke not a word, and he swore an angry oath. He strode up the stairs to Cuthbert's chamber, and my mother followed with trembling steps. They looked at the deserted chamber, and at last my mother's eyes rested on the open book. It was a Life of St. Francis, and the open page was a picture of the saint turning from his father, who was throwing up his arms as if in despair, while large tears were dropping from his eyes. The saint's eyes were turned and his hand pointed heavenward ; and underneath was written the text,

"Whosoever hateth not his father and his mother is not worthy of me."

My mother laid her finger on this page, and broke into bitter weeping and wailing. My father set his lips, and spoke never a word, but closed the book, threw it on the floor, and led me and my mother out of the chamber; then he locked the door, and put the great key in his girdle. From that day to this no one hath entered the chamber, nor dare any mention my brother's name before my father.

Nor from that day to this hath my mother dared in his sight to give a farthing to any of the begging friars, much as she had always been used to honour them, and often since as I have seen her eyes raised wistfully when we met any of the bareheaded Grey friars, and dropped with a sigh as no glance of recognition met her.

In good sooth this conversion of my brother did not work good for religion in our home, at least not at first. I do not think my father ever had too much love for the friars. Many a time I remember my mother checking him in some merry tale about their eating and drinking, and their easy life, looking at me, and saying with her pleading eyes, "Not before the child. It is not fit she should hear such things." Nevertheless he suffered my mother still to go to her morning mass, and to the Benediction with me. He himself always attended regularly the great Church services with her on Sundays and holidays, and entertained priest or friar freely at home. But after Cuthbert went, although he still would be present at the great services, his manner was changed, and now and then he chided my mother somewhat sharply if she was a little late in returning with me from the morning mass, and said he saw not much good in a religion which took wives from their duties, and children from their parents; and that he would not have his little maid brought up to be a nun, with downcast eyes and whining voice, with all the joy dried out of it.

Thereat my mother would sometimes gently weep; but she was a meek woman, and seldom made answer again. But in secret she would tell me that my father, although the best of men, had much to fret him, and would sometimes speak more strongly than he felt.

About this time, moreover, a thin large book, in English, began to be much on my father's knee in the evenings after his work was done. It was by Wycliffe. I knew not its contents then, but only knew it as the cause of many differences between my father and my mother; he reading many passages aloud with great glee, and she seeking some excuse at such times to send me to my games. The book did not interest me much, but the discussions did; and I used to play softly, murmuring to myself, as if I were quite busy with my puppets, but really listening to every word—for which deceit may I be forgiven!

I remember how one summer evening my father sat near the window to catch the last light, and tracing the lines with his finger on the book (for he was never a ready reader), and chuckling as he found some passages which he particularly approved. "Listen here, good wife," he said at length, unable to keep his satisfaction any longer to himself; "the good doctor saith, 'The institution of the friars' religion is a foul heresy put on our Lord Jesus Christ; for it saith that he lacked wit to teach his apostles and disciples the true religion;'" and then my father went on to say something about the book declaring that if the Pope were a sinful man he would be damned and sent among the devils, like any one else. But here my mother's patience was exhausted. Rising quickly, she laid her hand on his mouth and said, "Thou shalt not ruin our souls and thine own by repeating such blasphemies."

And she took me from the room and put me hastily to bed, her hands trembling all the time, and I not daring to ask a question.

Thus, I never knew the end of that debate. But that evening my mother came and knelt by my bed when she thought I was asleep, and said, in whispers, prayers to our Lord Jesus Christ, and our Blessed Lady, and every saint I had ever heard of, to keep us from the evil one.

And when I threw my arms around her as she was rising, her face was quite wet with tears, and she crossed my forehead and said,—

"Didst thou pray to sweet Cicely, thy patroness, and to the Holy Mother of mercy, and to the Lord Christ, and the Saints Matthew, Mark, Luke, and John, to bless thy slumbers, little one."

I murmured, "Yes," for I would have been quite afraid to sleep without, on account of the black fiends my nurse had told us of, if for no other reason.

"Then thou art in good keeping, darling," said she. "Pray, too, for thy dear father and for me. The words he read were not thy father's, Cicely," she said; "but perchance thou didst not hear them. If thou didst, pray to God, to thy patroness, and to thy guardian angel, to take them out of thy heart and out of mine."

I promised and tried, which was, perhaps, the reason that my perverse memory never forgot them; and that at last one day by way of breaking the spell, I got Cousin Richard to look in the book and tell me the rest.

Nothing clings to the memory like a thing half remembered, especially if we wish to forget it. The jagged edges of the broken thought seem so many points by which it holds on.

After that my father never read any of the hated book in my hearing.

When I was about sixteen years old, seven years after Cuthbert left, my father sent for my cousin Richard to help him in his business on the exchange.

The evening before he was to come my father drew me to him and said, stroking my cheek fondly,—

"Cicely, thou art a tall maiden now, and must do what thou canst to make thy father's house pleasant to strangers. Thy cousin Richard is a stranger in London, and we must not expect him to be like the gay, young, empty-headed city 'prentices. He was brought up as I was among the Yorkshire hills, and has been the very stay and staff of his widowed mother. With the good old English bow, I trow, he could match the cleverest among these Londoners, unless the Yorkshire lads are changed since my days. But if in speech and apparel he be not so brave as these young braggarts, albeit he studied a year at Oxenforde, we of the Goldsmiths' Company know how to tell gold from gilding, and thou wilt receive him civilly as thy father's kinsmen."

"In sooth, father," said I, "never before didst thou think it needful to enjoin me to be civil to any guest of thine. But it seemeth to me if my cousin Richard was the staff and stay of his mother, I had liever he had stayed with her."

"Nonsense, child," he said fondly, but hastily; "she hath other sons, and I have none. What thou hadst liever be cannot always be done. Thou hast had thy rule long enough over the household. Children may rule in fools' houses, but maidens must serve."

I said no more to him, but the whole willful heart in me was roused; and next morning, when he had gone to his business, I said to my mother,—

"Mother, my father is bringing this cousin Richard here to take Cuthbert's place. Wilt thou have it so? I never will."

Thus perversely I spoke, until I saw my mother's eyes filled with tears, and then I said,—

"I am in sooth, I fear, a naughty and willful maiden; but Cuthbert was so good and kind, I cannot bear that this Yorkshire cousin should be set in his place."

"Be patient, Cicely," said my mother, gently; and she added, with a sad smile, "Hath thy father opened Cuthbert's chamber? While he keeps thy brother's chamber sacred we may well keep his place sacred in the heart. Yet," she added, "we are growing old daily. Thy father needeth help, and ere long, may be, thou wilt need other shelter than thy father's roof."

"What other shelter, mother, can I wish for? Tenderest of fathers, and dearest of homes."

"It will not last for ever, Cicely."

I burst into tears and hid my face on her breast.

"And thou hast little vocation for a nun's life," she said, winding one of my curls fondly round her fingers.

A bright thought struck me. I murmured, "Cousin Richard is within the prohibited degrees, so that if he is to be to my father as a son, he can never be more than cousin to me."

"Thy father saith he is not," she replied. "I know

not. But receive him kindly, Cicely," she added, smiling, "as if he were."

Fortified by this hope, and by the fear of really grieving my father, I did receive my cousin Richard kindly, or, at least, civilly, when he arrived that evening. And although his green forester's tunic was not of the newest cut, and his dress was, moreover, sorely soiled by the sloughs through which he had ridden, and more especially by a large and deep puddle into which he had fallen in the street just at our door after dismounting from his horse, I did like something in his high open brow, and the merry kindliness of his large gray eyes, albeit he was not like Cuthbert.

We became friends, and might perhaps soon have become more had it not been for my father's premonitions. Cousin Richard suited my father marvellously well. Indeed, he had a way of making himself at home with most people. To my mother also he ever showed a gentle kindliness, which would have won her heart at once had it not been for his free speech on some subjects, and for his evident delight in the very same thin large English book which had been the subject of the difference I have related.

This came out in the following way.

One day when my father and Richard had been at the shooting in St. Giles' Fields, when they came back my father said,—

"Richard hath heard Dr. Wycliffe at Oxford, good wife; and he saith, of all the clerks and doctors he has heard he is the wisest, and is a man of such holy life his bitterest enemies can say naught against him."

"Yes," quoth Richard, "I heard him speak at Oxenforde five years ago, before my father's death, when it was thought I might have studied as a scholar or a man of the law; which," said he, somewhat sorrowfully, "now can never be. Yet would I not have missed those two years for much."

"But surely this Dr. Wycliffe saith very blasphemous and perilous things," said my mother.

"So say some of the friars, who have well-nigh made the university a waste by their arts," he replied, "tempting lads into their Orders against the will of their parents."

He had spoken eagerly, but here he checked himself, and said softly,—

"I mean not such as enter their religion as a good work to serve God, but merely those who choose it as a life of idleness and pride."

"Friars for love of idleness, or love of selfish religious gain, matters little to me!" said my father. "But what said Dr. Wycliffe?"

"I remember chiefly four things which he said," replied Richard, "because they were on matters which had troubled me. He said that true religion consists in faith, hope, and charity; and that true charity consists not in any outward rule or alms, but in loving God with all our heart and our neighbour as ourselves; not our kindred only, still less the monk his order—but our neighbour, the creature of our God. That love indeed is holiness; and Christ wished his law to be observed willingly, freely, that in such obedience men might find happiness. He said also that there is much vain babbling about mortal and venial sins; that only one sin is mortal, and that is *final impenitence*, resisting and sinning against the Holy Ghost to the end. He spoke also very fervently against men who 'chatter on the subject of grace as though it were something to be bought and sold like an ox or an ass, who learn to make a merchandise of selling pardons.' He said also, the homage paid to any saint is useless except as it incites to the love of Christ. For the Scriptures assure us that Christ is the Mediator between God and man; and hence, he said, many are of opinion that when prayer was directed only to that middle Person of the Trinity for spiritual help, the Church was more flourishing and made greater advances than now when many new intercessors have been found out and introduced.

My mother looked startled, and said,—

"Who honours the mother honours the Son."

"Dr. Wycliffe said, moreover," continued Richard, deep in the recollection of the doctor's discourses, "that the chief cause of the evils in the Church now is our want of faith in Holy Scripture. We do not sincerely believe in the Lord Jesus Christ, or we should abide by the authority of his word, especially that of the Evangelists, as of more importance than any other. Inasmuch as it is the will of the Holy Spirit that our attention should not be dispersed over a large number of objects, but concentrated on one sufficient source of instruction, it is His pleasure that the books of the Old and New Laws should be read and studied; and that men should not be taken up with other books, which true as they may be, and containing even scriptural truth, as they may by implication, are not to be confided in without caution or limitation."

"Hast thou anything against that, goodwife?" said my father.

"Nay," she replied, cautiously; "doubtless nothing can be better worthy of study for the scholar than the Holy Evangelists."

Emboldened by this admission, my father brought out his beloved book against the friars, which my cousin welcomed as an old friend.

Whereupon my mother rose, and said, "It was time we women prepared the supper." And the next morning, she said my cousin Richard was not without wit, but it was a pity he talked Yorkshire and meddled with matters too high for simple folk.

"But it matters little to us, Cicely," added she, "for Father Bennet saith he is surely within the prohibited degrees."

The next time we were alone, however, I asked my cousin Richard to tell me about that terrible passage in the book, that, knowing the rest of it, I might more easily get it out of my head. I knew he could find it easily by those words about the Pope.

He then read it to me: "Friars say their religion, founded of sinful men, is more perfect than that religion or order which Christ himself made, that is both God and man. This heresy saith that Christ lacked wit, might, or charity to teach his apostles and his disciples the best religion. But what man may suffer this foul heresy to be put on Jesus Christ? Christian men say that the religion or order that Christ made for his disciples and priests is most perfect, most easy, and most sure. Most perfect for this reason, for the Founder or Patron thereof is perfect, for he is very God and very man, that of most wit and most charity gave this religion to his dear worth friends. Also the rule thereof is most perfect, since the Gospel in its freedom, without error of man, is the rule of this religion. Also knights of this religion be most holy and most perfect. For Jesus Christ and his apostles are the chief knights of it, and after them holy martyrs and confessors. It is most easy and light; for Christ himself saith that 'His yoke is soft, and his charge is light;' since it stands all in love and freedom of heart, and bids nothing but reasonable things, and profitable for the keeper thereof."

Then followed the passage about the Pope.

"It is noble and true, cousin Cicely," said Richard. "Thinkest thou not so?"

I could not gainsay him. But when I told my mother afterward about these good words, thinking to comfort her with regard to my father, to my amazement she exclaimed warmly that it was a wretched book; "Father Bennet said so; and, indeed, what I had told her was enough to prove it, for did it not speak of Christ the Lord lacking wit and charity, and of the Pope being damned?"

In vain I endeavoured to convince her. Such methods of quoting books were then strange to me; although I have heard much of the same kind in religious controversy since.

But my mother forbade me ever to touch the book again. Wherefore after this, cousin Richard usually read to me at my spinning in the poems of Chaucer, which, in good sooth, I found more entertaining.

There were parts which he did not read to me, and although I could read English, he said it was better I should listen than read for myself.

Therefore we laughed and cried together over the book day after day, until the people seemed more real to me than our next door neighbours. "The Prioresse Madame Eglantine, with her dainty ways,

> "Her over lip wiped so clean,
> That in her cuppe was no ferthing sene
> Of grese, when she dronken had her draught;

letting no morsel from her lippes fall, ne wetting her fingers in hire sauce deep;" the service divine she sang so well, "entuned in her nose ful swetely;" the French "she spake ful fayre and fetishy, after the school of Stratford atte Bow, for French of Paris was to her unknown; her eyen gray as glass; her fair broad brow; her soft red lips," from which fell the sweet sorrowful tale of the martyred child; her "statelike manere, digne of reverence; hire conscience so charitable and piteous, she wold wepe if that she saw a mous caught in a trappe, if it were ded or bledde; the small hounds that she fedde with rosted flesh, and milk, and wasted brede, weeping sore if one of them were dead, or if men smote it with a yerde smerte, all conscience as she was and tendre herte. The monke with bridle jingling like a chapel bell, his bald head shining like any glass, and face as it hadde been anoint, who held the text not worth an oyster, that monks might not hunt and be out of cloister. The clerk of Oxenforde, on his horse thin as a rat, his face hollow, his coat threadbare, loving his twenty books at his bed's head better than richest robes, or fiddle, or psaltery. The franklin, with sanguine complexion, and beard white as a daisy (like my father's), whose table stood ready covered in his hall all day. The doctor of physic, clad in sanguin perse, and taffeta, who by his astronomy and magic natural knew the cause of every maladie, were it of cold or heat, or wet or dry. The sergeaunt of the lawe, ware and wise,

> "Nowhar so besy a man as he there was,
> And yet he seemed besier than he was."

The young squire with curled locks, who could make songs and dance, pourtraye and write, and had borne him well, in hopes to stand in his lady's grace. The yeoman forester, with his brown visage, his green baldric and his mighty bow. The merchant with a forked beard, clad in motley with a Flaundrish beaver hat. The friar who devoutly heard confession, an easy man to give penance; for if any man gave to the begging orders, he might be sure he was repentant:

> "For many a man hard is of his herte,
> He may not wepe although him sore smerte;
> Therefore in stede of weping and praieres,
> Men mote give silver to the poure freres.

The old knight, worthy man, who loved truth and honour, freedom and courtesy, who had fought in Christendom and in Hethenesse—in Prussia, Russia, Lithuania, Grenada and Algesira—had been at Alexandria when it was won—had been in fifteen mortal battles, and fought thrice in the lists for the faith, and aye slain his foe, yet

> "Of his port was meek as any mayde,
> And never yet no vilanie ne sayde
> In alle his lif, unto no manere wight;
> He was a very parfit gentil knight.

The ploughman, who loved God best with all his heart, at all times, were it gain or smart," "would thresh and thereto die and thereto delve for Criste's sake for any poor wight;" and his brother, the poor parson of the town, learned, benign, and diligent, "that Criste's Gospel trewely wold preche," "in adversitie full patient," as had often been proved, "to sinful men not despitous," but discreet to draw folk to heaven, yet able to "snibben sharply" the obstinate, were he high or low. We knew them all, Cousin Richard and I, and their tales always seemed as fresh and touching to us as to talk of old friends.

The parson and the ploughman, he told me privately, he believed to be portraits of Dr. Wycliffe and Piers Plowman, the pious poet. Thus, to me, Dr. Wycliffe's name was clothed in the charm of poetry and of unjust aspersion. I longed to see him devoutly teaching his poor parishioners at Lutterworth, readier far to give of his offerings and eke of his substance, than to curse for tithes; never failing, for any rain or thunder, to visit the poorest in his wide parish, "in sickness and in mischief," not on a jingling palfrey, but on his feet, with a staff in his hand—"a shepherd and no mercenary," and "teaching Criste's life, but first following it himself."

One evening, when I was with my mother in the kitchen, rolling pie-crust, and humming verses from Chaucer to myself, my father came in and told us how Dr. Wycliffe had been summoned before the bishops in St. Paul's, and Bishop Courtney and Lord Percy had chidden each other sharply, and the people had stood for their bishop, and there had been a riot, the white-haired parson, with his grave, powerful face, standing silent and fearless amidst the tumult.

Then, in a few months, came another summons of Dr. Wycliffe to answer for himself as a suspected heretic in Lambeth Palace Chapel. And from that meeting my father and Cousin Richard came back greatly excited, telling how the citizens had rushed into the chapel, fearing some harm should happen the brave doctor.

Sad, troublesome times followed, of disturbance and discontent, and through them all, I scarcely know how, kept coming up the name of Wycliffe. My mother said he was at the bottom of all the mischief; she had always known it would be so ; shake one stone and the rest will fall. Against Chaucer also she said many sharp things. Father Bennet, she said, told her he spoke many blasphemies against friars and priests, and was more than half a heretic himself, having in his youth, moreover, been guilty of beating a Franciscan friar in the open street—a fate, my father said, many of them well deserved. But my mother thought of Cuthbert; and thus altogether our home became rather sad, especially when Cousin Richard was away on long voyages for my father, which my mother much encouraged. These things pained and fretted me. My mother traced all our troubles back to Dr. Wycliffe, and my father to the Franciscan friars; and thus there was division in the household which I saw no way to heal.

At length, one spring, she persuaded herself and my father that I was paler and graver than a young maiden ought to be, and that the country air for some months was needful to set me up, so that he undertook himself to take me to his step-sister, the Franklin's widow, among the Yorkshire hills.

I was not very willing to go just then. Richard had just come back from a great journey, and had much to tell of foreign parts ; and although he had not by any means taken Cuthbert's place, with any of us (was not my poor brother's chamber still empty and locked ?) yet it was impossible for any place not to feel more home-like where he was.

But my resistance was unavailing. My father's fears were roused about my health ; he would not have his darling a pale, listless city damsel, he said. And so, one morning early in May, at three o'clock, we started by the Great North Road.

My mother had packed wonderful baskets of provision for us. We had two large baggage-trunks and two serving men, and Cousin Richard went with us as far as St. Albans for protection, because the roads near London were infested with thieves watching for merchandise; and although the monks of St. Albans undertook to guard them with armed retainers, and the wood, according to statute, was cleared away for more than a hundred yards on either side the road, my father had more faith in Cousin Richard's sword than in all the hired men-at-arms.

When we had passed the muddy way through Gray's Inn Lane, where the swine and the deep puddles often nearly threw down the horses in the dusk, it was delicious to mount the hills into the forest around the villages of Hampstead and Highgate. There Cousin Richard bade me listen to the nightingales that were singing to each other in the trees on either side,

> "The small foules making melody
> That slepen alle night with open eye."

And as the day rose, and we turned our horses' feet from the uneven road to the cool, soft, dewy turf, where the golden furze glowed above the countless tiny wild flowers, he reminded me how "April, with his soft showers, had pierced the drorght of March," and Zephyrus, with his soft breath, had "inspired in every holt and heath the tender croppes," while the young Sun was rejoicing in the heavens.

He spoke more than his wont, and was strangely blithe, I thought, seeing that I could say but little for fear of weeping. He had much to tell me of his mother's home among the Yorkshire hills, and many places to bid me be sure and see, and poor people to ask about, and bring him tidings of; and especially he bade me visit the old mansion near the village of Wycliffe, where Dr. Wycliffe was born.

We had no call to hurry, and it was rare pleasure to eat our bread and meat among the woods, with thrushes and blackbirds singing, and wild flowers welcoming us like smiles. I could not wonder any one should write verses who lived among the woods or fields, because it all seemed written and set to music for us there already.

Towards evening our converse grew more grave, and Cousin Richard spoke again of Dr. Wycliffe; how he had been very ill lately at Oxford, and the begging friars had come to him on his sick-bed and admonished him to repent; but he had raised himself, feeble as he was, in the bed, and said,—

"I shall yet live, and declare the evil deeds of the friars," so grimly and solemnly, that the poor friars could say no more, but left the chamber sorely discomfitted. He spoke also of Chaucer's Poor Parson's Sermon, and repeated many beautiful sayings from it concerning the goodness of God, and the love we owe to Christ who bled for us, so that I was sorry to see the hill of St. Albans, crowned with its fair abbey; and when we parted the next morning, after staying the night at the town, the good words still lingered in my heart, and gave me more courage to go on than I had the day before.

Yet was that day very different from the one before, and I trow my father thought me somewhat over-grave; for when he kissed me, as we parted for the night, he said,—

"Never be cast down, little Cicely. Thou shalt be at home again soon, and we will have merry days then. Richard loves thee well, and thou wilt know thy duty to me and to him better than to say nay."

"It is not to be thought of, thou knowest, father," I said.

"Why not?" he exclaimed, testily.

"My mother told me long since we are within the prohibited degrees."

"Prohibited cobwebs," said my father, angrily. "Kings can break through them for policy, and merchants for money. Besides, Richard is but my step-nephew; scarcely kindred at all, but that for his worth I like to deem him so."

MY SOJOURN IN YORKSHIRE.

THE home of my aunt, the Franklin's widow, was very different from ours. There were no carpets in it, brought by shipmen from Syria or Italy; no carved chairs, or boxes of perfume; no pictures, or silken hangings. But to me it was a perpetual delight to feel the fresh breeze come in perfumed with flowers and sweet new grass, or with the cows' breath, as they came home to be milked; to hear the bees buzzing their happy songs among the blossoms, and to watch the light, silent butterflies hovering about like fairy spirits. It was a busy home. The youngest child was not seven years old, and it was a new life to me to help my aunt about the farm, and take care of the children till they grew to love me and cling about me for tales and songs, and especially to hear about their brother Richard. It was wonderful how his memory was cherished.

My aunt's family knew very little about books; indeed, I never saw one but an old Anglo-Saxon Gospel of St. John, which had once belonged to an ancestor of ours, called Editha, whose name was honoured in the family, together with that of the Lady Marguerite who founded the convent by the river, as much as that of any saints. They had no books in the house, but my aunt had legends of our Saxon forefathers which to me were better than any books. It was strange to me who had scarcely ever heard the words Norman and Saxon, but instead only the common name English, to find the old distinctions still so clearly marked in the country. At my aunt's farm I heard strange merry tales and songs of Robin Hood, Friar Tuck, and Clym of the Clough, and other blithe foresters who held the woods against the "castle-men," and rescued their countrymen from the gallows, and exacted heavy ransoms from Norman barons. Merry men all they were, merry even in their revenge, and never fierce or cruel; with good bows, and clad in Lincoln green, who lived in good greenwood, with Saxon harp or song and dance, and Saxon priests to wed and bless them. (But in the legends of the castles these same merry foresters were transformed into reckless outlaws, highwaymen, and thieves.) At the farm also there was reverent memory kept of Saxon hero and saint, of King Alfred and Hereward of the Fens, of St. Oswald and Bishop Aiden, of the Abbess Hilda, of Boniface and Willibrord, of St. Cuthbert, the Venerable Bede, Guthlac the hermit, and St. Chad; names which at the castle, (although in the Roman calendar,) were little thought of. St. Cecilia, St. Agnes, St. Martin of Tours, St. Francis, St. Dominic, St. Clare, and many other foreign names, were the sacred household words there.

It was on the second Sunday after I came to the farm that I first saw the Lady Clare of the castle. The family of the Baron de Garenne frequently attended the Mass in the castle chapel, instead of coming to the village church. But this Sunday was a festival, and the stately train came down the hill from the castle. The Lady de Garenne and the Lady Clare, borne in a gay gilded litter, with silken curtains, met us at the church door. I noticed the sweet face of the young lady, and its gentle, calm expression, so different from the haughty bearing of her mother. And that afternoon, as I was visiting an old palsied man Cousin Richard had told me to inquire for, I met her again, carrying a little basket of dainties in her own hands, that the sick man also, she said, might keep the festival. She spoke very graciously to me, and from that time we met often—at the castle or at the farm, or at the convent school, where the village children were taught to spin, and say the Creed, the Paternoster, and the Ave Mary. She had a pleasant fancy that we must be friends, because two hundred years ago an ancestor of hers and of mine had loved each other dearly; and often we sat on their graves in the convent burial-ground — the stately monumental cross of the Abbess Marguerite, and the lowly slab which marked the resting-place of Editha, the daughter of Aldred, and Siward her husband.

The Lady Clare was different from any one I had ever seen in the world, or in Chaucer. When I watched the gentle stateliness of her manner, her pretty courtly ways, and looked at her broad fair brow, her soft red lips, or listened to her sweet rich voice, musical in common speech, and sweeter than convent-bells at evening across the water, when she sang psalm or hymn (the only songs she ever sung),—I thought she might be like the Prioress Madame Eglantine, when she told the sad tale of the little child who died for his love to Christ and His dear mother, and yet did say, *Alma Redemptoris mater*. "All conscience and tender heart" she seemed. And yet there was a depth and fervour in her dark eyes Madame Eglantine's gray eyes could never have had; there was no mere prettiness or pettiness about her, and she could never have made "small hounds" the joy or sorrow of her life.

Her sisters were married. Her parents wanted her to become abbess of the family convent founded by the Lady Marguerite, but she said the convent had become a mere idling-place to dream life away. She had spent six months there once, and she said the conversation of the nuns wearied her to death, with their small bickerings and small ambitions, their confections, their ailments, and their ceremonies. They thought as much of the making and materials of their nun's dress as her sisters of their court robes of state. They misunderstood each other, and found fault with each other, and had gossips enough in their small community to supply a city. If a pet bird or hound of the abbess fell sick, there were tears enough about it to bewail a child.

"A melancholy, hopeless, lifeless life," she said; "like what the old heathens used to feign of the dead,—a world of shades, where the only solace of the spirits was to live over again, in a dim, shadowy way, the fastings and the feastings of earth."

And then she told me the histories of St. Francis and St. Clare, her patroness—of their toiling night and day in the great cities, to succour the poor, and tend the sick, and solace the dying.

"That is the life I mean to lead when I am a nun," said the Lady Clare; "to lead a life as full of life as my sisters in their married homes, with joys as deep, sorrows as real, love as human: but not for myself—not for me and mine—but for Christ the Lord and his Church; serving his poor, nursing his orphans, solacing his sufferers—my name lost in His, my life lost in His. And this grace one day I trust He will bestow on me."

Thus we grew to love each other very dearly. I told her of the poor parson in the "Canterbury Tales," of the martyred child of St. Cecilia, and the holy Lady Constance, wife of King Ella of Northumbria, whom God led safely, with her babe, in the rudderless boat, through the salt sea. And I told her of my brother Cuthbert, and all I knew of the Poor Clares, the Minorite sisters, whose convent was in London, near St. Catherine's, by the Thames.

And she told me holy legends of St. Catherine, St. Agnes, and St. Marguerite, and especially of the holy Francis and St. Clare; and sang me Latin hymns, expounding to me their sense in English. Marvellously sweet they were from her voice, especially the new one by the Franciscan Jacopone, *Dies iræ, dies illa*, whose rhythm only spoken flows like a heavenly song.

Of the name most revered by cousin Richard, however, I dared never speak to her—namely, of Dr. Wycliffe. She dreaded it as much as did my dear mother, and crossed herself, and said her Franciscan confessor had told her he was a damnable heretic; which made me fear cousin Richard and I had been too hasty in taking up his praises, and that my mother, after all, might be right.

On my way home, however, I learned to think otherwise. My father had another brother, an aged priest of a parish in Leicestershire; and it was arranged that he should fetch me and Ethel, one of my aunt's daughters, to pay him a little visit before I returned to London.

My uncle was not exactly like any of the priests or friars in the " Canterbury Tales." He was, I thought, something of a compound of the Franklin and the Clerk of Oxenforde, if such a compound can be imagined; a homely, comfortable man, with a fat benefice, and a table always ready covered and open to all comers in his hall; yet withal a great lover of books, looking, it seemed to me, on men and women, and their history, as a kind of necessary but inconvenient interruption to his studies. His real kingdom was his library; his parish was a foreign land, into which he made a journey on Sundays and holidays, or whenever he was called to take the holy sacrament to the dying. In his house ruled supreme Mistress Margery, his mother's widowed sister. From him, therefore, I could get no solution of my difficulties concerning Dr. Wycliffe and the Franciscans. His studies did not, indeed, reach so far down as St. Francis. He could tell you every particular of the controversies between Athanase and the Arians, and the semi-Arians, the Sabellians, and the Samosatensians; but of Dr. Wycliffe he knew nothing whatever, except that he was the parson of the neighbouring parish of Lutterworth.

I had therefore to observe for myself.

My first sight of Dr. Wycliffe was at the cottage of a poor labourer of my uncle's, who lived on the outskirts of Lutterworth. As I was entering the door of the hovel with my little wallet from Mistress Margery's stores, I saw a tall figure coming up along the road from the bridge which crosses the river below Lutterworth. As he drew nearer, by his grave, powerful face, his long venerable beard, his tall white staff, his plain belted robe and sandalled feet, his slow steps, as of one weak from recent illness, I felt sure it was he Richard had so often described to me—the original of the portrait of the poor parson of the town.

I entered the hovel, gave the contents of my wallet to the sick man, and waited to see if the parson would enter. In a short time he came in, blessing the house and all in it, as he entered, with a faith and gravity which made me feel, "He has blessed me, and I am blessed."

There, by the bed-side of that poor sick man, I heard words such as I had never heard before, about sin and doom, and Christ and his passion, and God and his goodness.

I hid my face and wept quite gently, lest I should miss one of the precious words, until he once more prayed for a blessing on the sufferer and on me, and left.

I was very quiet all that day. All things around me seemed mere thin vapoury clouds compared with the great eternal realities of which I had been hearing.

After that I missed no opportunity of attending mass or preaching in Lutterworth Church with my cousin Ethel. Happily for me, the offices in my uncle's church were not frequent, and he preached only the four prescribed sermons annually, on the fourteen articles of the faith, the ten commandments, the two evangelical precepts, the seven works of mercy, and the seven sacraments. Mistress Margery knew little of any world but the rectory, and my uncle had not yet come down far enough in history to be aware of the suspicions against the doctor; and therefore they simply regarded me as a very religious maiden, who, my cousin Ethel told me, Mistress Margery suspected had probably been crossed in love, and would become a nun.

Dr. Wycliffe had only held the living four years (since 1376), and had hitherto passed half the year lecturing on divinity at Oxford.

There in the little church at Lutterworth, on the hill among the trees, I heard truths which made all life new to me. I heard him first on Christmas Day speak of the Child born to us, in whom we should have joy; of Adam's sin and ours; how the justice of God could not suffer him to forgive sin of his mere power without atonement, else must he give free license to sin both in angels and men, and then sin were no sin, and our God were no God; how the nature that sinned must be the nature to make atonement, and yet every man being bound to serve God to the extent of his power for himself, can have nothing beyond wherewith to make atonement for himself or others—wherefore the atoning Lord needed both to be God and man. Then he said how, if indeed this Child was to be born "*to us*," to be our joy, we must follow him in the meekness of his birth, in the meekness, righteousness, and patience of his life and death; that so this joy in the patience of Christ might bring us to the joy that shall ever last.

Again I heard him speak of the Passion of Christ, bidding men print it on their hearts; how it was most voluntary and most painful. *Most voluntary*, and therefore most meritorious; for with desire, the desire of his Godhead and his manhood, he desired to eat that passover, and afterwards to suffer. And *most painful;* for he was the most tender of men, and suffered in body and mind: and the ingratitude and contempt were most painful; for men who should have loved him most ordained for him the foulest death in return for the deepest kindness.

Beautiful it was also to hear him speak of the grace of God, and of all the good we have or do being his gift; so that "when he rewardeth a good work of man, he crowneth his own gift."

Of other severer and darker matters, also, Dr. Wycliffe preached. Of Antichrist; of false friars and priests; of the "two days of judgment"—man's day and God's day; of the poor, fallible, reversible judgments of men; and of the sure, righteous, eternal doom of God.

He spoke also of the source whence all his preaching was derived—the holy Word of God—which should, he said, be in every man's hand in English, by God's grace, before many years had passed. It was this which occupied him in all his leisure at the rectory, when he was not preaching or visiting his sick and aged parishioners.

Dr. Wycliffe was translating the Holy Scriptures into English. Of all his works this seemed to me the most undoubtedly right, and the one which all Christian men must most approve. For what can be dear to Christians as Christ's own words? And if the Venerable Bede had translated the Gospel of St. John, which I had seen at the farm, for the lay people of his day, and died finishing his work, as they say, and been held a saint, why should it not be a saintly work for Dr. Wycliffe to do the same for us poor English men and women of these days, who can read neither Bede's Saxon nor the Church Latin? Alack! and it seems to me that work, more than any other, which draws down curses on his memory, because, as they say, "he hath turned the jewel of the Church into the sport of the people, and the choice gift of the clergy and divines he hath made for ever common to the laity."

I stayed nearly two years at my uncle's rectory. The country was disturbed. Wat Tyler and the Kentish men had risen against the young King Richard, or, as they said, against the king's evil counsellors; and it was not until the insurgents, who had assembled to the number of forty thousand on Blackheath, close to London, were dispersed, that my father held it safe to fetch me home.

Thus I had ample opportunity for hearing "the evangelical doctor" preach; and what was, if possible, better, I procured, by spending all the money I had left, a copy of such of the Gospels and other books of the New and Old Testaments as were already translated—"God's law written in English for lewd (lay) men."

For in the little town of Lutterworth at that time there were many scribes working at multiplying copies of the English Scriptures. Some of them also divided their time between copying the sacred manuscripts and going about among the villages and cottages preaching to any who would listen; in churchyards, farm-houses, market-places, "poor priests," like their master, the poor parson, enlisted in the same work, preaching as, he said, Christ did—now at meat, now at supper, at whatever time it was convenient for others to hear him. Once I heard Dr. Wycliffe in the pulpit saying these words: "The Gospel telleth us the duty which falls to all the disciples of Christ, and also how priests, both high and low, should occupy themselves in the church of God, and in serving him. And first, Jesus himself did indeed the lessons he taught. The Gospel relates how he went about in places of the country, both great and small, in cities and castles, or in small towns, and this that he might teach us how to become profitable to men generally, and not to forbear to preach to people because they are few, and our name may not in consequence be great. For we should labour for God, and from him hope for our reward. There is no doubt that Christ went into small, uplandish towns, as to Bethphage and Cana of Galilee; for Christ went to all those places where he wished to do good. He laboured not for gain; he was not smitten with either pride or covetuousness."

When I went home that evening, I repeated these words to myself again and again, and to my cousin Ethel, that I might never forget them (not being able to write); because they made me feel, as I never felt before, that Christ the blessed Lord went about teaching on this very earth, in a country like ours, among little towns and villages, and poor lay people like us. And they made me feel also that *all* the disciples of Christ, not priests only and friars, but I, even, a simple burgher maiden, was called in some way, in my humble quiet place, not only to listen but to tell to those around me the good tidings of great joy.

The next day a messenger came on horseback to the rectory from the bishops who had met in London, warning my uncle and all the clergy around Lutterworth, as they valued their everlasting salvation, to have nothing to do with the notorious heretic Wycliffe, silenced in that year at Oxford for his damnable doctrines.

My uncle started up as if from a dream. "Dr. Wycliffe notorious, and a heretic!" he said, "a man whom bishops have thought it worth while to meet to censure? What can it all mean? Is he an Arian or a Sabellian, or can he, perchance, have been tainted with the notable heresy of the Monophysites? In these days the whole world is Catholic and orthodox. A heretic is the next parish to me? One would think one were living in the days of Athanase."

Mistress Margery's view of the matter was, to my grief, more practical.

"See," she said, "how little we simple folk can judge. Here are all the poor people around revering Dr. Wycliffe as the holiest parson in the country; and here have Cicely and Ethel been running to his preachings day by day. Never enter the doors of that church again, children," she added irrevocably; "and let it be a warning to you both all your lives, never to desert your parish church. See what perils you have escaped! you might have become tainted with some foul heresy without knowing it!"

Mistress Margery believed that heresy was a thing to be caught like the plague; and never again were we suffered to approach Lutterworth.

Instead, we had a new series of sermons from my uncle, departing in this emergency from his ordinary church form, against all the heretics of the Oriental Greek and Latin Churches as far as the time of St. Augustine; but when he reached this period, to our infinite relief, the insurgent peasants had been dispersed, and King Richard and good Queen Anne of Bohemia had been right loyally received by the citizens, and my father came to take us back to London.

And with us went the copies of what had been written for me at Lutterworth, of portions of Wycliffe's English Bible.

CUTHBERT'S TALE.

LAMBETH, 1420.

ONCE more in prison, but no more in darkness,— never more in darkness. Under my feet the ground is firm. I stand on the rock whereon the Church is built. Over my head the sky is clear. I see the way open into the sanctuary of sanctuaries, and in its depths of light, Himself the Light of Light, I gaze in faith on the Only-Begotten, the Lamb of God, the Priest of man, the Pardoner, without money and without price. Around me in uplandish towns, in forest hamlets, in lonely homesteads, in crowded cities, I see the lost sheep lost no more, returning to the fold, following the good Shepherd, listening to his voice, obedient to his call,—obedient even unto death.

There is little chance of my escaping now. There are statutes enough against heretics in England now, and tribunals enough to condemn them, and informers enough to betray, and stakes enough to burn.

Such changes the last thirty years have wrought; and yet I hold the last thirty years the best and most prosperous England has ever seen.

For, once more God's yea and amen, the blessed Saviour's "verily," has gone forth into the world, and He teacheth in men's homes and hearts, who speaketh with authority, and not as the scribes.

Thirty years ago, on the morning when I heard in the prison of the Minorites that sweet voice chanting the "Dies Iræ," and awoke once more to the desire of life, I looked through my prison bars, and recognised spreading out before me the familiar levels of Goodman's and Spital Fields. My prison was on the outskirts of the city, and once beyond the walls, I had no doubt but that I might reach my home.

Heretic hunting being by no means such a keen and familiar pursuit in England then as now (when the condemned heretic's property is divided between the tribunal which convicts him, the place where he is convicted, and the crown), I effected my escape without much difficulty, only laming myself in my descent from the prison window. It was midnight when I contrived to limp through the dark and uneven streets to the door of my old home.

The old servant, who opened the door at my knocking, said, like Rhoda in the Acts, "It is his ghost," and again shut me out into the darkness.

But in a few minutes my mother came and folded me in her arms, and sobbed, and said,—

"I always knew thou wouldst come back."

My father made little ado; but his voice faltered as he took a great key from his girdle and said to my mother,—

"Mother, there is the key of the lad's chamber."

But Cicely, now grown to a tall, fair woman, would have roused the whole neighbourhood to rejoice with us, had I not stopped her by saying,—

"Let not a soul know I am here, and wait to hear what I have to tell before we know if it is safe for you to receive me at all. I have escaped this night from the prison of the Franciscan friars, where I have been lying for weeks under charge of heresy."

My mother turned pale as death; but my father grasped my hand, and said,—

"The friars will need to turn all their abbeys into prisons if they would seize all the good men they call heretics. Where didst thou learn to hate their evil deeds?"

"In Italy," I said, "I found the book for reading which I was thrown into prison."

"Have Dr. Wycliffe's writings then reached even to the Pope's own land?" said my father.

I was bewildered. I had never heard Dr. Wycliffe's name. It was Abbot Joachim's Everlasting Gospel and the heresy of the Spiritual Franciscans that had brought me into trouble.

My father's countenance fell as he heard this; but the colour came back to my mother's face.

A feast of welcome was prepared for the wanderer, although without the music, and the dancing, and the calling the neighbours together. In a few hours my old chamber was ready for me, and I was asleep on the old bed.

The pain in my lamed leg awoke me, and strange it was to wake in the old familiar room, and look up into my mother's face as she sat watching beside me.

"Night and day I have prayed," she said, "to see thee once again before I die. Tell me, my son, can God have answered my prayers in anger, and sent thee back to me in judgment? I have loved every Grey friar for thy sake, Cuthbert, since thou didst leave us. Tell me those words last night were but an ill dream. Thou art no heretic; thou never wilt be, promise me, my son."

"I would not be a heretic, mother, indeed," I said, "if I could tell how to help it. But would to God I were no friar. And how God hath answered thy prayers, in sooth I know not, for I know not what prayers reach him, nor how he answers any, such confusion, and hypocrisy, and unbelief, and lying have I seen since I was in this chamber last; such luxury among friars sworn to poverty,—such pride, and mockery, and intrigue." For my heart was very bitter, and I could not hide it from her.

"But at least," she said, catching at her last straw of consolation, "thou art no Wycliffite. It is not from that perilous tongue of Wycliffe that thou hast learnt to dislike the friars?"

"No," said I, "I have seen them myself."

She said no more. The hurt in my leg pained me more severely. And the next day my father insisted on my seeing cousin Richard, who, in his voyages to foreign parts, had picked up some skill in leech-craft.

We soon understood each other. To him I could pour out the burdens of my heart as I could neither to my mother nor to Cicely. He seemed to understand it all; but he said,—

"Be of good cheer. This gulf of darkness has a bottom. This sea on which you are tossing has a shore; and what is more, the ship in which you are tossed has a Pilot."

And he went and fetched me a manuscript, and read:

"And anon Jesus compelled the disciples to go up in to a boat, and go before him over the sea, while he left the people, and when the people was left, he stied (went up) alone into a hill to pray; but when the evening was come he was there alone, and the boat in the middle of the sea was schogged (tossed) with waves, for the wind was contrary to them; but in the fourth waking of the night, he came to them walking above the sea. And they seeing him walking on the sea were distroubled, and said that it is a phantom, and for dread they cried, and anon Jesus spake to them and said, Have ye trust I am; nyle ye dread.

"It is the fourth waking of the night with your cousin," he said, "and the boat is tossed, but it is no phantom which speaks to you through the darkness and the storm." And he read on:

"And Peter answered and said, Lord, if thou art, command me to come to thee on the waters.

"And he said, Come thou, and Peter gede down from the boat and walked on the waters to come to Jesus, but he saw the wind strong and was afeard, and when he began to drench, he cried, Lord, make me safe, and anon Jesus held forth his hand, and took Peter, and said to him, Thou of little faith, why hast thou doubted, and when he had stied in to the boat, the wind ceased, and they that were in the boat came and worshipped him and said, Verily thou art God's Son."

I could scarcely account for it. I lay still quietly weeping as of old when my mother told me some touching sacred history. Doubtless I was weak with my hurt, and with prison fare, and with long anguish of mind. But it was long since tears had risen to my eyes. And this was no tale of woe, no story of wrong and agony to harrow the heart, no appeal such as the Friars' Preachers make on Passion Week or on Martyrs' Festivals,— appealing with quivering voices, clasped hands, and streaming eyes, to the blood-stained crucifix, the pierced side, the nailed hands and feet, until the people sobbed, and wailed, and beat their breasts, as I had seen them often in Italy. Richard's voice was calm and steady, the story was cheerful and quiet, the words of comfort very simple and very few. Yet could I do nothing but cover my face for shame at these childish tears and weep, so deep did the soft, slow-falling words pierce into my inmost heart.

"Thou of little faith, why hast thou doubted? have ye trust I am!"

"Verily, *verily* thou art God's Son."

The verily ı had longed for had come to my heart at last.

Richard made no sign that he observed me, but read on:

"And when they had passed over the sea, they came in to the land of Genaser, and when men of that place had known Him, they sent in to all the country, and they brought to him all that had sickness, and they prayed him that they should touch the hem of his clothing, and whoever touched were made safe."

In a deep, grave voice Richard continued:

"Then the scribes and the Pharisees came to him from Jerusalem and said, Why break thy disciples the traditions of elder men? For they wash not their hands when they eat bread."

I laid my hand on the book to stop him, and begged him to leave me for a while.

Of scribes and Pharisees, and washing hands and traditions of elders, I had heard enough in those bitter ten years.

What wonder they should carp and babble now, when the voice which calmed the winds, the hands that made Peter safe on the sea, the presence which healed all who touched, would not silence them? But with the hushed waves, the echo of whose raging was in their ears, couching at His feet quiet as a tamed steed at its master's touch, with the healed sufferers pressing joyfully around Him, with the sense of a Divine Presence striking every heart into awe, they could still talk of washing hands, and cups, and plates!

But what to us was the strife of tongues any more than the strife of winds, since through it all came that voice, "I am. Nyle ye dread."

I know not how long I lay still alone, scarcely thinking nor praying, asking nor remembering, but simply resting, resting my whole soul, as Peter rested his whole weight on that unfailing Hand.

For weeks during my recovery I fed on those divine words from the precious manuscripts Cicely had brought from Lutterworth, as Richard or Cicely read them to me, or as I tried to sit up and could read them to myself.

Many changes have come on me since then. The confusions in the world and in the Church have not passed away; but in my heart from that time to this there has been, instead of a chaos, a great calm; instead of man's "Peradventure," Christ's "Verily."

"Verily, verily, he that heareth my words, and believeth on Him that sent me, hath everlasting life."

"Verily thou art. Thou art the Saviour, the Son of God."

By degrees the audience at those readings increased. Cicely, and Richard, and Ethel; and now and then Margery, the faithful old servant; and after his day's business my father; and at first half hesitatingly, but at length more regularly than any one, my mother.

"Even Dr. Wycliffe would not surely dare to falsify the holy evangelists," she said, at first, to excuse herself for listening, until the divine histories wrought their own work on her poor troubled heart, and she ceased to wonder at anything, unless it was why the priests and friars had not given this book to the people long before.

"Books written," she said, "by St. Peter and St. Paul; words spoken by the blessed Lord himself; and such words—so deep, so pure, so simple, so divine—children might understand them; dying men, too feeble to grasp anything else, might grasp them; hardened sinners, too hard to feel anything else must feel them;—and to keep these back from the thirsty multitudes, and give them instead such tales as the friars tell!"

"Tales," chimed in my father, "to which wise men will not listen, and maidens should not, and which no man can believe; tales of phantoms and devils, of saints whose holiness consisted in transgressing the fifth commandment, and whose best works were wrought by their bones when they were dead;—because, forsooth, they are 'safer for the lay people!'"

"Histories," said Cousin Richard, "which certainly never end with 'Nyle ye dread,' since their chief aim is to make men dread, and to wring from terrified consciences wealth for the Church. With too many of them, at least!" he added, "but, thank God, not with all."

Thus God's word, which in Dr. Wycliffe's first presenting of it had caused so much division and trouble of heart in our household, at last in its own pure light made us to be of one mind in the house. And, in good sooth, "there was great joy among us," as of old in the city of Samaria, where the same glad tidings reached.

Some good man says, God first gives his children food, and bids them rest; and then, when they are strong enough, he sends them forth to the battle. For who, in this world of ceaseless holy war, would wish to be always a babe, and never to endure hardness as a good soldier of Jesus Christ?

When I recovered, it was decided that I should throw off my Grey friar's frock, as no longer either safe for me nor to my mind.

Our decision was hastened by some news Cicely heard.

She had always felt sure, from my description of the voice and the hymn which I had heard that morning in the Minorite prison, that it was the Lady Clare who sang it. And at length, one day, she found access to the convent of Poor Clares, and actually saw the Lady Clare, and tried to speak to her of the Book of God we had all grown so dearly to prize; but when the nun heard of the name of the translator, she crossed herself and would not listen to another word, but implored Cicely, as she valued her salvation, to flee from that heretic's poison as from the plague, "for," said she, "heresy is busy among us now, even in the holiest places."

And then she told how, not many months before, a Franciscan friar had escaped from the prison of the Minorites, on the charge of holding terrible errors, and could nowhere be found, so that many believed the devil himself had spirited him away.

Cicely's heart beat very fast, but she said nothing; only as she left soon after, something in the Lady Clare's look piercing the calm of her grave, nun-like bearing, reminded her of old times, and she said,—

"Sweet Lady Clare, are you then at rest and satisfied here, and is all as you hoped?"

"All can never be as we hope, Cicely," was the sad reply, "on earth. But if the world penetrates even here, I may surely find my Saviour here, and serve Him in every sick and suffering creature whose loathsome wounds I dress, in His name, seeking to lead them to Him."

They said no more, but Cicely verily believes that the Lady Clare and Dr. Wycliffe are working (unknown to each other) for one Master and one end.

After this no time was lost. I journeyed at once to Lutterworth, and there, for two years, till he died in his parsonage in 1384, I had the great blessing of learning of Dr. Wycliffe, copying the Holy Scriptures among his scribes, and being trained among his "poor priests."

Since then I have journeyed through the country north and south; in uplandish towns such as were Cana and Bethphage, in places of the country both great and small, in cities and castles, wherever men could be gathered and would listen, the little band went forth from Lutterworth, with sandalled feet and simple dress, content with such fare as the poorest were ready to share with us, remembering the words of our Lord, "Behold the crowes: for they sow not nether reap, to which is no cellar nor barn, and God feedeth them: how much more ye be of more price than they." And in the bosom of our robes we bore the precious jewel, the new English Bible.

The seed, the incorruptible seed of the word is sown; the Sower, the Son of man, has been with us; the Spirit, the Living Water, has watered it; and now I know of a surety it shall never more be rooted out throughout England.

Chiefly in the homes of franklins and burghers, craftsmen and ploughmen of the old Saxon stock, I think it has taken root; and in this I greatly rejoice, for although the headsman's sword may be sharpened, or the traitor's gallows may be erected for a few noble heads among us, what search can find out the countless lowly hearts in farm, and cottage, and city, which the good tidings have reached? Thank God for the welcome given to his word in castle and court. Had not even the Queen, the good Lady Anne of Bohemia, the Bible in her own language and in ours, and has not the truth spread through her attendants from England into Bohemia; Saxon or English lips once more, as in the days of Boniface and Willibrord, proclaiming the faith to Europe, confession here met by confession there, fire here answered by fire there? Thank God for the noble and the mighty, though

17*

not many; but let us thank Him even more for the many, the great multitude which no man can number, not noble, not mighty, "the things which are not, bringing to nought the things that are."

Lord Cobham dies alone—dies because he is too high to be suffered to live a heretic. But Badby the tailor, burned in 1409 at Smithfield, represents hundreds of humble, thoughtful men, of plain Saxon sense underlying their devout Christian aspirations, who, like him, "believe in the Omnipotent Trinity, but cannot receive the twenty thousand gods in the consecrated hosts on all the altars in England;" and, if called upon, although loving life and valuing earthly good, yet can, like him, be seduced by no promises of royal pensions nor dread of direst death-pains to say they worship for their Lord a thing "created by the priest" instead of the living God, Creator, Incarnate Redeemer, life-giving, all-present Spirit.

Yes, this "heresy" is everywhere; for the book of God which teaches it has penetrated everywhere. The bishops and judges speak of the numbers of the Lollards as countless — multiplying continually — five hundred being apprehended in a short time in the diocese of Lincoln alone, among the fens, old haunts of Saxon piety and refuges of Saxon freedom. In London, in Norfolk, at Hereford, at Shrewsbury, at Calais, informers betray them, and stakes reveal them to the eyes of all. But there are more yet than these informers can search out or the most zealous judges manifest.* Once more the Church is beginning to believe in the true Vicar of Christ, the Comforter, the Teacher, the Paraclete, for

* Foxe, on the authority of Spelman, says, that in those days scarcely two people could be found together and not one of them a Lollard or a Wycliffite.

the sake of whose coming it was expedient that even the incarnate Christ himself should for a season in visible presence depart.

The poor may-bes and peradventures of the scribes are passing away before the calm, divine "I Am." Once more the Verily and Yea and Amen of God is sounding through the world, through the Word of life breathed into men's hearts by the life-giving Spirit.

Once more to Christian men life has glorious ends, and death is but a more glorious beginning.

CICELY'S TALE.

YORKSHIRE, 1420.

WE have left London, and are living, Richard and I, and our boys and girls, in the old farm among the Yorkshire hills.

Times are much changed since I was a child. Subjects were openly discussed in my father's house in London which now scarcely may be mentioned above a whisper, even in lone country-houses such as this.

Thirty years ago England had never seen man, woman, nor child burned on account of religion. In 1390 came the cruel statute of King Henry the Fourth, *de heretico comburendo*,—soon afterwards proclaimed a terrible reality by the burning of William Sawtree, parish priest of St. Asyth's in London, as a Lollard,—the first heretic ever burned in England.

In 1417 good Lord Cobham died at St. Giles' Fields. Among the bushes there they cleared a space for his gallows, condemning him to die as both a traitor and a heretic. He met his slow death of agony and shame fearlessly, as a soldier should who had served King Henry well, and Christ better. The priests cursed him as he suffered, but the people wept and prayed. And Richard said no doubt both curses and prayers reached their own place ; the curses bringing back fire and bitterness to the hearts which breathed them, from the accursed one who delights in them ; the prayers bringing down blessings on the martyr and on the praying people from God.

Shortly after Lord Cobham's death, my brother came back from Bohemia, whither he had gone to help about the translating of certain of Dr. Wycliffe's writings, and brought us an account of the most Christ-like patience and death of the martyrs John Huss and Jerome of Prague at Constance in 1415.

And not many months after that Cuthbert died in prison at Lambeth, in the Lollards' Tower. Richard and I visited him often in prison. One day his countenance had more than even its wonted peacefulness, and he told us how there had come back to him that morning in the early twilight, as if chanted once more, as once he had heard it by the rich voice of the Lady Clare, the words of the Latin hymn—

> Recordare Jesu pie
> Quod sum causa tuæ viæ
> In me perdas illâ die.

And then, as if it were an antiphon from the other side of the choir, these words—" My sheep hear my voice, and I know them, and they suen (follow) me, and I give to them everlasting life, and they shall not perish without end, and none shall ravish them from my hand ;"—and these, " Death, where is thy victory ? Death, where is thy prick ? But the prick of death is sin, and the virtue of sin is the law; but do we thankings to God, that gave to us victory by our Lord Jesus Christ."

The sigh, he said, was answered by the promise and the song; the trembling human aspiration of the hymn by the joyful divine Amen of the Holy Scriptures.

"Happy those," said Richard, "who like Cuthbert begin the song of thanksgiving on earth;—yet happy also those who, like your mother and the Lady Clare, although with downcast eyes and trembling lips, breathe that sigh to the pitying Lord; for it shall surely turn to the song in heaven."

Dark as the times seem, Richard saith it is the day and not the night that is coming. And he tells our boys,—in the evenings when the doors are closed and the bolts are drawn and all the house is still, and from its secret niche in the wall he takes out Dr. Wycliffe's prohibited Bible and reads it to us,—that the days may yet come when England will glory more in Wycliffe, the first Reformer, and in Wycliffe's Bible, the first translation of the Holy Scriptures published among the people, than in all the victories of King Henry in France. But this the boys find hard to believe.

BOOKS PUBLISHED BY
M. W. DODD,
506 Broadway, New York.

JUST PUBLISHED:

Chronicles of the Schönberg-Cotta Family. By Two of Themselves. 1 vol. crown 8vo, beautifully printed, $1 50.

To those unfamiliar with the history of Luther and his times, the title of this unique work may not sufficiently indicate its character.

The design of the author is to so reproduce the times of the Reformation as to place them more vividly and impressively before the mind of the reader than has been done by ordinary historical narratives.

He does this with such remarkable success, that it is difficult to realize we are not actually hearing Luther and those around him speak. We seem to be personal actors in the stirring scenes of that eventful period.

One branch of the Cotta family were Luther's earliest, and ever after, his most intimate friends. Under the title of "Chronicles" our author makes the members of this family (which he brings in almost living reality before us) to record their daily experiences as connected with the Reformation age.

This Diary is fictitious, but it is employed with wonderful skill in bringing the reader face to face with the great ideas and facts associated with Luther and men of his times, as they are given to us by accredited history, and is written with a beauty, tenderness and power rarely equaled.

"A book of unusual attraction and merit, where the interest never flags, and every page is full of gems. The work might justly be termed "A Romance of the Reformation." The various incidents in the life of Luther are portrayed with a graphic beauty and truthfulness rarely equaled. * * * *
Albany Times.

"This is a book of extraordinary interest. The Cotta Family received Luther into its bosom when he was the "beggar boy," and he cherished the warmest affection towards its various branches. The story from first to last is remarkable for its artlessness and tenderness, and it chains the reader's attention to the close."—*Am. Theo. Review.*

"The prominent scenes, from the time of Huss to the death of Luther, are painted before us, and we read them with such interest as even D'Aubigné can scarcely create. The book has all the fascination of a romance."
—*Evangelical Repository.*

"The family history which it contains, if read by itself, would be regarded as one of the most successful portraitures of domestic life that has ever been drawn, each character being delineated and preserved with striking distinctness, and some of the characters being such as the reader will love to linger over as he would over some beautiful portrait drawn by a master's pencil."—*N. Y. Observer.*

M. W. Dodd's Publications.

PULPIT ELOQUENCE (History and Repository of); *Deceased Divines;* containing the Masterpieces of Bossuet, Bourdalone, Massillon, Flechier, Isaac Barrow, Jeremy Taylor, Chalmers, Robert Hall, M'Laurin, Christmas Evans, Edwards, John M. Mason, etc. With DISCOURSES from the Fathers and the Reformers, and the marked men of all countries and times, from the Apostles to the present century; with Historical Sketches of Preaching in each of the countries represented, and Biographical and Critical Notices of the several Preachers and their Discourses, by Henry C. Fish, D. D. Two volumes, 8vo, $7 00.

It is believed to contain a very complete *history of preaching*, and of the great *pulpit orators;* and to embody an amount of *Christian eloquence*, and a great *variety of topics*, such as was never before presented in anything like the same compass. More than *eighty different preachers* are here represented; each by a brief sketch, and by his *most celebrated discourse.* Under the Greek and Latin pulpit, their are eight discourses under the English, twenty-two; under the German, ten; under the French eleven; under the Scottish, nine; under the American, sixteen; under the Irish, four; under the Welsh, three. It will be seen that *more than thirty are from foreign languages.* The *translations* are uniformly from high sources.

"The purpose of this massive work will commend itself to clergymen and to all admirers of the highest style of eloquence. It aims to present the characteristics of pulpit oratory, in all ages of the Christian Church, by furnishing specimens from the most celebrated and influential men of each period. The idea has been carried out with wonderful completeness. Such a body of homiletic literature, embracing so great a variety, and so instructive indications, has never been brought together before. . . . . The interest and value of such a collection can hardly be over-estimated."—*Evangelist.*

"We have felt, in glancing through these splendid and massive volumes, as though walking in a gallery of statuary, along the reaches of which stood, each on his pedestal, the mighty pulpit orators of other centuries and generations. And as we paused before each, to read the name inscribed, and to study the form and features, the statue warmed suddenly into life, called back the long-silent voice, and, with lifted hand and glowing lip, repeated the strong arguments that wrestled so overmasteringly with the minds of their day, and now held us wrapt listeners."—*Congregationalist.*

"Even a layman would be justified in recommending it unhesitatingly and without reserve, as an invaluable treasure to every man of taste, and as of especial and indispensable importance to ministers of the gospel and to the Christian public."—*Evening Traveller.*

"The historical information communicated in these volumes will, of itself, more than repay the expense of their purchase."—*Bibliotheca Sacra.*

"We regard these volumes as scarcely less valuable to the intelligent layman than to the aspiring clergyman. They are filled with the most eloquent and powerful appeals which human minds have addressed to their fellow creatures in the interests of religion, and constitute an enduring record of the highest order of eloquence."—*Com. Advertiser.*

M. W. Dodd's Publications.

PULPIT ELOQUENCE of the Nineteenth Century.

Being supplementary to the History and Repository of Pulpit Eloquence (deceased divines); and containing Discourses of Eminent Living Ministers in Europe and America. Accompanied with Sketches Biographical and Descriptive. By Henry C. Fish, D. D. With an Introductory Essay by Prof. Edwards A. Park, D. D. One large volume, 8vo. Illustrated with seven large Portraits from steel, $4 00.

Nearly sixty of the most distinguished Preachers of the present day are here introduced, about forty of whom belong to foreign countries. The Discourses have been almost uniformly prepared expressly for this work, or selected and designated by their authors themselves. They are, therefore, no ordinary productions; but will be esteemed worthy, it is believed, of being placed with the "Master-Pieces of Pulpit Eloquence" of other ages. The materials of the Biographical Sketches have in all cases been derived from responsible sources.

As indicative of the character of the work, it may be stated, that, under the German Pulpit, such men as Professors Tholuck, Julius Müller, Nitzsch, Drs. Krummacher and Hoffman, Court Preachers to the King of Prussia, will be found; under the French Pulpit, Drs. J. H. Merle D'Aubigne, Gaussan, Malan, Grandpierre, and the celebrated Adolphe Monod (deceased since the preparation of the work was commenced); under the English, Melville, and Noel, and Bunting, and James and the like; and under the Scottish, Drs. Hamilton, Cummings, Buchanan, Guthrie, Duff, Candlish and others.

The American Pulpit is represented by eminent men in each Evangelical denomination, selected with great care, and after wide consultation. Most of the Discourses in this department appear in print now for the first time.

"Our readers will remember the noble volumes of which this is a supplement, and how cordially we commended them to their delighted study. The present volume is worthy to go with them as a memento of the living, who teach and preach Jesus in many nations.

"Those who own the former volumes will hasten to add this to their treasure, and those who have failed hitherto to procure them will find themselves doubly tempted now."—*Congregationalist.*

"The biographical sketches are compiled with care, and, along with an outline of the history of each individual named, contain brief critical discussions of their merits as preachers and as divines. These criticisms are, so far as we can determine, just and discriminating. Altogether, this volume, like its predecessors, is a highly valuable and acceptable contribution to our religious literature, and will be an acquisition to the library of any reading man, whether he be a minister or layman.—*Christian Times.*

"Whether it be considered in reference to the felicity of its selections, the fidelity of its sketches, the amplitude of its range, or the general impartiality and good taste that mark its execution, it is worthy of all praise, and the author has fairly entitled himself to the gratitude not merely of his own generation, but of posterity."—*Puritan Recorder.*

M. W. Dodd's Publications.

CRUDEN'S COMPLETE CON-
CORDANCE to the Holy Scriptures; or, A Dictionary and Alphabetical Index to the Bible. By Alexander Cruden, M. A.

By which, I.—Any verse in the Bible may be readily found by looking for any material word in the verse. To which is added—

II.—The significations of the principal words, by which their true meaning in Scriptures are shown.

III.—An account of Jewish customs and ceremonies illustrative of many portions of the Sacred Record.

IV.—A Concordance to the Proper Names of the Bible, and their meaning in the original.

V.—A Concordance to the Books called Apocrypha. One vol. 4to. Price, $4.

To which is appended an original Life of the Author, illustrated with an accurate Portrait from a Steel Engraving.

The only *genuine* and *entire* edition of the complete work of Cruden—the only one embracing those features of it which Cruden himself and the Public, for more than a hundred years, have regarded as *essential* to its completeness and inestimable value, is the edition published by the subscriber.

It is believed to be the most accurate Edition, now in existence, of the original work, as it came from the hands of the author; and is the only American edition having any fair claim to his name. In its *complete* form it has ever been regarded as immeasurably superior to any other work of the kind.

"Cruden's Concordance, in its unabridged and *complete state*, is invaluable to the biblical student, and the abridgements which have been made of it furnish no idea of the thoroughness and fullness of the original and complete work."—*Rev. Thomas De Witt, D. D.*

"Cruden's Concordance has been the companion of my whole life, both as a theological student and a minister; and it is the last book, with the exception of the Bible itself, that I would consent to have pass out of my hands."—*Rev. Wm. B. Sprague, D. D.*

"In its complete form, as published by Mr. Dodd, I would earnestly commend it as the book that should find a place in every family by the side of the Bible. I am acquainted with no work that can be a substitute for it."—*Rev. J. B. Condit, D.D., of Auburn Theological Seminary."—Auburn, N. Y.*

"In reply to yours, I can only say, that if I possessed but two books in the world, they should be God's Bible and Cruden's Concordance."—*Rev. Gardiner Spring, LL. D.*

"I have made use of Cruden's Concordance for many years, and have always regarded it as a monument of industry, and an indispensable assistance, in its *complete* form, to the study of the Word of God."—*Rev. Professor Goodrich, D. D., of Yale College, New Haven.*

"No English Concordance can take its place. It is equally precious to the Minister of the Word and the earnest reader of the Scriptures, of any sort or condition of men."—*Rt. Rev. Bishop McIlvaine, D. D.*

"The value of Cruden's Concordance, *unabridged* and *entire*, I consider as incomparable and indispensable."—*Rev. Samuel H. Cox, D. D.*

"No book has aided me more in the study of God's Word—enabling me to compare Scripture with Scripture, and interpret Scripture by Scripture. I believe its usefulness both to laymen and ministers can hardly be overrated."—*Rev. Bishop Janes, D. D.*

"Cruden's Concordance, in its original state, I consider above all price to the student of the Scriptures."—*Rev. Francis Wayland, LL. D., President of Brown University.*

JUVENILE BOOKS

PUBLISHED BY

M. W. DODD,

506 BROADWAY, NEW YORK.

JUST PUBLISHED:

Amy Carr, by Caroline Cheesbro. 1 vol. 16mo. 3 Illustrations, - - - - $0.85

"No stilted language, no startling incidents, all is simple and true to nature. This little book is written by one who looks on life with sad but kindly eyes, and children with a warm, yearning heart for their present and future well-being. A photograph of "life as it is." You have not to look to the end for the moral. Instruction, moral and religious, is woven like a golden thread through the whole fabric. A sweet melody, as from a better sphere, sings in your heart as you read, and lifts it toward celestial harmonies."—*Rochester Democrat.*

Robert the Cabin Boy. By H. K. P., Author of Mary Alden, etc. 16mo, illustrated, 85

"The interest with which our author has invested the history of this homeless orphan child of the sea, and the important lessons of instruction conveyed as the reader is induced to follow him in after years, will be certain to make the book about 'Robert the Cabin Boy' a universal favorite."

Glenarvon; or, Holidays at the Cottage. A beautiful Scotch Story. Illustrated. 18mo, - 65

"This is a delightful book. Its stories, drawn from Scottish life, are interspersed with interesting anecdotes and episodes, illustrating historical and scientific truths. It conveys the best moral and religious lessons adapted to the youthful mind, and told in such a manner as to engage the attention."—*Am. and For. Ch. Union.*

Henry Willard; or, the Value of Right Principles, by C. M. Trowbridge. Illustrated, - 65

"A story of a boy who learned from his pious parents *always to do right*, and who, though an orphan when quite young, and often sorely tempted, maintained his integrity, and eventually won many warm friends, and exerted a good influence over others."—*Presbyterian.*

M. W. Dodd's Publications.

The Little Savoyard, Wonderful Phials and other Stories. Translated from the French by Anna. 18mo, - - - - - $0.65

> If any one can read the story of the Little Savoyard and not have the sensibilities deeply moved, and the kindliest feelings of the heart brought into exercise, we are greatly mistaken. This and the other stories embraced in the volume make it one of great interest to the reader.

Heroes of Puritan Times, by Joel Stoughton. With an Introduction Letter by Joel Hawes, D. D., - - - - - - 65

> "This is a book of decided interest. The times to which it relates, the characters it describes, the stirring events which it sketches, and the noble sentiments which it illustrates, lend it a peculiar charm."

Honey Blossoms for Little Bees. A beautiful Juvenile. Illustrated, - - - 65

> "A beautiful book with a *sweet* title, and what's more a pretty story, in large type and short words, with beautiful pictures to help the little reader to understand."

The Deaf Shoemaker, and other Stories. By Philip Barrett. Illustrated. 18mo, - - 55

> "The author of this charming little book understands what will interest children, and how to adapt his style and language to their taste and wants. We cordially recommend it to a place in every Sabbath-School and family library."—*Advocate and Guardian.*

Fred. Lawrence, or, The World College. By Margaret E. Teller. Illustrated, 18mo, - 55

> "This interesting story shows how a youth may make a man of himself in spite of many disadvantages, and the embarrassments of poverty. He is cut short in his course of study by the necessity of providing a livelihood for his widowed mother and sister; yet contrives to make himself a scholar, and push his way to wealth and an honorable position."—*Church Times.*

Winter in Spitzbergen; a book for Youth, from the German of C. Hildebrandt, by E. Goodrich Smith. Illustrated, - - - 65

> "A book of surpassing interest for young people. Those who have been charmed with Robinson Crusoe will be delighted with this. It gives an account of the manner in which three lonely castaways spent a winter in the dark, frozen, and desolate polar regions of Spitzbergen, and how they were at length providentially delivered. A capital book to be read aloud around a winter fireside."—*Baptist Memorial.*

The Old Chest and its Treasures, by
Aunt Elizabeth. A most attractive volume of several hundred anecdotes and stories. 12mo, $0.90

"A collection of more than two hundred striking incidents and anecdotes, illustrative of moral and religious truths. It is an excellent book for the family, and especially the young."—*Christian Observer.*

Sunday Sketches for Children, by a
Father. Illustrated. 18mo, - - - - 65

"These are admirable sketches, naturally and strikingly drawn, and will be read by the children with pleasure and profit."—*Christian Chronicle.*

Shadows and Sunshine, as illustrated in the
History of Notable Characters, by Rev. Erskine Neal. 18mo, - - - - - 65

"A book in which various characters are made to teach, and from whose chequered experience much which is valuable may be derived. We can heartily recommend it."—*Religious Her.*

Stories for Young Americans. By
Prof. Joseph Alden.

The Example of Washington. With Portrait,	40
The Old Stone House. A Story of 1776,	40
Fruits of the May-Flower,	40
Stories and Anecdotes of the Puritans,	40

"Prof. Alden's juvenile books are in many respects patterns of publications for the young. They have a purity, simplicity, and gravity of style, that must do much towards forming mental and moral characteristics of the best model."—*Religious Rec.*

By Charlotte Elizabeth.

Personal Recollections and Memoir,	65
Posthumous Poems,	65
Judah's Lion,	65
Judæa Capta,	65
The Deserter,	55
The Flower-Garden,	65
Count Raymond of Toulouse,	65
Conformity,	40
Falsehood and Truth,	40

M. W. Dodd's Publications.

Sovereigns of the Bible, by Eliza R. Steele, author of "Heroines of Sacred History," etc. With illuminated title and fine illus. 12mo, $1.50

"We have here the scattered facts in the lives of the kings of Israel and Judah skillfully arranged in continuous narratives, which are highly instructive. The book is an important contribution to our general biblical literature."—*Albany Argus.*

The Russell Family, by Anna Hastings. Illustrated. 18mo, - - - - - 55

"A very beautiful and instructive story from real life, illustrating the power of a Christian mother, and the sweet influences of the domestic circle."—*New York Observer.*

Minnie Carlton, by Mary Belle Bartlett. A beautiful Story for Girls. Illustrated. 18mo, - 65.

"The subject of this narrative is the eldest daughter of a household forced by the death of her mother to take charge of it. The pledge given to her dying mother to train the little ones to meet her in heaven is conscientiously fulfilled, and the lessons of her example, prudence and piety, rewarded by the most cheering results, bringing light and joy to the household, will scarcely be read without deep and grateful emotion."—*Evang.*

Uncle Barnaby; or, Recollections of his Character and Opinions. 65

"The religion of the book is good—the morality excellent, and the mode of exhibiting their important lessons can hardly be surpassed in anything calculated to make them attractive to the young, or successful in correcting anything bad in their habits or morals."

The Finland Family; or, Fancies taken for Facts. A Tale of the Past for the Present. By Mrs. Susan Peyton Cornwall, - - - - 65

"The Finland Family belongs to the very best class of religious tales. It is full of the gentlest and sweetest sympathies, and at the same time commends the culture of the firmest and most steadfast principles."—*Ch. Intelligencer.*

Frank Forrest; or the Life of an Orphan Boy. By David M. Stone. Illustrated. 18mo, - 45

"It inculcates the most impressive lessons of virtue and religion, and the intense interest of the story will rivet the attention of the children; thus securing a happy influence on their hearts."—*Journal of Commerce.*

Poetic Readings for Schools and Families, with an Introduction by J. L. Comstock, M. D. Illustrated, - - - - - 65

"We cordially recommend to all young readers this charming collection. It is executed with soundness of judgment, delicacy of taste, and great range of research; no school ought to be without it."—*Home Journal.*

www.ingramcontent.com/pod-product-compliance
Lightning Source LLC
Chambersburg PA
CBHW051244300426
44114CB00011B/879